Alexander H. Japp

Days with Industrials

Adventures and Experiences Among Curious Industries

Alexander H. Japp

Days with Industrials
Adventures and Experiences Among Curious Industries

ISBN/EAN: 9783744661621

Printed in Europe, USA, Canada, Australia, Japan

Cover: Foto ©Suzi / pixelio.de

More available books at **www.hansebooks.com**

DAYS WITH INDUSTRIALS:

ADVENTURES AND EXPERIENCES AMONG
CURIOUS INDUSTRIES.

BY

ALEXANDER H. JAPP, LL.D., F.R.S.E.

AUTHOR OF

"INDUSTRIAL CURIOSITIES," "GOLDEN LIVES," ETC. ETC.

With Numerous Illustrations.

LONDON:

TRÜBNER & CO., LUDGATE HILL.

1889.

Ballantyne Press
BALLANTYNE, HANSON AND CO.
EDINBURGH AND LONDON

PREFACE.

SOME of these chapters, in a condensed form, have appeared in "All the Year Round," "Good Words," "Gentleman's Magazine," and other periodicals. Favourable opinions were expressed of them in various newspapers and reviews; and the author trusts that his friendly critics may have no reason to change their opinion of them now that they are brought together. All that remains for the author to do is to thank the Editors of the various magazines for making it possible for him to reprint them in this form.

CONTENTS.

—◆◆ —

APPENDIX.

DAYS WITH INDUSTRIALS.

I.

QUININE AND ITS ROMANCE.

MANY a romance could be written of botanists in their
self-denying devotion to plants and flowers. Linnæus's
life is one ceaseless heroism, in which his love of certain
plants amounted almost to worship. His falling down on
his knees on Putney Heath, when he first saw the gorse
in bloom, and thanking God for having created so beautiful a flower, is widely known, and poets have vied with
each other in setting the incident to fitting verse. Of an
earlier botanist the same or nearly the same story is told,
so that we can only suppose that in this department of
science sentiment of a certain kind asserts itself more
readily than in some others. At all events, the records
are alive with instances of perseverance and devotion,
such as cannot be surpassed, if they can be equalled, in
other walks. When Jussieu, the famous French botanist,
for example, was bringing a seedling of the Lebanon
cedar from Syria to Marseilles, the ship ran so short of
water that the passengers were limited to half a glass

A

a-day. Jussieu shared his half with his plant; and, thanks to his self-denial and his generous enthusiasm, it reached Paris in safety, and lived to be a hundred years old and eighty feet high.

But it is in the case of plants directly associated with the art of healing that we can find the most exciting records; for here the chivalry and heroism are fed, so to speak, from a double source: the desire for the extension of scientific knowledge, and the passion for the welfare of mankind. The thirst for knowledge and the impulse of beneficence support each other; and the man of science becomes a minister, a missionary of love and healing, claiming our admiration in the one aspect, our love and our gratitude in the other.

There is no tree whose story is more interesting than the chinchona or quinine-yielding tree. Jussieu, too, figures prominently in its history. Unfortunately, his devotion and self-denial did not avail him in this case as they did in that of the cedar, else the chapter we are now to write would not have been so deeply interesting, so stirring, because so full of adventure. "The many fail, the one succeeds," sings the Laureate, and the record of failure, as in so many other instances, is more fascinating than that of easily achieved success could possibly have been. It has been said, indeed, that the story of the efforts to achieve the naturalisation of the chinchona tree in different countries, so as to insure a plentiful and continuous supply of the invaluable bark, is perhaps the most striking in the records of scientific travel.

All know the virtues of quinine, and many have good cause to think of it gratefully. The medical practitioners

of temperate climates have found in the various preparations from the chinchona tree valuable remedies for many
severe and trying diseases; but in the tropics they have
been simply indispensable in the treatment of malarial
fever and other affections common there. No one would
have thought of going on a long journey in India without
a bottle of quinine in his valise, and it is not too much to
say that if deprived of chinchona bark we could not keep
a European force in India, and even native troops and
police would have to be withdrawn from various unhealthy
stations at which they are now placed. Livingstone and
other travellers in Central Africa have celebrated the
manifold virtues of quinine; and one of the most exciting incidents in the records of more recent travel is that
of Schweinfurth, the great German explorer, in Africa
among the Monbuttos and Pigmies, when he lost almost
the whole of his property by fire—scientific instruments
among the rest. But the most important of all to him was
his quinine, as he tells us; and how often he thought of
it with regretful sorrow, and with fear in the remarkable
journey which, stripped of everything, he nevertheless persevered in, preserving his measurements and a knowledge
of latitude by carefully pacing and counting his paces as
he walked. Thomas de Quincey, in his "Confessions,"
magnifying the merits of his favourite drug, opium, while
as yet he had not felt its woes, speaks of ecstasies "having
become portable, and might be corked in a pint bottle;
happiness bought for a penny and carried in the waistcoat-
pocket, and peace of mind sent down by the mail." So
quinine enables us to say that health and joy in malarious
eastern latitudes may be carried about corked up in a

little phial, and what proves a more powerful agency than an army of doctors in the corner of a knapsack.

Strange it is that the chinchona trees—natives of the mountainous forests of South America, should be of such importance in the maintenance of our Eastern Empire, in the opening up of interior Africa, and indirectly in the extension in these parts of civilisation and Christianity! Stranger still, however, that a plant whose rare virtues had been practically known for centuries (for doubtless the medicine men of ancient Indian tribes had found out that virtue was to be extracted from the chinchona bark) should have been left so long neglected, or but very partially applied to mitigate sufferings that had smitten down annually thousands on thousands of men and women. Mr. Markham, it is true, infers from the fact that no reference is made to it by Inca Garcilasso nor by Acosta in the lists of Indian medicines, that it was unknown in the time of the Incas, but the fact of its absence then might be accounted for in another way.

Notwithstanding the great and permanent importance and interest of the subject, we believe that few comparatively have followed the steps and stages by which this invaluable specific has been made more and more available; and we shall therefore try to retell clearly and concisely the leading facts in its history; since, so far as we are aware, they have till now lain practically buried in reports, in blue-books, and in big tomes, from which we shall carefully extract it.

I. THE SEARCH FOR PLANTS AND ATTEMPTS TO NATURALISE THEM.

In the year 1639 the wife of a Spanish Viceroy of Peru returned to Europe from that country; and having been cured of fever by the use of a tree-bark, she was wise enough to bring some of it home, with the intention of distributing it among the sick on her husband's estate, and making it generally known throughout Europe. The bark powder was not unfitly called Countess' powder (*Pulvis Comitessæ*), and by this name it was long known to druggists in Europe. Mr. Markham tells us, in his Memoir of her,[1] that the good deeds of the Countess are even now remembered (and no wonder) by the people of Chinchon and Colemar in local tradition. A goodly number of species of the tree have been named after this beneficent lady, and their growth in an extending zone in the East will surely for ages keep her memory green.

Jesuit missionaries who afterwards returned from South America also brought with them some supplies. The lady was the Countess of Chinchon; hence the scientific name, Chinchona. The Jesuit missionaries gave to it the more popular name of " Jesuits' Bark." *Quina* was the native name of the bark, which, of course, is the original of quinine, which has been retained for perhaps one half of the medical preparations from the bark. Little or nothing was, however, scientifically known of the tree which produced the bark till 1739—a whole century after its first introduction into Europe. La

---

[1] A Memoir of the Countess of Chinchon. By Clements R. Markham. London: 1874.

Condamine and Jussieu, who were then on an exploring expedition in South America, after not a little trial, obtained plants with a view to having them sent to the Jardin des Plantes in Paris. Unfortunately, the whole collection perished in a storm at sea near the mouth of the river Amazon. Unfortunate it surely was, for fully another century passed before anything effective and practical was done to introduce or naturalise the tree in Europe, or in suitable climates in the Eastern dependencies of England, from which supplies might be assured; and this notwithstanding the fact that the French chemists, Pelletier and Caventon, had in 1820 developed true quinine from the bark. The first living chinchona trees ever seen in Europe were some *Calisaya* plants raised at the Jardin des Plantes in Paris from seeds collected by the well-known Frenchman, Dr. Weddell, in his first journey to Bolivia in 1846; though in 1835 Dr. Forbes Royle, then Superintendent of the Botanical Garden at Seharunpore, had become thoroughly convinced of the possibility of the profitable culture of the chinchona tree in India, and had earnestly urged the Government to make efforts to introduce the plants on the Khasia and Neilgherry Hills, at that date and afterwards in 1847, and again in 1853 and 1856. Nothing came of it, though Dr. Grant, the Apothecary-General in Calcutta, had earnestly supported the proposal in 1850.

While all this was going on, however, some gentlemen interested had not been idle, and, though they went a warfare on their own charges, and had no definite connection with any government, they were anxious all that in them lay to aid governments, as will be seen.

Mr. George Ledger, whose name will ever be honoured in this relation, as indeed it is inseparably linked with one of the finer kinds of bark which has been named after him, made an expedition in the Valley of Santa Aña, Department of Cuzco. Mr. Backhouse was his companion. The expedition wholly failed, and indeed had a fatal termination. Mr. Backhouse was murdered by the Indians, all the supplies were stolen, all the bark that had been collected with great labour was destroyed, as well as seeds and plants; some sixty pounds of gold dust was missing. Mr. Ledger escaped; but he estimates his losses at some £1500, and that of his brother Arthur at £700. In 1861 Mr. Ledger sent an expedition into the Bolivian wilds, with the double object of obtaining seeds and plants of the chinchona and alpacas of various kinds. This expedition was more successful; and in 1865 Mr. Ledger was enabled to present a portion of the seeds and plants of some valuable species to the Government of India and the Government of the Netherlands. In the letter to Mr. J. E. Howard, from which we have already quoted, Mr. Ledger says: "Surely, after the success attending the seeds sent in 1865, the Government of India and the Government of the Netherlands should award me some compensation for the losses I sustained in the search." Mr. Howard, remarking on this letter and other points, says, "The superiority of Ledger's *Calisaya* is beyond doubt."

In 1852 Dr. Falconer, then Superintendent of the Botanical Gardens at Calcutta, urgently repeated the recommendation that had been so often made, and with more success. The Court of Directors of the East

India Company were induced to procure and send out six plants of *Chinchona calisaya.* Five of these precious trees reached Calcutta alive, and were at once placed in the Botanical Gardens. Here they received all possible care and attention, but they did not thrive. After a short time they were sent to the hill station of Darjeeling, where they all died in the ensuing winter. The first experiment in chinchona culture in India was, therefore, a disappointment,—how deep a disappointment was only known to those—medical men and others— who realised fully what was at stake in the future.

Meantime the Dutch, always alive to interests of this kind, awoke to the great importance of the chinchona culture, and happily having a very suitable field for it in Java, they sent out the botanist Hasskarl to Peru in 1852 to collect plants and seeds. He also encountered many difficulties and dangers in his wanderings, not a few of which arose from the jealousy of the native bark-gatherers—cascarilleros, as they are called, who managed to infect the whole people with the idea that their trade would be ruined, if chinchona trees were allowed to leave the country.

Some difference of opinion seems to exist regarding the results of M. Hasskarl's efforts and explorations. On one side we are told that he had not any local knowledge of the wild regions where he travelled, neither had he any acquaintance with the language of the natives; that his avowed intention was chiefly to find seeds of *Calisaya;* but that, unfortunately, he entered the chinchona zone at a point where neither that nor indeed any valuable species grow; that he collected the seeds of the species he found believing them to be true *Calisaya;* that he did ultimately penetrate into a *Calisaya* region, and remained in it a short time, but that he trusted too implicitly a native collector who led him to believe that he was collecting the true *Calisaya,* when he was in fact gathering a worthless species; and that the twenty cases landed in Java did not contain one plant of any valuable variety of *Calisaya.*

On the other hand, the Dutch authorities have a very different account to give. They say that M. Hasskarl, though he did not know the Quichua language, had thoroughly learned Spanish, and that his knowledge of botany and science was so great as to have rendered next to impossible some of the errors with which he is credited; that he had lived for years in Java, and was accustomed to a tropical climate, and in dealing with natives; that he did land in Java seventy-eight *Calisayas* alive, with other valuable varieties; and that, *if he was deceived,* the climate of Java, which is undoubtedly very favourable to the chinchonas, transformed them! But the same could hardly apply to Holland. In 1855, Weddell, the famous French traveller and botantist, we are told, paid a visit to the Botanical Gardens at Leyden, and saw there the *Calisaya* plants, which M. Hasskarl had sent from Sardia. As soon as he saw the young plants he exclaimed, "La vraie *Calisaya,* rien que cela, il n'y a pas le moindre doute." "In 1874," Mr. Moens of Java says, "I sent a case of dried specimens of our chinchonas to that great quinologist, Mr. Howard. Amongst the specimens were some of the *Calisaya* varieties reared from seeds obtained from M. Hasskarl's original plants."

Mr. Howard writes me about them: "No. 1 may and indeed must be, a rather fine kind. No. 2 is a form of *Calisaya*, which I do not at present recognise. No. 4 resembles more my specimen of *C. calisaya vera!*" It is thus certainly incorrect to say that M. Hasskarl's mission was a failure as regards securing any specimen whatever of *Calisaya*. But it is undoubtedly the fact that the cultivators both in Java and Holland had many difficulties at the outset: and that their assiduity and perseverance alone secured the good result in the end; and owing to the strenuous efforts of the cultivators there the undertaking has in Java become a success commercially and otherwise.

No further action worth noting was taken by the Government of India till the year 1858, when, owing to influential representations, it was decided, with the sanction of the Secretary of State for India, that a competent collector should be sent for a couple of years to South America to explore the forests, and to procure young plants and seeds of the best kinds. The necessity for such a measure has, as we have hinted, long been fully recognised by scientific and medical men, as it was well known that the collection of the bark in South America was carried on in the most reckless and extravagant manner. Systematic regulations for the working of the forests did not exist—each collector did what was right in his own eyes. Grave fears were, therefore, felt more and more lest the supplies of bark should become limited or even cease for long periods. There was also the risk of the price of the bark being at any moment raised to such a point as to restrict its use, and in fact, put it altogether beyond the reach of the poor. Chemistry, unfortunately, not having yet discovered any efficient substitute.

The choice of the Indian Government fell on one who fully justified it. Mr. Clements Markham, who volunteered to direct the mission, was appointed. He knew Spanish well, and had some acquaintance with the Quichua tongue, and also possessed a fair knowledge of the country. If not a professed botanist, he was a quick observer, and certainly gifted with discrimination of character, as the work done by those he had associated with him afterwards fully proved. With no little skill and forecast he organised a threefold expedition, the sections of which began their operations simultaneously in 1860, fully five years after the beginning of the Dutch experiment. Mr. Markham himself undertook to collect seeds of the *Calisaya* or Yellow Bark tree (the most valuable of the chinchonas) in the forests of Bolivia and Southern Peru, where alone it is to be found. He arranged that Mr. Pritchett should explore the Grey Bark forests of Huanaco and Humalies in Central Peru; and 'that Messrs. Spruce and Cross should collect the seeds of the Red Bark tree on the Eastern slopes of Chimboraza in the territory of Ecuador.

Mr. Markham applied himself to his perilous task with characteristic caution, tact, determination, and ardour. In addition to difficulties from the nature of the country and the lack of transport, he had to contend against the jealousies of the native collectors, whose spirit had already been aroused by the efforts of M. Hasskarl, and who regarded all inquiry and examination as an interference with their rights and vested interests. They regarded the trade in bark as their monopoly, and were not inclined to be intruded upon under any pretence. And then plants are bulky and need considerable space in packing, if they are not to be injured or destroyed. When all this is borne in mind, some sense of the arduous nature of the task Mr. Markham had taken in hand will be realised.

The cascarilleros, or bark-collectors, spend their whole lives in the woods, and have been known to lose themselves and have never again been heard of. This gives some idea of the wildness and extent of the quinine-producing forests of South America, which may be roughly said to lie in a belt stretching from 19° S. latitude to 10° N., following the line of the Andes over an area of more than a thousand miles. They grow on the sides of the mountains, or in the ravines between the mountains. The scenery is described by travellers in that region as magnificent. The deep indigo of the sky, with the icy peaks of the Andes clearly defined against it, fill the higher portion of the picture, while below are narrow gorges down which rush glittering cataracts, and across which are hung slender bridges made of rope and twisted branches of trees.

The paths down the sides of these gorges are very narrow and precipitous. Sometimes a traveller riding on a mule down one of these ridges has one leg touching the side of the mountain, while the other hangs over a precipice.

The sides of the hills, even at very high altitudes, are

covered with wild flowers, many of which have long been naturalised in England. A profusion of ferns form a graceful background, and serve to show out the brilliant colouring of the lupins, verbenas, calceolarias, fuchsias, and begonias with which these hanging gardens abound. A large portion of the Andean region is capable of cultivation, and in ancient days there is no doubt that it was cultivated by the Incas to a great extent.

The general calmness in the air of Peru contrasts strangely with the frequent disturbances of the earth. The Peruvians often say that in their country thunder comes from below. At Lima the slight shocks of earthquake which are felt daily are thought nothing of by the inhabitants. The whole ridge of the Cordilleras facing the Pacific is studded with volcanic peaks, and there are no less than twenty-four distinct volcanos in the range.

In Humboldt's " Travels " we read interesting accounts of this curious Trans-Andean country. In his excursions through the mountains he frequently had to cross vast chasms by native bridges. One of these he mentions particularly, which was formed of ropes manufactured from the fibrous roots of the *Aguava Americana*, only three or four inches in diameter. The weirdness and solitude of these regions are intensified by the song of a bird, which is ceaselessly heard but seldom seen, and which possesses a low, melancholy, wailing note of such an oppressive character that it has been called *Alma perdida*, or the Lost Soul. It is said that there have been cases of lonely bark collectors who have been driven mad by its continual melancholy wailing.

In this wild and trackless region Mr. Markham laboured

for many months, exposed to peril from wild beasts, and also to the enmities of the native bark-gatherers, and groaning under the manifold difficulties of land transport. The collections he made at such risk and labour were exposed to so many trials that unfortunately much of the fruits of his courage and industry was lost; but enough came safely to hand to form the beginning of the great chinchona plantations of India, of which we shall speak particularly under another head. Towards the end of 1860, cases with samples from Mr. Markham and his party began to arrive at Calcutta.

On his return journey, Mr Markham, as was almost to be expected, found the jealousy of the people aroused by rumours which had got abroad as to the nature of his mission. To return along the road he came by would have simply insured the destruction of his plants, and possibly involved injury to himself, so he had to resort to a stratagem. And surely never was such stratagem more fully justified by the nobility of the cause for which it was brought into play. Mr. Weir was sent back by the old route, and Mr. Markham himself proceeded with the plants in a straight line towards the coast, through an unknown country, and without a guide.

Let the reader for a moment pause and try to realise what this implied in a wild, mountainous, and in great measure roadless region. Let him then think how hard it must have proved with only personal accompaniments. But Mr. Markham had his precious seeds and plants— bulky impedimenta—to carry with him. After much hardship he arrived at the town of Vilque, with his plants in good order. A few more marches brought him to the port

of Islay. But where his difficulties ought to have been
ended, the worst and most trying were only begun. The
custom-house authorities having discovered what the
plant-case contained, would not allow them to be shipped
without an order from the Minister of Finance. This Mr.
Markham had himself to go to Lima to procure, leaving
his plants behind him to the tender mercies of those not
likely to lose a chance of injuring them, and fancying
they were doing their country, if not God, good service.
We can well imagine what Mr. Markham's feelings must
have been on that needless and wearisome journey, and
amid the formalities and polite excuses of officials. All
this caused a delay of three weeks, but Mr. Markham
had succeeded by his tact and careful explanations. On
the 24th of June the cases were at last embarked on
board a steamer bound for Panama, but not before a
scheme had been set on foot by some patriotic Bolivians
to kill the plants by pouring hot water on them through
holes to be bored in the cases. None of the more
valuable chinchona trees, and certainly none of the
Calisayas, can stand frost, but they can as little stand
boiling water. Her Majesty's steamer *Vixen* was at this
moment lying idle at Callao, and could have taken the
plants straight to Madras, with every chance of saving
them alive. But it is hardly the style of the various
departments of our public service to work hand in
hand and eye to eye; and probably it would have been
regarded as an infringement of all the "traditions" of
the service that a ship of war should have been used not
only to forward the arts of peace, but the arts of healing,
by which men, both of the navy and the army, were to

be so directly benefited. Truly, even in these days of advanced culture, organisation, and perfection of machinery, it may still be said, "With how little wisdom the world is governed." Instead of this being found possible, Mr. Markham was compelled by his orders to take his plants to India, *viâ* Panama, England, the Mediterranean, and the Red Sea, and thus expose them to transhipments and alterations of temperature, which ultimately killed them all. Whether they died from hot water or from exposure to frost, the result was the same, but most likely from the latter; for against malice, up to a certain point, watchfulness will suffice to guard you, but against stupidity in high places as in low scarce any amount of care or caution, of heroism, devotion, self-sacrifice, will suffice; as Schiller so well put it—so well, indeed, that Heine plagiarised the idea without acknowledgment—

" Mit der Dummheit Götter kämpfen selbst vergebens."
("Against stupidity the gods themselves struggle in vain.")

While Mr. Markham had been thus fighting hopelessly against awful odds, Mr. Pritchett was collecting seeds and plants of the chinchona species producing grey bark, in the forests near Huanco, in the northern part of the same territory, and was successful in bringing to Lima in the month of August a collection of seeds and half a mule load of young plants of three species—*Micrantha*, *Peruviana*, and *Nitidia*.

Mr. Spruce, six months before Mr. Markham had sailed from England, had left his home in the Quintenian Andes, and had fixed on Limon as the most suitable headquarters. He had made a good collection, and had arranged to go to Loxa, south of the Ecuador Territory, to procure seeds of the pale or crown bark. This arrangement, unfortunately, was frustrated through Mr. Spruce's serious illness. But in July 1860 Mr. Spruce was joined at Limon by Mr. Cross, who had been sent out from England with Wardian cases to receive such plants as might be secured. Here the work was carried on vigorously and successfully. Mr. Cross established a nursery at Limon, and there put in a number of cuttings of the red bark tree. Mr. Spruce now searched for seeds. Mr. Cross ultimately succeeded in taking his cuttings safely to India, while Mr. Spruce's seeds were sent to India by post. It is from the results of those journeys mainly, if not entirely, that our plantations in certain parts of India and Ceylon have been made, and if the immediate fruits of these perilous journeyings and labours did not appear adequate, we must all surely feel grateful that by care and scientific treatment the tree has now been brought to such health and productiveness at various points in our dominions.

II. NATURE AND HABITS OF CHINCHONA TREES.

The genus Chinchona includes as many as thirty-six species, but only about a dozen of these are found available for yield for medical purposes.

The following are the more prominent : their scientific and popular names are set side by side :—

Crown bark = *Chinchona officinalis* and varieties.
Red bark = *Succirubra.*
Yellow bark = *Calisaya* and varieties.
Grey bark = *Nitida, micrantha,* &c.

B

The Loxa Crown Bark, the *Cortex* chinchona *pallidæ* of pharmacy, which was the first bark brought to Europe in the seventeenth century, is now fallen into disrepute, most probably owing to its having been collected from a very young wood. Study of the habits of the tree, and methods of improved treatment gradually attained, have done much to bring into view species which at first were not held in great favour. And the efforts and experiments of the Dutch in this direction both in Java and at home must be gratefully recognised in regarding the broad result.

The tree itself is a beautiful object, as any one may see by a glance at the photographs of sections of plantations given in Mr. Howard's elaborate and valuable " Quinology of the East Indian Plantations." It has a delicate small flower in close clusters, and at certain seasons its fragrance fills the air for a considerable distance. The leaf-forms vary considerably in the different species, from a form approaching to heart-shaped to a purely lance-headed figure, as the name *lancifolia* applied to one variety may be taken to indicate. This is perhaps the most elegant of the whole—its lines are so delicate, tapering softly at once towards the point and towards the stalk; while the leaf of *C. officinalis* and *C. grandiflora* more incline to something of a trowel-shape.

The *succirubra* or red-bark tree is more of an umbrella-shape than the others, and the aspect of the leaf more that of our plane-tree. Some of the trees are more marked as the yielders of pure quinine, others of all the alkaloids in a mixed state.

Science, too, while it has made us more and more

acquainted with the peculiar habits and needs of the tree, has done not a little to render its own classification inexact, since hybridisation has been found of the greatest value. Mr. Howard presents, in his " Quinology," most careful analysis of the different barks ; but he admits that, owing to hybridisation and other causes, the attempts to classify barks according to a too precise system, " would certainly end in confusion."

The medicinal virtues of the bark depend on the presence of one or more of four alkaloids—quinine, quininedine, chinchonine, and chinchonidine. All of these have been subjected to rigorous trial, and found nearly equal as regards their value in the treatment of malarial fever and allied diseases. The alkaloids do not exist in a free state in the bark, but in combination with tannin, such as is found in oak bark and other barks, and extensively used in the process of tanning leather. All the four alkaloids are found present in most species of the bark ; but some varieties of the tree contain a much greater proportion of alkaloids than others, and some are more remarkable than others for producing a much greater proportion of one particular form of alkaloid. *C. succirubra,* we learn, yields far the largest amount of alkaloids as a whole ; but *C. officinalis* and *C. calisaya* the largest per centage of quinine. The young trees —that is, trees prior to their sixth or seventh year— contain but a small proportion of the alkaloids, which moreover is present in them in almost uncrystallisable form. They are, therefore, of little commercial value. Experience in India year by year has gone to show that this holds true of all the species, and most true of the most valuable species, in a quinine-producing light. Even up to the eighth or ninth year the active principles continue to increase in quantity and to improve in quality. No doubt much has been lost in former years through lack of knowledge of this fact; for much young bark was cut down too early, with the result of weakening the producing power of whole plantations permanently later. This the quinological gardeners will avoid in the future, of course, with no end of gain, though with much deferred return of outlay. It will thus be seen that the chinchona planter cannot expect any return of money invested for the long period of eight years. This fact must always place the chinchona industry at a great disadvantage. The culture of tea and coffee begin to be remunerative at much earlier stages, and are, therefore, more likely to find favour with capitalists. But we should not omit to say that some of the elements of success in treatment are even yet not wholly known, and further acquaintance with the subject may remove some of these difficulties. Facts are grasped and made familiar, somewhat to the disadvantage of chinchona with planters, while it is not always as distinctly grasped that we are still in the dark on some vital points. For example, barks of one district are sometimes devoid of quinine, while those of the same species from a neighbouring locality may yield $3\frac{1}{2}$ to $4\frac{1}{2}$ per cent. of sulphate of quinine. This seems at first sight a small proportion; but even the flat *calisaya* bark, which is the favourite, and is most often offered in the drug trade for pharmaceutical purposes, contains generally only from 5 to 6 per cent. of quinine. The thick, flat red bark contains 3 to 4 per cent. of alkaloids, and with a large proportion of colouring matter. The quill red bark of the Indian plantations is a fair drug, some of it yielding 5 to 10 per cent. of alkaloids, more than a third of which is quinine, a fourth chinchonidine, and the remainder chinchonine and quininedine. The Pitayo bark is very valuable: it is the chief source of quininedine.

In their native habitat the chinchona trees all grow at a height of from 2500 to 9000 feet above the level of the sea, and in an equable but comparatively cool climate. High temperature, we learn, favours the formation of chinchonidine, and diminishes that of quinine. Deprivation of light favours the increase of the total amount of alkaloids in a bark. Mr. Broughton, the moment he guessed at this law, made a very beautiful experiment. He covered the stem of a chinchona tree with a shield of tinned plate, and the stem of another with black cloth; his object being to keep the bark in darkness without impeding the free access of air, or protecting it from the heating influence of the sun's rays. The results were that, after ten months' protection in this way, the amount of the total alkaloids was increased about 2.8 per cent. in each case; and Mr. MacIvor's experiments in the same direction have conclusively proved that bark renewed under moss contains a larger amount of total and crystallisable alkaloids than ordinary bark. This has given rise to the now widely accepted "mossing" system, of which we shall speak in detail under the next head.

Luckily for the multiplication of the plants, the most valuable species of chinchona are with strict care and attention easily developed from cuttings. This is especially true of *C. calisaya* and *C. succirubra*, both fruitful in quinine; and under due adjustment of heat, light, and moisture, can in this respect be depended on. Stock plants are therefore established from which cuttings can be taken. The quality of which Dr. Lindley speaks in the following passage is thus found powerfully present in the chinchonas :—

"It is known," he says, "that plants possess some quality analogous to animal irritability, to which, for want of a better, the name of excitability has been given. In proportion to the amount of excitability in a given plant is the power which its cuttings possess of striking. The great promoter of vegetable excitability is heat. Therefore the more heat a given plant has been exposed to, within certain limits, the more readily its cuttings strike root." "The young wood," he says, "of trees growing in the open air will not do for cuttings; and yet if these same trees are forced in a hothouse, their cuttings are almost sure to succeed."

In all other parts of the tree the amount of alkaloids is insignificant compared with the bark, as that is really the only place of deposit of the alkaloids from the sap; and the fact of this deposit is mainly due, according to the great German chemist, Herr Flückiger, to a peculiarity in the formation of the *liber*. Some species of the trees differ from others in respect of their habitat in relation to genuine producing capability: crown barks are adapted to a higher elevation and red to a lower, as in their native habitat. For some members of the *Calisaya* family a great elevation is essential. Some of these planted at an elevation of 7300 feet above the sea seem to have adopted a more luxurious habit than some at lower elevations. Mr. Howard, indeed, declares it a useless attempt to cultivate these trees below 4000 feet above the sea-level. The *Officinalis* species, which stands high for its yield, is also one of the most hardy, and a peculiar observation has been made on this species. In the third generation a sort of *atavism* is to be noticed, the produce having returned almost exactly to the first, and having on the Neilgherries of India rather surpassed the quantity of alkaloid yielded by the first generation on the mountains of Uritusinga, its native habitat. Mr. Frècul, a French chemist, discovered that when isolated each of the two fundamental parts of the branch may give rise to the production of either wood or bark; and certainly one of the most instructive and interesting of the very beautiful and carefully executed coloured illustrations in Mr. Howard's book of the various barks is that of the third crop of renewed bark and its junction with the old bark.

III. Cultivation in India.

We have already done something to recount the difficulties and perils which were encountered in exploring the remote mountain forests of Ecuador, Huanco, and Caravaya; we now come to speak specially of the methods resorted to, and the various measures for the successful naturalisation and culture of the tree in India. The Neilgherry Hills, in the Madras Presidency, was selected as the most suitable locality for the first experi-

ments. These hills, most readers will remember, lie
between the eleventh and twelfth parallels of north latitude, and run out in an eastern direction from the plains
of Coimbatore from the chain of the Western Ghauts,
and may be regarded as a gigantic spur of that vast
range. The crest of the Neilgherries is not by any
means a flat plateau. It consists rather of a series of
green undulating hills, with ravines here and there,
usually very well wooded and well watered. The elevation of this upper region ranges from 6000 to 7000 feet
above the sea-level, and enjoys a climate cool and exhi-
larating. The thermometer ranges from about 42° to a
little under 70°. In the central portion of the plateau
the rainfall, as we learn, averages about 60 inches, but
on the western side it is heavier, and the air during a
great portion of the year is constantly moist. The soil
is very fertile, and abundantly produces European fruits,
cereals, and vegetables, as well as tea and coffee.

In selecting sites for chinchona plantations, due attention was paid to the requirements of the plants in the
matter of elevation—the facts as to different needs in
this respect in different species being as we have already
noted. Two localities were accordingly chosen : one a
little under 8000 feet on Dodabetta, near Ootacamund,
and another at an elevation under 6000 feet at a place
called Neddiwattum, on the north-western side of the
range. The Dodabetta site was set apart for the growth
of the crown barks, while that at Neddiwattum was
devoted to the red, yellow, and grey barks. The chinchona plants and seeds, as they arrived from South
America, were placed in the hands of Mr. M'Ivor, the

Superintendent of the Neilgherry Botanical Gardens. As it was felt advisable to multiply the chinchonas quickly, both practical plans of propagation were had recourse to by seed and by cuttings. By great care and skill not only were the plantations at Dodabetta and Neddiwattum rapidly stocked, but others were before long opened at Pykarah and Mailkhoondah. Private individuals also entered the field about the same time, and chinchona-planting was for some years regarded as a most promising investment.

But the special risks and the slowness of return, which we have already referred to, led to most of the planters abandoning it. Meanwhile the Government, slow to move, but fortunately also slow to retreat from a scheme once set in progress, determined to carry the work to a successful issue. The results have been satisfactory beyond the most sanguine expectations. At the close of the official year 1872–73 there were 1,170,029 chinchona trees of various ages on the Government estates, cover-ing an area of 1222 acres, on which the expenditure up to that date had been a little under £65,000. This gives a mean cost of about £53 per acre, and against this, of course, has to be set the value of bark utilised in India for the manufacture of alkaloids, and of consignments sold in London. During the period which has elapsed since that stock-taking, progress has been equally steady, and there are now several million trees in culture.

In spite of the ascertained drawback in chinchona culture as regards speedy commercial result, it needs to be stated, with all emphasis, that some gentlemen, whose names deserve to be held in honour, did not fail bravely to face loss of time and fortune in their efforts to naturalise the plants in various parts of India. Among these Colonel Nassau Lees stands prominent. In his plantations in the Kangra Valley chinchona had an extended and patient trial. Colonel Lees threw much spirit into his efforts to introduce the plant. From Java, Ceylon, and the Neilgherries he provided himself with seeds or seedlings of all the leading species, and he imported from Scotland a trained gardener to superintend the cultivation. He was also supplied by Mr. Markham with seeds of *C. pitayensis*, a species which thrives well at high altitudes on the Andes, and which it was hoped would thrive in the comparatively severe climate of the Kangra Valley. For some time the prospects of success seemed moderately hopeful, but ultimately the majority of the plants succumbed to frost. The results were almost identical in the North-West Provinces.

IV. Methods of Barking and Preparation in India.

By scientific men, and those who had at an early stage interested themselves in chinchona culture, it had for years been strongly felt that the extraordinary recklessness of the Peruvian bark-collectors must eventually greatly lessen the supply to be obtained. Indeed it was seen, as we have already said, that there was a great risk that at any moment the price might suddenly be raised to such a point as would render quinine beyond the reach of the great mass of the poor, more particularly in certain parts of India, where it is almost essential to life.

The Peruvian bark-hunters thought only of present gain, and cared nothing for the future. They therefore stripped the trees standing; and the consequence was that as soon as they were deprived of their bark they were attacked by myriads of insects, which penetrated the stems and soon killed the trees. Their practice, therefore, involved the destruction of each tree felled for its bark, and no measures were ever taken by the owners of either public or private forests to secure supplies by any conservancy or re-planting. When the cascarilleros came upon a tree which had accidentally been thrown down, so great was their carelessness that they would actually strip the upper side of its bark, and then, rather than take the trouble to turn over the trunk, they would leave it to rot in the ground, and pass on to supplies which they could procure with even less exertion. Under this method it was inevitable that the area of supply would in course of time, at the best, become narrowed. The consumption of bark in Europe and the East went on steadily increasing, and as a natural result prices rose, and fears even began to be entertained that the supply would ultimately fail alto-gether. This was the fear involving so much to the whole world, which formed the spur that impelled the noble men, whose doings and sufferings we have very faintly outlined, to secure at all hazards seeds and plants from which, in favourable soil and climate, a supply might be insured independently of the native region of the tree. The same consideration weighed with the cultivators in India, who soon, by thought and experiment, discovered more economical and scientific methods of barking and after-manufacture.

In this they had ceased to follow the good example set them by the Jesuits, and it should be said in fairness that so long as the Jesuits had influence and power, wise consideration was paid to conserving the trees. The Jesuits even enlisted superstition on their behalf in this matter. Mr. Ledger, whose acquaintance with the Peruvian chinchona forests is very intimate, and who, on various visits, dwelt for long periods in the country, closely studying the people as well as its botany, natural history, and trade, in a letter to Mr. J. E. Howard, writes :—

"Whenever bark trees were cut down or 'stripped,' not a particle of the smallest branch was lost. Moreover, they imposed the moral obligation, appealing to the superstition of the Indians, thereby compelling the cascarilleros or 'cutters' to plant five cuttings in the shape of a cross ·.·· for every tree destroyed. I have repeatedly seen these plantations: always, when passing them, my Indians would go down on their knees, hat in hand, cross themselves, and say a prayer for the souls of the 'Buenos Padres.'"

At first the method employed in India for barking was to cut down the tree very near the ground, precisely as is done in ash or withy coppices in England. If this was carefully done, a rapid growth of young wood immediately sprang up, and in the course of five or six years the saplings were ready to be felled again. This was called coppicing, and in some circumstances may still be found advisable, and practised in circumstances where, as Dr. Bidie, a good authority, has said, firewood is a desideratum, but Mr. Howard very decidedly declares against coppicing in ordinary circumstances.

Another method, more economical and more efficient in every respect, is now in use. This method permits the bark to be removed periodically without cutting down the tree ; and, indeed, by a very simple device, draws precisely the chemical elements that are wanted more liberally into the bark. This is the " mossing process," and we are sure that our readers will be interested in the account of a method so simple, and so admirably calculated to secure the end sought by very slight means. Though we have not ourselves seen it, our account is drawn from varied reliable sources. Mr. M'Ivor, with whom the idea originated, tells us that in this, as in so many other beautiful processes of culture, man only follows a hint of nature. His idea of artificially applying moss to the bark of chinchona plants originated in the fact that the best chinchona bark of commerce is invariably overgrown with moss (or lichen).

About a year or eighteen months before the bark is ready for removal, the trunk of the tree is covered with a thick layer of common tree moss, collected in the neighbouring forests. It is fixed in position with twisted bark till it grows and becomes attached by natural adhesion to the tree. When the eighteen months have expired the bark is thus removed. The workers are divided into gangs of five men each—two *barkers*, two *mossers*, and a man to split and roll up bast into balls. The first operation is the removal of the covering of moss, which is very carefully treated with the view of being used again. The barkers then, with their pruning knives, remove the bark in longitudinal strips, from 2 to $2\frac{1}{2}$ inches wide, and from a point as high up as they can conveniently reach. Between every two of these strips a portion of bark of the same width is left to carry on the circulation, &c., as the tree would die if completely denuded of so large a portion of its protective covering. When the bark has been removed it is found that the surface of the wood is covered with a gelatinous-like substance, the cambium of botanists. This consists of young cells from which future additions to the bark and wood are derived.

The greatest care is taken to avoid inflicting any injury on this, as it is found that a denuded surface is very slowly and imperfectly renewed. When carefully preserved, however, the gaps in the bark are perfectly filled up.

As soon as the barkers have finished their task the mossers begin their work. This consists in re-applying a thick covering of moist moss to the trunk, which afterwards is carefully and continually kept moist. A good authority has given this account of the process :—

"At certain seasons of the year the bark can be separated from the tree with great ease. It is accomplished in this way. A labourer proceeds to a tree, and, reaching up as far as he can, makes a horizontal incision of the required width. From either end of this incision he runs a vertical incision to the ground. Then, carefully raising with the knife the bark at the horizontal incision until he can seize it with his fingers, he strips off the bark to the ground and cuts it off. The strip of bark then presents the appearance of a ribbon more or less long. Supposing the tree to be of 28 inches in circumference, the labourer will take nine of the above ribbons, each 1½ inches wide. He will thus leave, after the tree has been stripped, other nine ribbons still adhering to the tree, each somewhat broader than the stripped ribbon and at intervals apart, occupied by the spaces to which the stripped ribbons have adhered. As soon as he has removed his strips, the labourer will proceed to moss the trunk all round, tying on the moss with some fibre. The decorticated intervals will thus be excluded from light and air; and this is one of the capital points in the system. The mere exclusion of light and air from a stem partially bared acts in two ways: it enables the healing process to be rapidly set up in the same way as plaster does in the case of a wound in an animal organism; and it has the further curious effect—it increases the secretion of quinine in the bark renewed under its protection. At the end of six months or more, the bands of bark left untouched at the first stripping are removed, and the intervals they occupied on the trunk are mossed. At the end of twenty months, on an average, the spaces occupied by the ribbons originally taken off are found to be covered with renewed bark much thicker than the natural bark of the same age, and this renewed bark can be removed, and a fresh renewal again be fostered by the moss."

On being taken from the trees the bark is laid to dry in rough sheds fitted up with open shelves made of split bamboo. These sheds are erected in any convenient place near the spot where the trees are being cut. When the bark has dried as far as is possible without artificial heat it is carried off to the drying-house, a masonry building (near the factory) fitted up with shelving and supplied with arrangements for keeping charcoal fires lit. If the drying-house be kept well closed the bark is speedily and thoroughly dried, and without being exposed to a temperature high enough to affect its chemical constitution. When well dried, it can be stored without danger of deterioration.

In his report to the Government of Madras, Mr. Markham had directed the special attention of Government to the importance of finding out as soon as possible the best way of dealing with the anticipated produce of the Government plantations, so as to secure the avowed object of Government in undertaking the cultivation at all. Had pecuniary profit been that object, it would probably have been best secured by arranging to send the bark to England for sale, and by continuing to purchase quinine in the usual way, trusting to reduce its price by increasing the supply of bark. But it is extremely doubtful whether, under such an arrangement, a cheap febrifuge would ever have been brought within the reach of fever patients so poor as the agricultural population of India, a population who, for ages accustomed to look on oft-recurring fever as part of their fate, have become too apathetic to be prepared to pay much for relief from it. The object of Government is that an efficient febrifuge shall be available by purchase in every corner of India, that it shall become part of the stock-in-trade of every village shopkeeper, and that it shall be purchasable at not more than a rupee an ounce. At the period in question quinine was available by purchase only in a few of the larger towns where there is a European population, and even in such places it costs from six to ten rupees an ounce. It was, of course, supplied to all Government dispensaries, but only to a limited extent, the supply for a year being, as a rule, really equal to the actual demands for a few days. The dispensing of so costly and scarce a drug gave rise, it was believed, to much sharp practice among the lower officials at dispensaries and hospitals, and a doze of the coveted febrifuge was probably, as a rule, unattainable to the very poorest of the patients. Mr. Markham suggested that, instead of sending the bark to England to be sold, a febrifuge should be prepared from it at the Government plantations which should contain the alkaloids in a rough form, and should be saleable at a cheap rate. He recommended the preparation called quinium, a product which (while an effectual febrifuge) would not be bought up by speculators as a source of quinine, it being unsaleable for manufacturing purposes. Quinium is made by treating pounded bark with slaked lime, and the resulting lime product with alcohol. Mr. Markham considered that a competent chemist should be got from England and located in the Neilgherries, whose functions should be to work out the whole subject of Indian quinology. His recommendation coincided with others which had been made to the same effect, and was subsequently strengthened by the verdict of the Alkaloid Commissions. In October 1866, Mr. John Broughton, then Dr. Franklin's assistant at the Royal Institution, London, was appointed. The results of his researches and efforts were valuable.

c

V. Preparation of Alkaloids, &c.

One of the most improved and widely accepted methods of manufacturing the chinchona alkaloids consists in precipitating the alkaloids in an insoluble state, and subsequently separating them from the mass of impurities with which they are mixed by solution in alcohol. Mr. Broughton thus describes the process adopted by him, and followed with the greatest success:—

"The bark, in long strips, exactly as taken from the tree, is placed in a copper pan with $1\frac{1}{2}$ per cent. of sulphuric acid for *trunk bark*, and about 1 per cent. or less for *prunings*, and a quantity of water that has already been used for the fourth extraction of nearly spent bark, and is boiled for an hour. The liquid and bark are then separated by strong pressure in a screw-press, the former falling in a wooden vat placed underneath. The squeezed and nearly dry bark is again boiled with liquid that has been used for a third boiling of other bark, and another half per cent. of acid is added. After an hour's boiling, it is again squeezed. It is then boiled with a liquid that has come off nearly-spent bark, again squeezed, and finally boiled with water. During these four boilings, the bark after each squeezing diminishes greatly in bulk, and becomes almost pulp, so that it occupies far less room in a pan at the third boiling than it did at first. The order in which the several liquids used in extraction are employed depend on the qualities of bark under manufacture; but it is so arranged as to obtain finally a liquid containing as much alkaloid as possible in solution; and also, that as far as possible the bark should be

exhausted of alkaloid. The liquid is now evaporated to
about one-sixth of its bulk and allowed to cool. It is
then decomposed by neutralisation with lime, which pre-
cipitates the alkaloids, decomposing the quino-tannates
and sulphates with formation of insoluble lime-salts. The
powdered lime-precipitate is then packed in an ingenious
inverted cone-like vessel, with a receiving vessel below it.
Alcohol is poured on till, by passing through the precipitate, the lower vessel is about third full. A fire is kept
up to certain heat under the lower vessels. By the skilful
use of copper condensers, &c., the vapour rises and becomes liquid; and this process is kept up till a small
amount of alcohol, by constant circulation, has dissolved
the whole of the chinchona basis without any waste of
spirit or alkaloid."

VI. Amorphous Quinine, &c.

The chinchona industry in India was instituted with
the avowed object of providing at a cheap rate an abundant supply of a remedy for fever, the great scourge of
the people of India. So far this object has been attained. So long ago as 1859, the Quinologist sent to
the Medical Department of Madras, for trial in hospitals,
a preparation of the plantation barks, which has since
been known locally as Amorphous Quinine. This name
is not very appropriate, as the substance so designated
does not consist of quinine only, but contains the several
alkaloids, in the exact proportions in which they occur
naturally in the bark. The term mixed or amorphous
alkaloids would therefore have more properly indicated

the chemical character of the preparation, but the other was adopted in deference to the prejudices of the native population, as they were to some extent already familiar with the properties of quinine.

The substance known as amorphous quinine is prepared by a very simple process, is supplied at a moderate cost, and furnishes the active principles of the bark in a state of sufficient purity for all ordinary medical purposes. As furnished to the hospitals, the preparation is a greyish powder with a bitter taste, really insoluble in water, but rendered quite soluble by the addition of a little acid. With the view of thoroughly testing its power as a febrifuge, supplies of it have from time to time been sent to civil hospitals in the most feverish districts of the country, and the results have invariably been highly gratifying. It is not for a moment asserted that it is quite equal to the European-made crystallised preparations of the alkaloids, but then the cost of the latter has hitherto been such as to place them quite beyond the reach of the lower classes of the population of India.

And quite recently a great step has been made, as we believe, in the extraction from the bark by the heads of the plantations at Sikkim. At first the *Succirubra*, or red-bark tree, was planted there almost exclusively, but of recent years these have given place to *Calisaya*, to the extent of about a million trees, as it was found that, though the red bark contained a comparatively small portion of quinine, with large proportions of chinchonidine and chinchonine, it was more difficult to extract the alkaloids from it, and that the yellow bark, or *Calisaya*, could be more economically dealt with in this respect, and dealt with on the spot, instead of being sent away. Experiment in the hands of Dr. King and Mr. Gammie, the superintendent there, has led to the discovery of a pro-cess of extraction by means of stirring the powdered bark in a fluid which contains fusel oil and kerosine oil, with a small proportion of caustic soda or lime, when either sulphate of quinine or chinchona febrifuge can be ob-tained by varying the after-process. This promises to be one of the greatest steps in the development of a cheap and steady supply of the chinchona alkaloids which has yet been made, and we can only wish it suc-cess and general application.

So important to us does this discovery seem in view of a cheap and steady supply of quinine that we must find space for Mr. Gammie's clear and beautiful descrip-tion of the process included in a report made last year to the Government on the condition of the quinine production :—

" 1. In order that the oil may speedily and effectually act on the chinchona bark, the latter is reduced to a very fine powder by means of Carter's Disintegrator; and to get the powder of a uniform fineness, it is passed through a scalper, which is a machine commonly used for sifting flour. The scalper is in the form of a box enclosing a sloping, six-sided, revolving chamber, covered with silk of 120 threads to the lineal inch. It is driven at the speed of about thirty revolutions to the minute. Any particles of the powder which may be too coarse to pass through the silk meshes drop out at the lower end of the revolving chamber and are again passed through the Disintegrator.

" 2. A hundred parts of the finely-powdered bark are then set aside to be mixed with 8 parts of commercial caustic soda, 500 parts of water, and 600 parts of mixture composed of one part of fusel oil to four parts kerosine oil. If the caustic soda be of inferior quality, a little slaked lime (about 5 parts) may be used in addition to the eight parts of caustic soda; or caustic soda may be altogether omitted, and 15 parts of slaked lime may be used instead of it. The caustic soda is dissolved in the water and mixed with the bark. Then the oil is added, and the whole is kept thoroughly intermixed in an agitating vessel. Should lime be used, it is mixed in fine powder with the dry bark before adding the water and oil.

" 3. The agitating vessels in use at Mungpoo are barrels with winged stirrers revolving in them vertically, and with taps on the sides for drawing off the fluids. The first stirring is carried on for four hours, and then the whole is allowed to rest quietly in order that the oil may separate out to the top of the watery fluid. When the oil, which has now taken up the greater part of the alkaloids, has cleared out, it is drawn off by a tap placed just above the junction of the two fluids. The oil is then transferred to another agitator, and is there thoroughly intermixed with acidulated water for five or ten minutes, the mixture being again allowed to rest for the separation of the oil. It will now be found (if sufficient acid has been used and the stirring has been thorough) that the alkaloids have been removed from the oil to the acidulated liquor. The oil is again transferred to the bark mixture, and is kept intermixed with it for two

or three hours; the oil is again drawn off in the same
way, washed as before in the same acidulated liquor;
and this process is repeated a third or a fourth time, or
until it is found, by testing a small quantity of the oil,
that the bark has been thoroughly exhausted of its
alkaloids. Each stirring subsequent to the second, need
not be continued for more than an hour. The quantity
of acid required to take up the alkaloids from the oil
will entirely depend on the quality of the bark operated
on. If the bark contains 4 per cent. of alkaloids, about
2 lbs. of either sulphuric or muriatic acid mixed in
twenty gallons of water should be sufficient, and so on
in proportion.

"4. The after-treatment of the acidulated water containing the alkaloids depends on the product desired,
and on the kind of acid that has been used. Should
sulphate of quinine be desired and sulphuric acid have
been used, the liquor is filtered (if necessary), heated
and made neutral by adding a very weak solution of
either caustic soda or liquor ammonia. It is then
allowed to cool, and as it cools the crystals form out.
These crystals are afterwards separated from the mother
liquor by draining through a cloth filter. After they
have been thus obtained, the crystals are dried. They
are next dissolved in about fifty times their weight of
boiling water. The resulting liquor is filtered hot through
a little animal charcoal. On cooling after filtration the
crystals again form out, and they are separated as before
from the mother liquor by filtration through a cloth.
The crystalline mass obtained by filtration is then placed
in small lumps on sheets of white blotting paper stretched

on slabs of plaster of Paris. By this means they are practically dried. They are afterwards thoroughly dried by being laid on blotting paper in a room heated to about 10 degrees above the temperature of the open air.

" 5. If chinchona febrifuge is wanted, the alkaloids are exhausted from the oil by muriatic acid, the solution being neutralised and filtered in the same way. On an excess of caustic soda solution being added, the alkaloids are precipitated. After standing some hours the whole bulk of liquor and precipitate is passed through cloth filters; and when the alkaline liquor has drained off, the precipitate is washed with a little plain water, dried, and powdered. The powder is chinchona febrifuge ready for use."

So far, then, the benevolent object for which the chinchonas were introduced has been attained—a benevolent object, for the Government of India has always repudiated the idea of wishing to make quinine a source of profit, but only a means of obtaining for its subjects a full and cheap supply of a valued specific. There are several million trees growing luxuriantly on the government estates, and a process in operation by which a cheap and efficient preparation of the bark may be supplied to the fever-stricken masses. It may safely be said that at least 60 per cent. of the deaths once resulting from fever in India are now prevented by the extensive use of this valuable febrifuge.

The extension of chinchona plantations is confined almost entirely to the Government enterprise. Private efforts have not been successful to any great extent. In Ceylon, over large spaces, the quinine-bearing trees have of late years been rooted up to make room for tea and coffee, because of the quicker and far greater return derived from these wherever the soil and climate are found suitable.

And chemistry promises at length to supply a substitute—at least so far as the heat-reducing powers in fever are concerned—in some of the anti-febrine elements derived from the wonderful coal-tar substances. How far the medical profession will find these in every respect potent to replace quinine as a febrifuge, time will tell. Some say that the coal-tar anti-febrines have all the specific action on the constitution which quinine has, without inducing the headaches and swimmingness certainly in some constitutions induced by its large or continuous prescription. But the interest of quinine and its story remains; and for India and the East, at all events for a long time, quinine is likely to hold an important place.

II.

CURIOSITIES OF CANARY CULTURE.

I. Origin of Canaries.

It is a great thing with those who pique themselves on race and breeding to say that they "came over with the Conqueror." The canary-birds can claim a considerable antiquity, and also came over with the Conqueror, though not Norman William. The first hint that can be found in Europe of the forbears of our yellow favourites, who "discourse sweet music" to us winter and summer alike, is in Spain, where we are told that in 1478 some specimens were brought by Henry the Navigator, on his return from one of his voyages, during which he had landed at the Canary Islands. Though very unlike most of the canaries we now see in cages (for in colour they rather resembled the linnet, a grey shading into green on the breast), they soon were sought after for their song, and high prices were paid for them by the Spanish doñas. The Spanish bird-fanciers soon began to breed from them ; and as only the cocks, or singing-birds, were for some time brought to Europe, they now and then conveyed some of the cocks to the Canary Islands, to act as decoys for the female birds. It is said that these travelled birds were very healthy.

The Spaniards were carefully reticent about their Canary song-bird, and for a long period canaries were to be had only from Spain at high prices.

The birds were found pretty widely distributed in the Canary Islands; but they were met with in greatest numbers in the western mountainous parts, the thickly-wooded localities that abound on that side being especially suited to their mode of life. They were never found on the mainland, but were met with scattered over the Azores, and in still more limited numbers in the Madeiras.

The first writer of any note who made mention of the canary-birds was Gessner, in 1555. He called them *Canariam Aviculam*, also translated sugar-birds, and praised highly their very lovely song. Later on (in 1599–1609) Aldrovandi wrote upon them, and in 1622 Olina likewise wrote a work about them, which was published at Rome. Olina recounts that a Spanish ship, with thousands of canary-birds on board, bound for Leghorn, was wrecked on the Italian coast, and that many of the birds that gained freedom fled to the island of Elba. The climate agreed with them there, and they increased rapidly, but soon began to be so eagerly sought for that they were exterminated there. Up till this time the Spaniards had kept secret their methods of breeding and training the bird; and though a considerable trade in canaries had sprung up, the prices, especially for good specimens, were still very high. But now the Italians obtained numerous specimens of the bird from Elba, and applied themselves to breeding and training him, and, not being so exclusive as the Spaniards, the canary-birds of Italy quickly spread to the north—first to the Tyrol and then to Germany.

It was in the Tyrol that the canary found the most eager and appreciative welcome; and in the market-town, Imst, in Oberimthal, where there was a considerable community of miners, there was developed such skill in breeding and training that it soon became the centre of the traffic. Spindler says that many circumstances united to produce this result. First of all, the Oberimthalers had the rarest tact and patience, as well as a love for the little feathered folk; and next, they were very fond of wandering abroad and turning an honest penny, which they could do in the sale of the yellow favourite.

Trade-clubs, or companies, as we would say nowadays, were formed to develop the canary culture, and completely to organise the traffic. Every member contributed from 70 to 100 ducats, and the sum-total was spent in procuring from all parts—from Germany and Switzerland as well as from Italy—the very finest specimens of young birds for instruction and training. When these had been trained, at a certain date, somewhere between the second and the tenth of August, the bird-dealers took their departure to different parts, with their precious burdens on their shoulders. The event was celebrated by a festival, after which the procession set forth with the chaplain's blessing, and with musical accompaniment, till at a certain station the roads separated, when each group went on its own way, to divide still more farther on.

A very picturesque sight the procession must have

been. The guild, in their own costume, which consisted of blue and richly braided jackets, the breast ornamented with silver buttons; short leather hose, with sewn devices; red scarf round the body, and green hat on the head. On his shoulders each man bore the feathered burden in a basket of peculiar form, suited to the purpose; and at their head marched the far-travelled leader, begirt with a sash adorned with peacocks' feathers, and his travelling stick decorated with ivy and flowers, as a sign of his special dignity.

The fearless wanderers not only traversed the whole of the German kingdom, but also Holland, Belgium, France, and Russia; indeed Turkey, Armenia, and Syria were in great part visited by these enterprising bird-rearers.

For nearly a century this went on; and if in Imst the highest possible song-powers of the bird were not developed, much was done to increase his beauty of form, of plumage, of colour, though as yet, it must be confessed, our familiar yellow bird was not in existence. That was a work of time and care, and illustrates well Mr. Darwin's doctrine of selection, as we shall soon see.

Often the adventurous and enterprising bird-sellers came back with a good return, but the results were not uniform. There were bad years as well as good years. The year 1740, we learn, was a particularly good canary year. But owing to causes which we cannot enter into here, the mining at Imst altogether failed, and bad years almost ruined the bird trade. The consequence was that the centre of the canary trade was transferred by the removal of the bird trainers to St. Andreasberg in the Harz, which still holds its pre-eminence in this respect, though the title of the Tyrolese bird, still often given to the canary, tells that the earlier efforts at Imst have produced their own effect. But the Oberimthalers, while they remained at Imst, gave precedence to development of colour and form over singing in their training. The most gifted birds were, of course, taught to pipe and whistle, and sing songs, and play tricks; but the bird's proper song remained more or less a secondary thing. The excellence of the canary, in their view, lay in his being a chamber ornament or toy. Portraits exist to bear this out. On the Sunday reception of women of position the bird was perched on the right hand when visitors were received, and women who wished to be of importance had their portraits taken in this manner; and it belonged to good manners to make inquiry after the health of the yellow darling, and to bring him a little bit of sugar.

II. Culture and Training.

The original colour of the birds, as we have said, was grey, merging into green beneath, somewhat resembling the colours of the linnet; but by various devices, intermixture with other birds among them, canaries are now to be met with of various colours, and in almost every degree of shade and combination, and thus presenting innumerable differences. With regard to the yellow colour and its testimony to Mr. Darwin's theory of selection, it is said that after domestication in Belgium, Germany, and England, the birds threw upon the feathers small patches of yellow or lighter colour, and by carefully matching those birds that bore the largest number of these spots, they at length obtained bright and uniform colour, more closely resembling those of pure yellow, called " clear " birds in the present day. But the application of the phrase " canary colour," to indicate a special shade of yellow, though general, is not justified by the facts. Canaries of pure breed are to be found of many colours ; whole breeds are green ; and, by feeding on pepper and other seeds, canaries have been produced of cinnamon and coffee colour, and even of red ; and, in the very beautiful Lizard variety, the bird, though yellow in the crown, is elsewhere shaded and spangled in the most lovely manner.

From the Tyrolese bird, the Teutonic people—the Dutch, the English, and the Germans—have created three quite distinct breeds. The Dutch altered principally the figure ; the English principally the colour ; and the Germans especially developed the capacity for song.

(1.) *The Dutch Canary.*—The Dutch canary, as we now see him, is a yellow bird, with a little head, and a dull expression of face. He remains very slender in the bones, and is from six to seven inches high, thus certainly a third higher than the German canary. He is plentifully provided with tuft of feathers, and possesses a specially grotesque plumage, the breast and back feathers being very long and peculiarly curled. In like manner open feathers grow in a straight line from throat to breast, and this is called *jabot.* The feathers on the shoulders are strongly erect and curled, and are called epaulettes. If the epaulettes are very strongly developed the bird is called *Prompeter.* If the feathers of the breast are also very strongly developed, and form a neck ruff, then the birds are advanced to the title of Lord Mayor. The French appear to have especially liked these Dutch canaries, for they have further bred and developed them. From this circumstance they were extensively named Parisian canaries.

(2.) *The Belgian Canary.*—The so-called Belgian or Brussels canaries are a small variety of the Dutch, with close plumage and peculiarly arched back, which is named cat's-back. They have thereby a pronounced comic air, and the popular voice significantly calls them "undertakers." By breeding together those of the greatest length and with certain conformation of neck and shoulder, something almost approaching to deformity has been reached, which with the fanciers is accounted beauty.

(3.) *English Canary.*—The English adopted the Belgians, and have bred them up still further and characteristically, but without the cat's-back. The colour is bright gold-yellow; the head is like a snake's, flat, broad, and angular. The shoulders are quite erect—the chief point consists in the silk-like texture of the feathers. They are considered to be the most elegant of all birds. The most incredible alterations on the original bird have now taken place in England. Here they have bred birds which no novice would any longer take for a canary. The Dutch breeders devoted their attention to the alteration of the form and special points of plumage, but still retained the yellow colour, while the English, together with alterations in the form, have dealt with the feather peculiarity. Birds double as large as a German canary have been produced in England, the honours as to size having been carried off by a famous Manchester breed ; and by means of feeding on pepper and other seeds, &c., birds of different hues—copper, gold-yellow, brown, green, and even of red colour—having been produced. There are some birds with such strong tufts of feathers that the eyes are covered over. The Norwich crested variety looks almost as though it wore a cowl or cap. Other families are formed like the swallow, with almost regular black spots on the olive-green back, and these are named lizards. We shall refer to the more famous English breeds under another heading. There are such varieties of pretty cross-breeds that it is beyond our space even to name them here. It indicates the extent of the business that there exist societies of breeders in London and Manchester which issue periodical journals.

(4.) *The German Canary.*—But, while honour must be done to the Dutch, Belgians, and English for their remarkable achievements in modifying and perfecting form and feathers in the canary, to the Germans, particularly to the people at St. Andreasberg in the Harz, belongs the credit of studying the song-qualities of the bird as well as its imitative powers, and of developing them to the highest pitch. The musical endowment of the canary and his wonderfully melodious note-organ mostly attracted and captivated them. It is true that the Dutch and English coloured birds sing also ; but their twitterings can hardly be compared to the songs of the Hartzers. Bull-finches and gold-finches had for long been kept by the St. Andreasbergers. In the spring those who had leisure would wander for days in

D

the woods listening to the songs of the finches, and after much thought and concern, would spend further days in catching those with the best and fullest notes. The liking for thrushes, too, was great among them. Almost before the door of every house there hung a thrush in wicker cage. But the finches had become the great favourites. He who did not have his finch was thought to be worth nothing, and the poorest people would often strain and save till they were able to give four or five dollars for a good specimen. It was difficult to subdue this liking for finches and thrushes, and the canary-breeders at first had certainly a difficult task in hand from this propensity of their neighbours. For every singing-bird, and more especially the canary-bird, is attentive to strange song. But it was not well that the nobler singer should run the risk of hearing the loud-sounding *shaff, shaff* of the finch; and therefore canary-birds could not well be trained near finches. The German canaries have, therefore, not reached their perfection of song without great effort and pains. Nearly every hour of the day was devoted to the birds by the trainers. From September onward, indeed, the trainer did not leave the chamber where the birds were night nor day.

Out of every disadvantage profit is born to perseverance and skill. The canary-trainers learned, from the presence of other song-birds, to isolate their birds more and more; and in this isolation they were led to a closer and more thorough study of individual character and temperament, and thus learned some of the secrets of the craft which for so long a period has made them pre-eminent in their strange industry. They found out, not only how to guard their birds from coarser notes, but how to inspire them to higher efforts by emulation and the force of trained example, and by the use of darkened bowers or boxes during a special period of confinement, in which the trainer is seldom, as we have seen, for an hour absent from them, night or day.

The method of training thus developed deserves a somewhat more detailed explanation. First, as soon as the young birds are independent and can be taken out of the nest, they are brought into a flying-room in order that they may have free-play and exercise, to strengthen the body and to widen the chest. After the moulting, which the bird easily overcomes, as he only changes the down feathers and not the quill feathers, the song-passion becomes stronger. The music-leader several times a day exercises the young birds. They sit quiet, close beside each other in a row on the poles, and listen intently. Then they break forth and exercise their throats —each intent only on himself and his own study. At first, of course, the voice is awkward and harsh, but a little of this exercise makes the single tone clear and well heard. They soon become bolder, and try to increase their *repertoire.* The quieter the birds remain when sitting, the more profitably they exercise, and so much more promising, of course, is the after-training.

But the disposition of individuals is very various, and needs close study. Any birds with bad voices or bad inclinations must now be removed, as there is danger of their infecting others with the same fault. Now the bird inclines to wax strong and violent in voice ; but the aim of the Harz trainers is to get a low, soft note. At this point the little students are separated, and put each into a cage by itself. At first the narrow space appears to surprise and be painful to the bird, hitherto accustomed to a free flight; but their pliant nature soon adapts itself to the new circumstances, and they exhibit increased zeal for learning. Their perseverance is remarkable. There is even something touching to see how they will set themselves again and again to master a difficult song, until they finally succeed with it, and then with pride they repeat and repeat it. A certain amount of darkness is felt to be desirable for them. The birds are now placed so that they hear but do not see one another, as this is found to enable the learner more fully to concentrate his powers on the one song. This darkening has been for fifty years recognised by the St. Andreasberg trainers as an indispensable means of attaining the best result—a quiet, soft, continuous song. Without this help we would not to-day possess such perfect performances from the canary. The nightingale, as every one knows, sings her sorrowful lays "more musical, more melancholy," in the darkness of the night, or in the mild twilight of the moonshine, while her song by day appears unrestful, shorter, and more broken up and disconnected.

And it is not necessary to commiserate the birds in their twilight homes or darkened bowers; they keep very well, and recompense the care spent upon them by their song, which is also an expression of bodily satisfaction. The song informs us that the little dweller in the dark bower feels cozy. Only exceptionally quiet specimens can bear the full daylight without drawback, and these are proportionately few.   If even the best birds are suddenly or in an imprudent manner placed in the sun, they immediately become louder, the melodiousness is lost, and they begin to shriek or scream.   After the birds have passed through certain stages of training, they are placed in lesser or greater proximity to those of similar endowment, according to the judgment and practice of the trainer.   After Christmas a final decision is formed on the whole ; but, in spite of all the pains, a considerable number remain immature, and of these a certain proportion are sure to fall off at the next moulting. The most excellent of the after-breed the trainer, of course, keeps for himself, in order always to improve his stock, and hence the difficulty of procuring a bird of the very highest class.   The German trainers have thus reached their high perfection by careful attention to these points :—(1) Only the singing-birds of purest tone are used in breeding ; (2) the young are most exactingly trained, and (3) by careful feeding with pure oil-seed and judicious introduction of egg-diet ; and (4) the wise use of the dim-light boxes or bowers, by means of which the birds are at the right time effectively guarded against anything foreign or extraneous to the desired song.   The essential elements of this song may be thus described :—

(1.) In soft, delicate trilling and warblings, which have a more chirping, more flute-like, or more hollow-sounding character, and are connected in more or less rapid succession to each other with so-called rolls.   These rolls often resemble deep sounds bursting wave-like from the breast. (2.) In hollow pipes and flutes ; and (3.) in lively tones. The hollower, the deeper, and more melodious the tones—the more sung with the deep throat and closed bill—the more connected, the longer, and more various the song, the more valuable the bird. The deep, soft flute-tones are a very valuable element, and are considered to be especially beautiful when they fall in the height of tone at the end of the song. But the flute-notes, as they fall on the ear, do not belong to the song proper, but represent rather fitting interbreaks and characteristic ornaments. Such birds as are distinguished by these deep, soft flute-tones are called by the Germans "glücken," and also "nachtigallen-schlagen," that is, sweet or nightingale toned. The purity of breed is of the greatest consequence; for one of the most trying obstacles to the trainer are what are called bad *Lock* tones, so-called "adjectives," which are partly original sounds, and represent partly back-strokes in earlier impure breeds.

The throat of the canary is thus a most wonderful organ—perhaps the most wonderful in nature—and not for compass alone, though its compass is great—in some cases three octaves. A great error trainers have often committed is the tendency to make the canary merely imitative. They use for instruction and stimulus bird-organs and roll-pipes. A clumsy, unintelligent exposition is the only result of this. The St. Andreasberg people knew better; and their one great merit is, that they have developed the wonderful performances we marvel at out of the natural song of the bird. The song of wild canaries is still to be heard, so that comparison is possible, and has been made by experts, with this result. Only by their methods could the song, in spite of its high development, have preserved at basis its natural freshness and richness. The young bird has introduced to him nothing that is strange or really artificial, but he sings in the speech of his people—of course selected, and of a high degree in culture. His song thus shows soul and intelligence; it abounds in homely tones; he makes the tone swell up, fall, and swell again and change independently of art. In gloomy weather he sings quietly, low, and plaintive; in sunny weather the song becomes less tranquil, more joyous, penetrating, resonant. Song is the speech of the bird, and they must learn to speak well just as man must learn it.

It is seldom, as we have said, that the trainers will part with the very finest specimens, and only at extraordinary prices. It is the smaller wares alone, as the dealers say, that are offered in the open market; therefore it is that so many persons keep canaries, and yet so few know how a canary ought to and can sing. The very demand for the birds, now extending to America and Australia, has had bad effects upon the training. They are now too much taught in mass, without seclusion or individualisation. The money profit has risen more and more into importance, and the work of training is more and more descending into a trade. St. Andreasberg could not, of course, remain altogether outside this influence, and its effects are already seen there. The superior breeds are getting fewer in numbers, and the ordinary ill-taught ones increase. A good authority says that the only chance for the St. Andreasbergers is to return to their old customs and traditions, or else the St. Andreasberg birds will

speedily be worth no more than other birds. St. Andreasberg has been described as the canary Mecca, which
every lover of the canary must visit once in his lifetime ;
but if it is to maintain its pre-eminence it must in some
measure return to the old ways.   It has some 3000
inhabitants, with 476 houses.   There are about 250
breeders, who produce from 17,000 to 20,000 singing
cocks per annum, which may represent an income of
200,000 marks, or about £10,000, and to this must be
added the incomes of the women for the little baskets
or cages that are made for sale to contain the birds, and
the visits of strangers on account of the canaries.   The
society of canary-breeders there has also established a
journal for breeding and trade.

That the bird sings well does not, of course, arise from
the fact that he is bred in the Harz, but that he is bred
from the old Harz race.   Where the brood-bower has stood
is a matter of indifference ; the method of breeding is
everything. Good canaries of the Harz race are now bred
throughout Germany, especially in Berlin, Hanover, and
the Rhine, and something has also been done to improve
the breed in some points.   There are breeders in Berlin
who come close up to the celebrated breeder Tute, in
St. Andreasberg ; and a breeder like Peter Erntges, of
Elberfeld, St. Andreasberg does not any longer possess.
That the trade grows is evident enough.   In 1882 singing canary cocks were exported from Germany to New
York, 120,000 ; to South America, 10,500 ; to Australia,
5600 ; to South Africa, 3000 ; to France, 30,000 ; to
Belgium, 30,000 ; to England, 30,000 ; to Russia, 30,000 ;
to Austria, 30,000. But only the song-birds are exported.

The taste of the English and Dutch for breeding most other nations do not share. Nevertheless, it should be mentioned that the Japanese and Chinese have made a beginning, and that the Chinese production may by-and-by effect competition in the song-birds. Herr Reiche, a great authority, says respecting America :—

"From New York to California, from Canada to the Mississippi—everywhere, within the past few years, the canary-bird has made good his footing. Fresh, voiceful, warbling, rich in tone, he has made lovers and friends in all parts. He fills with delicious sounds the drawing-rooms of the foremost ladies, and, again, the solitary wood is penetrated by his notes as he sings, hanging in his cage at the door of the log-hut. Everywhere he enters he knows how to conquer the affection and companion-ship of all classes—in royal chambers of state, in the mansion, in the lowly cottage; and he is pre-eminently the darling of the little ones. He sings nearly the whole year, and if the storm rages and the snow falls, and we must want the songs of other birds, he sings for us in his loveliest strains. His maintenance is therefore cheap."

But America, which thus shows its love for and its appreciation of the canary, has as yet shown little eager-ness or tact in training him; and the large export to America is thus accounted for.

III.—English Varieties.

We have given this somewhat extended sketch of the German training because of later years the expert trainers in our country have borrowed more and more from

the Germans. And though it can still be said that
no variety of the English canary can quite match the
German for song-power, great improvements have been

ENGLISH BREED (LIZARD).

made in this respect, without sacrificing the beauty of
the plumage, in which, again, the German birds are,
compared with the English, admittedly deficient. And,
again, the German birds are more sickly; at all events,

they do not thrive well in England—either the air or the feeding does not suit them, and in moulting-time they sicken and lose singing power or die off. For those who are not experts probably a Norwich or a

LONDON FANCY.

Yorkshire bird, well trained, will be found the best, as they are hardiest. The Yorkshire and Scottish birds, too, have secured a high place of late years, and are good singers.

To most people it will be a surprise to learn that a

trade so extensive in these birds has existed for centuries; and it may also surprise them as much to know
that in England some of our favourite breeds—such as
the London Fancy, the Lizard, and Cinnamon, and

ENGLISH BREED (CRESTED NORWICH).

others—have been known for so long a period that no
details of their introduction or first appearance can be
found.   In a work dated 1709 as many as twenty-eight
varieties are named, comprising nearly all those known

at the present time. The following are the leading marks of the more celebrated varieties :—

(1) The clear Norwich, all yellow; (2) the Norwich uneven-marked or ticked; (3) the Norwich even-marked, which has a dark mark round each eye, called "spectacle eye-marks," the smaller wing-feathers and lower portion of the legs dark; and (4) the crested Norwich, which has a dark crest or cap and the small wing-feathers dark. Then there is (5) the London Fancy, all clear or yellow, save the whole of the wing and tail-feathers, which are black. The Lizard (6) is clear yellow on the crown, the breast streaked from the neck downwards, and the back beautifully spangled, the spangles increasing in size as they descend; wings and tail black, but fringed with light; legs and beak black. The Manchester Coppy (7) is entirely yellow and large; it has a golden crest, tufted over the beak—a magnificent bird. The Scotch Fancy (8) is very long, the wings and tail so falling from the shoulder as to form a curve or half-moon, and is entirely yellow. The Yorkshires (9) are hardly so deep in colouring as the Norwich, more of a lemon colour, but are longer than Norwich birds, straight in the back and longer in the neck. The phrase "mealy" merely indicates a certain lightness of colour.

Bird-exhibitions during the past twenty years in England have done much to stimulate progress in canary culture and training; and in connection with these the name of Mr. Barnesby should be mentioned.

IV.—Treatment.

All farinaceous seeds are dangerous for the voice of the canary, and some are bad for his health. They invariably make the voice light, harsh, and shrieky. Only oleaginous seeds should be given, and the best is ripe, scalded summer rape-seed—that is, the seed which is sown in spring, not the winter rape-seed which is sown in autumn. The milder and sweeter his tastes, the more esteemed the bird becomes. Winter rape should on no account be given. So, at all events, says Herr Richard Metzdorf, a good authority, from whose instructive and entertaining German we have culled some facts and suggestions. There are certain firms which cultivate the summer rape-seed expressly for the canaries, and who thoroughly weed and ripen it. The bird does not naturally care so much for this seed as for some others, and will, save in exceptional circumstances, eat no more of it than it requires for sustenance. Small mixtures of poppy and lettuce seed are admissible. The canary-seed, so called, acts very injuriously on the bird, if given in any quantity, and so does hemp-seed. The finer-bred birds should get neither of these, for it makes them violent and screechy. The German trainers will have nothing to do with hemp-seed; some of the English allow a *little* of it.

But a clever singer cannot do on rape-seed alone, and, as a strengthening food, a knife-pointful of hard-boiled egg, with some biscuit, daily, or every other day, suits him. A steady singing bird, indeed, is not to be kept in good condition without egg-food. It is the only food which gives the bird steadiness, and is at the

same time as favourable for the voice. Birds thus partially fed on egg have a *meltingness* in the organ and a
very melodious strain in song. Only if given in excess it
makes them violent, like so many other things ; and therefore it must be given very judiciously, and with due
regard to the individual requirement. One bird can

TYROLESE CANARY.

bear more, being more passive and requiring stimulus ;
another, more active, susceptible, will require less to
effect what is wanted. Egg, with a little maize-meal, or
sugar, baked after the receipt of Mr. Peter Erntges of
Elberfeld, known in the trade as maizena biscuit, is very

good, and may be easily obtained.   In moulting-time the heads of marigolds, but not the leaves, are much recommended.   It is needless to say that all the points respecting cleanliness, watering, &c., which are important as regards other cage-birds, are also to be very jealously attended to in the case of the canary, if you wish your bird to be well in health and to sing at once with vigour and with softness of tone.

The love of the canary-bird and delight in its sweet singing are thus very old, and there is no doubt that it is growing—one good fashion, at least, in which we follow our forefathers.   In this conviction we may be permitted to leave this interesting subject by quoting the following beautiful stanzas from the pen of Robert Leighton, a fine poet, who died too young :—

> " Overhead in the lattice high
>   Our little golden songster hung,
> Singing, piping merrily,
>   With dulcet throat and clipping tongue ;
> Singing from the peep of morning
>   To the evening's closing eye.
> When the sun in blue was burning,
>   Or when clouds shut out the sky :
> Foul or fair, morn, eve, or noon,
> Its little pipe was still in tune.
>
> " Its breast was filled with fairy shells
>   That gave sweet echo to its note,
> And strings of tiny silver bells
>   Rang with the pulsings of its throat ;
> Song all through its restless frame,
>   Its very limbs were warbling strings :
> I well believe that music came
>   E'en from the tippings of its wings ;
> Piping early, late and long,
> Mad with joy and drunk with song,
> Oh, welcome to thy little store,
> Thy song repays it o'er and o'er."

III.

ALL ABOUT RICE.

"One half the world," it is said, "knows not how the other half lives." One half the human race have rice for their food-staple, and yet we in this part of the world know on the whole very little about rice, its history, its mode of culture, its many varieties, and the processes through which it passes before it is placed upon the table. We see it in the shop or in the store at home, and it is one of the "familiar good creatures" of our life; but if we knew more of it we should esteem it more highly, and probably extend our use of it largely. At the present time, when, owing to various influences, the supply of native grain is so limited, it may be more than usually interesting to be made somewhat better acquainted with the merits of a staple which for the last twenty years has been rapidly making way on the Continent, but which has not yet by any means got the position it so well deserves amongst us. Our interests and its claims are luckily identical; and therefore we have the more faith in our right to request our reader's close attention, particularly if he is a social reformer, concerned for economy and the comfort of the masses. We shall therefore try to begin at the beginning, and follow the rice from the first to the last.

E

Rice is a cultivated variety of aquatic grass, bearing when in the ear a nearer resemblance to barley than any other of the English corn plants, and it reaches about the same height. The seed grows upon separate pedicles like the oat, each springing gracefully upwards on a hair-like stalk from the main stem. The seed is enclosed in a rough yellow husk, which in some varieties terminates with an awn, or beard, like barley; other varieties are awnless.

There is little reason to doubt that the rice-plant is of Indian origin, for in India it is now found growing in a wild state. Tradition says it was introduced thence into China about 3000 B.C., but its use and introduction into Europe are far more modern. It was first introduced into Spain by the Moors as recently as the twelfth century. The derivation of the word from the Sanscrit, *vrihi;* Tamil, *arisi;* Arabic, *aruz;* Latin, *oryza;* Italian, *riso;* English, *rice*, very probably suggests the route in which the cultivation of the plant has extended from its Indian home. It is certain that rice was not known in Italy in Pliny's time, 60 A.D. In describing the foods of India he says:—"But the most favourite food of all these is rice, from which they prepare 'ptisan' (pearled or clean rice), similar to that made from barley in other parts of the world. The leaves of rice are fleshy, very like those of the leek, but broader; the stem is a cubit (18 in. high), the blossom purple, and the root globular, like a pearl in shape." (Book xviii. chap. 13.)

This description clearly proves that Pliny had never seen the plant itself. He goes on to say, "Hippocrates, one of the famous writers of medical science, has devoted a whole volume to the praises of 'ptisan,' the method of preparing which is universally known." Pliny does not give rice among his list of plants cultivated in Egypt, but Wilkinson considers it was cultivated in the Delta; and the pictures in the Theban tombs of the cultivation and manufacture of a grain where the processes are the same as to-day practised in India in rice cultivation confirm Wilkinson's opinion.

The Karens (an aboriginal race in British Burma) have an account of the Creation, which is of undoubted antiquity, and to this effect:—"The Father, God, said, 'I love these, my son and daughter; I will bestow my life upon them.' He took a particle of his life and breathed into their nostrils, and they came to life and were man. Thus God created man. God made food and drink, *rice*, fire and water, rattle-elephants and birds." (Forbes's "Burma," 1878.)

Rice has perhaps more cultivated varieties which differ more from each other than any of the cerealia. The Karens have names for forty varieties. Dr. Moon mentions one hundred varieties growing in Ceylon. Besides these, there are the different kinds growing in China and Japan and other parts of the world. They are of every colour, from ivory white to coal black. The grain varies in shape from cylindrical to globular. Some varieties are sweet, some oily, some soft and chalky, others hard and translucent.

With reference to the mode and time of growth, there are four main varieties in cultivation—common rice, early rice, clammy rice, and mountain rice. Common rice, the variety cultivated in British Burma, is the strongest plant and gives the largest yield, for one crop about twenty-five-fold, and takes six months from ploughing to harvest. Early rice grows mostly in China and India, and takes three or four months to mature. Mountain rice grows on the Himalayas, sometimes pushing its way through the snow, and without irrigation reaching maturity in ninety days. Clammy rice (*Oriza glutinosa*) has the advantage of being able to grow on wet or dry land, and ripens in about five months.

The rice-plant is distributed over the earth as high as the 45th parallel N. and the 38th S.

It is the main crop of China, Japan, Burma, Cochin China, India, Madagascar, Java, and Italy, and is extensively cultivated in North and South America..

Wild rice is still eaten as a luxury on the Madras coast; it has a small white grain, very sweet; it grows on waste marshy lands. The only reason it is not cultivated is because it returns so small an increase as compared with the cultivated varieties of the same plant.

Although rice was introduced into Italy so lately as the thirteenth century, its cultivation on the rich meadows of Lombardy, watered by the Po, and other similar flat lands, has so increased that the Italian rice-crop of 1879 amounted to no less than 500,000 tons. It is the most profitable crop to the cultivator of any that is raised in Italy; but the same unwholesome effect of malaria from irrigated lands is experienced there as has proved so fatal in Carolina, and the Government has found it expedient to place its cultivation under great restrictions. This circumstance, together with the extra taxation on rice, would have destroyed any other culture save one that offers the only means of profitably cropping swampy and marshy lands.

Rice-culture in Carolina and Georgia and the adjoining States, which attained to such a high degree of excellence, dates only from about the year A.D. 1700. White rice was introduced from India by Mr. Dubois, Treasurer to the East India Association, and the red rice was brought from Madagascar. It is said that it was taken by accident by a sea-captain, who gave some of the "paddy" to a Mr. Woodward. After its value was discovered the captain was handsomely rewarded for the service he had done the country.

The rice, by careful selection and cultivation in trenches—instead of being sown broadcast—has made the Carolina plant so famous that the seed has been exported to Java, Madras, Spain, and Italy, and some of the finest modern varieties of Indian rice are grown from Carolina seed.

Since the American war and the abolition of slavery the rice export trade from America has practically ceased. The crop in 1870 was only 73,000,000 lbs., against 250,000,000 lbs. in 1850. This is because the free negroes object to work in the swampy rice-fields, associated as they are with fever, malaria, and sickness.

The cultivation of the varieties of common and early rice throughout India and China are very much alike.

The fields are carefully levelled and divided into squares, surrounded by low embankments about eighteen inches wide, and the same height, which fall gradually from the level of the source of supply to that of the drainage-cut, which carries off the surplus water. In some instances, as in Southern India and China, crops are raised which depend in the main on artificial irrigation—the water being raised by manual or animal labour from a tank or river, but generally the natural fall of the country is taken advantage of to save this extra expense.

The fields are cleared of weeds; then, when the rains have begun, they are ploughed or scratched with a simple wooden plough while they are a foot or more under water, the ploughman and his buffaloes being sometimes knee-deep in slush.

The "paddy" intended for seed is placed in large baskets under water for a few days to let it germinate. When it has sprouted and is known to be good, it is sown broadcast on the surface of the water by men who stand upon the embankments on those fields that are to be used as a sort of nursery for the rest of the land. Probably this process is referred to in Ecclesiastes: "Cast thy bread upon the waters: for thou shalt find it after many days."

When the young rice has pushed its way through the water, and is about eight inches high, the labour of transplanting from the nurseries to the rest of the farm lands must begin.

The plants are pulled up, roots and all, and piled in large baskets and taken to the fields where they are to be finally transplanted. The operation is generally carried on in the midst of heavy rain, the labourers standing up nearly to their ankles in water and slush, and the stooping posture all day long makes the work very arduous. They protect their heads and bodies with a sort of umbrella or thatch made of palm-leaves. Thus attired, the worker presents rather a comic appearance when seen for the first time, looking from behind not unlike a crab or tortoise walking on its hind-legs. The women and children are engaged in planting out, and half the village will turn out to plant for *Tulsi Das* one day, and *Hurri Pandoo* the next, and so on, each helping the other in proportion till the whole of the fields are planted.

The transplanting process is thus described :—

" A bundle of seedlings being laid across the arm of each person, all standing in a row, a couple of the young plants are disengaged from the bundle with the right hand and stuck in the ground, or rather mud, in rows about a foot apart, with the same distance between the plants. Sometimes a forked stick is used, with which the plants are deftly drawn from the bundle and planted with a slight thrust in the soft soil ; this obviates the fatigue of the stooping posture when the hand only is employed. The operation proceeds at a rapid pace, the seedlings being put down almost as fast as one can count. After the transplanting no further care is given to the crop until it begins to ripen ; no weeding is ever thought of, nor is any manure ever applied to the ground before planting ; all is left to nature." *

Archdeacon Grey, in his book on China, has given the following very picturesque description of a rice-field at the various stages :—

" So quickly does the rice-plant grow, that in the course of a few days the whole country presents a rich green appearance. Perhaps one of the most charming scenes

* Forbes's " British Burma, 1878," page 104.

on which I ever gazed was the vale of Manta, in the island of Formosa, seen from the slopes of one of the neighbouring mountains when the rice-plants were putting on the fresh green of their early growth. . . .

" After the rice has been planted the farmer must see that his lands are well supplied with water, for a scarcity of that element would prove fatal. In general the rains, which fall at such seasons in heavy showers, are enough for this purpose. The labourer must watch the plants carefully lest they should be destroyed by noxious weeds. A labourer who observes a weed growing in close proximity to a plant immediately removes the latter, so as to destroy the weed, after which he replaces the plant. It is the duty of other labourers to gather a kind of worm, like our common earth-worm in form and size, and said to be very destructive to the rice-plant. These worms are not thrown away, but conveyed to the various markets, and sold to ready purchasers as a delicate article of diet. There is also an insect resembling a grass-hopper by which the rice-crops in China are often in danger of being blighted or destroyed, and which flies about in large numbers.

" When the rice is ripe unto harvest—generally in the month of June, *i.e.*, one hundred days after it was first sown—the reapers come upon the field. Each reaper is provided with a sickle, which bears a strong resemblance to the reaping-hooks in use in Great Britain. In some of the agricultural districts reapers gather only the tops of the ears of rice. To this mode of reaping grain a reference is made in the Book of Job (xxiv. 24), where it is written, ' They are taken out of the way as all other, and cut off as the tops of the ears of corn.' And again in Isaiah (xvii. 5), 'And it shall be as when the harvest-man gathereth the corn, and reapeth the ears with his arm; and it shall be as he that gathereth ears in the valley of Rephaim.' According to this mode the ears are cut off near the top, the straw being left standing. As it is cut the grain is bound into small sheaves, each of which is placed on the ground in an upright position. In this position, however, the sheaves are not allowed to remain for any length of time; they are threshed then and there by labourers, who take them in their hands and strike them with force against inner sides of tubs, into which, of course, the grains fall. Certain kinds of rice, however, cannot be threshed in this way; and it is customary for the labourer to carry the sheaves of this rice to the homestead on bamboo rods, so that they may be threshed there by flails. The threshing does not take place in a barn, but on a threshing-floor, with one of which every farm is provided. Before the sheaves are laid on this floor it is very carefully swept. To this careful cleansing of the threshing-floor an allusion is surely made in the Gospel of St. Matthew (iii. 12), where St. John the Baptist describes our Lord as one ' whose fan is in his hand, and he will throughly purge his floor, and gather his wheat into the garner.'

" According to the Book of the Prophet Isaiah (xxviii. 27) and the Book of Ruth (ii. 17) this mode of threshing grain is very ancient. It would appear, however, that the Hebrews principally used the flail in threshing small quantities of grain, or for lighter kinds, such as vetches, dill, or cummin."

We must, however, introduce one or two details omitted by Dr. Grey. The rice-fields are weeded once or twice before harvest; all the villagers help each other, as they do at transplanting, so as to complete the whole of each field at the same time. The fields are kept covered with water until about fourteen days before harvest, when the supply is cut off and the grain ripens and turns yellow.

Perhaps one of the finest sights earth can show is often to be witnessed when the rice ripens, though it is a great grievance to the husbandman: flocks of birds, green parroquets, and crowds of other varieties come in such immense numbers, that were the crops not closely watched from early morn till night there would be little left to repay the cultivator for his labour. Boys are perched up in small pigeon-house-looking structures on the top of bamboo poles some sixteen or eighteen feet high, for protection from wild beasts. Here they scream and yell all day long, besides having loose bamboo rattles attached to cords, at different parts of the field, tied to one rope, which they pull occasionally. Even this is not always effective; for instance, Carolina rice cannot be grown in Burma because it ripens some six weeks sooner than the general crop, and the birds manage to carry off so much of the isolated patch, when they can get no other, that its cultivation has in consequence been abandoned in the few cases in which it has been tried.

In British Burma rice can be so cheaply cultivated, and the land is so well adapted for its growth, that this has in the last thirty years become the centre of the rice-supply of the whole world.

The rainfall is so heavy that the whole country is inundated completely from one range of hills to the other. The only traffic that can be then carried on is in boats. The villages are built either on piles or on elevated clumps of land, and cattle are stabled and grain stored, and the people live, during the rains, in a condition not unlike that which existed in the time of the lake-dwellings.

The heavy rainfall flooding the whole country enables the cultivator to dispense with those expensive husbandry operations—such as levelling the fields, making embankments, &c.—which are so necessary in other countries. The Burmese do not even observe the rotation of crops or manure the land. On the other hand, they crop the land only once a year; while in China and parts of India three crops are gathered—two of rice and one of other grain. It is common, indeed, in many parts to take two crops of rice off the same land in one year. Mr. Crauford, a good authority, says that he has seen fields which have produced two crops a year from time beyond the memory of any living person, and that in some particularly favourable spots they manage to get six crops in two and a half years.

The Burmese main crop consists of varieties of the "common rice" that ripens in six months. It is sown about June, and gathered in December following. The nursery grounds are sown on the higher land at the beginning of the rains, before the ground is ready for the main crop. When the plants are about eight inches high they are pulled up, roots and all, and tied in bundles, and carried by the boatload to supply those cultivators who are ready to plant out their land. The "paddy" lands are prepared for being planted by being lightly ploughed with a wooden plough, while they are under water, after the rains have set in. The crop is reaped with sickles, but only the top of the stalk with the ear is cut off; the straw and stubble are left standing till spring-time, when they are burnt, which gives the land in Burma the only manure it ever gets.

After harvest the grain is carted to the dry earthen threshing-floor, and either stacked or threshed out then and there, sometimes, in China and Japan, with flails; but generally, as in Burma, it is trodden out by oxen. The "paddy" is laid in a circle in the centre of the threshing-floor, and the oxen, tied together in line, are driven round the heap, the herdsman following with a stick, still singing on his way, as in the old harvest scenes depicted on the Theban tombs some three thousand years B.C. And, still carrying out ancient command, they do not muzzle the ox that treadeth out the corn.

The "paddy" is then stored in granaries, which in Burma are raised on piles some feet above the surface of the ground, built of bamboo wattle and daub. In China, where grain is very extensively stored throughout the empire as a provision against famine, the granaries are larger and of solid masonry. From them seed is lent to indigent farmers in the spring-time, to be recovered with interest after harvest. The Chinese mix the ash of the burnt husk with the stored "paddy" to preserve it from weevil, for which it is said to be effective.

The "paddy" is next shelled by being passed through

a small pair of millstones or cylinders of the same shape made of hard wood, set on end, grooved in the working surface. These work at such a distance apart as serves to remove the husk by friction without breaking the grain. And they are generally made large enough to require three or four men, who work them by means of a long handle or connecting-rod attached to the upper cylinder.

The grain and chaff are separated by being dropped together from a height in a light breeze, recalling the description in the 1st Psalm, of the ungodly who "are like the chaff which the wind driveth away." Or the grain is tossed up on bamboo trays with wooden shovels against the wind. In China, Japan, and Burma, however, the winnowing-machine, made on the English system by Chinese carpenters, is rapidly replacing the older method; just as in the Burmese and Cochin China rice-ports the European steam machinery for shelling and winnowing is daily diminishing the quantity of the hand-cleaned article.

After the rice is shelled, the inner skin adhering to the grain must be removed, which is done by pounding it in a wooden or stone mortar with hard wood beaters, until the friction has entirely removed the outer skin.

This process must not be confused with that of pounding or pulverising in a mortar. The pestle or beater is of another shape, and the mortar holds a larger quantity of grain at a time, so that the impact of the beater will not break it. It is referred to in Proverbs xxvii. 22 : "Though thou shouldest bray a fool in a mortar among 'grain' with a pestle, yet will not his foolishness depart from him." Had our translators known the mysteries of rice and barley milling, they would not have translated the word as "wheat," which means literally "decorticated grain," or, as Herodotus and Pliny call it, "ptisan"—a process never applied to wheat.

There were in 1877 forty-five steam rice-mills in British Burma, which are mainly worked for the preparation of cargo rice, *i.e.*, four parts by measurement of husked rice to one of paddy, in which condition most of the Burmese crop is shipped to Europe. These mills have lately been introducing machinery for making "cleaned rice." This enables them to supply the Burmese with cheaper rice than they can clean by hand, besides supplying direct a large foreign trade which, until lately, was in the hands of the English millers.

There are few busier scenes than the port of Rangoon in the height of the shipping season. What with the cargo boats coming down the rivers bringing "paddy" to the mills, the coasting dhows and steamers taking away the cleaned rice to the Straits, China, and India, and the large sailing ships and steamers loading for Europe and Australia and America, the people have a busy time of it. The mills work night and day, and no one who has seen the Burmese labourer running along with a two-hundredweight bag of rice on his shoulders, working in a hot sun and for long hours, will preach the usually accepted rubbish that mankind cannot labour and thrive on a diet mainly composed of rice.

The rice-milling process of the English rice-mills in London and Liverpool is but a modification and repetition of the processes already described, carried out with greater detail and with self-acting machinery. The five-part cargo rice is brought from Burma in two-hundred-weight bags; these are unloaded at the docks and carted to the mills.

They are emptied into a bin, whence the rice is elevated by an endless band called an elevator, with small cans attached, to the top-storey of the mill, and passed through a sieve to free it from sticks, stones, straw, and sometimes a rupee or a broken bangle.

Then it passes through the shelling-stones. They are large millstones, six feet in diameter, revolving 120 revolutions per minute, dressed hollow in the centre and flat for twelve inches at the rim, where they are set the length of the grain apart, so that as the rice passes through this narrow space the husks may be cracked off with the least possible breakage to the grain itself. The chaff, meal, and rice from this process pass through a screen to remove the meal; then a fan or winnowing-machine is used to take out the chaff, and the rice is ready for being "barley milled."

The barley-mill, as its name implies, is a modification of the well-known machine used throughout Europe for making "pearled" barley. It consists of a circular cheese-shaped stone, four feet in diameter and two feet wide, which revolves very quickly inside a slowly revolving wooden casing covered with fine wire-netting. About five-inch space is left on all sides between the stone and the casing, which is partly filled with rice, and the machine is started.

After barley-milling, the rice is again elevated to the

top of the building, and passes down through two or three polishers. They are inverted conical wooden drums about four or five feet in diameter and six feet deep, covered with sheepskin with the long wool outside. They revolve about two hundred revolutions per minute inside a fine wire-covered casing of the same shape, which is firmly secured in its place, leaving small space between the woolly surface of the drum and the casing. As the rice passes through this space the meal adhering to it is driven through the wire and the rice is polished.

It is then winnowed once or twice to remove any remaining husks, and it finally passes over a sieve which is kept moving with a quick kind of shake, and which is set at a slant from top to bottom and with holes graduated in size. Thus a separation is effected into whole rice, and middling broken, and small broken rice, known as "smalls."

During the twenty-five years from 1854 to 1879 the increase of consumption is something altogether marvellous, and (taking into consideration the liability to fluctuate) it has been marked and steady, as any one who notes the following figures will at once perceive :—

In 1854 the total quantity of rice exported from Burma was 69,820 tons, all of which was Akyab rice; in 1862 it was nearly trebled, being 191,861 tons, of which 64,785 were Rangoon, 98,751 were Akyab, and 28,325 Bassein. In 1870 the increase, though not so great as that of the former eight years, was still considerable, the total being 294,673, of which 170,306 tons were Rangoon, 80,295 Akyab, 34,206 Bassein, and 9866 Moulmain; showing that while the Akyab had decreased by 18,456, the Rangoon had considerably more than doubled its total number of tons. During the next nine years (1879) the totals are 594,500, showing an increase of 524,680 tons for twenty-five years.

In all probability the time is not very distant when the bulk of Burmese rice will be conveyed to European ports by the rapid and safe agency of steam vessels. It seems that about five-sixths of the rice imported into England is shipped from Burma, the quantity of rice shipped from the ports of India being comparatively small.

During the year 1880 the exports from Burma into Europe reached 617,000 tons, viz. :—

To Great Britain	315,000
To the Continent	302,000
	617,000

It would thus appear that the people on the Continent are more of a rice-eating race than we are in Great Britain, as the former consume nearly all that they import, whereas a large proportion of the imports into Great Britain are again exported in its cleaned state to different countries. It is calculated, indeed, that nine-sixteenths of the crop sent to Europe is disposed of on the Continent.

We shall now glance very shortly at some peculiarities of the different kinds of rice. Patna rice takes longest to boil; it is hard and brittle. Java is similar, very highly finished and pretty to look at. Carolina is like Java in appearance, but hardly any is now imported to England. That sold as such is either Java or " Paris

F

dressed" rice, *i.e.*, some other rice polished with beeswax to make it look like Carolina. Waxed rice seems a
curious thing, yet it is now in the market. It appears
that one or two per cent. of beeswax adds a peculiar
lustre to rice, and makes it look so pretty that the Dutch
are profiting much by preparing it for English use. So
much favour, indeed, does this waxed rice receive over
the plain and genuine article that Carolina rice is actually
sent over from England to Holland to be waxed, and
is returned to England in its "transformed deformed"
condition to be sold at a high price as the finest Java.
So much do appearances avail in such matters, and so
gullible is the English public even in the all-important
matter of food. Much that has been written against the
food value of rice (which in reality shows only the necessity of a *mixed* diet) may be disposed of by showing the
estimation in which it is held as a food by the people
who eat it. In Southern India a working man indicates
his prosperity by telling how often he can afford to
eat rice, "once or twice daily, or weekly." Or to take
larger statistics, the Burma export during the last
thirty years has increased by £9,000,000, and the
Italian crop last year was valued at £5,000,000. If
the proof of the (rice) pudding is in the eating, these
figures showing the increasing popularity prove a great
deal.

The consumption in England, as we have seen, is
small as compared with that on the Continent. Here
it competes with potatoes ; people do not like to pay
twopence per pound for rice when potatoes are a penny,
but some shrewd housewives have found out that pota-

toes at the same price as rice are four times as dear, and here is the scientific proof of it :—

	Water.	Flesh-formers.	Starch, &c.	Total Food.
Rice . .	13	6.5	80	86.5
Potatoes .	75	1.4	22.6	24.0

This shows that 1 lb. of rice contains $3\frac{1}{2}$ times as much food as 1 lb. of potatoes. Taking into account the loss in peeling potatoes, 1 lb. of rice is worth 4 lbs. of potatoes; and, as rice absorbs three times its weight of water in boiling, the 1 lb. of rice, costing 2d., when boiled equals 4 lbs. of potatoes, costing 4d., in bulk and weight, and exceeds them in food value.

Hassall states that rice is the most easily digested food known; it will disappear in the stomach in one hour. The smallness and regularity of its starch-grains probably give rice this valuable property of being so easily digested. It is, therefore, very remarkable that rice flour, the most valuable of all the farinas in food value, cheapness, and digestibility, which is so much used in America and in France as food for invalids and infants, where it is known as Crême de Riz, is almost unknown in England for the same purposes. Its value may be seen by the following table :—

	Flesh-formers.	Starch.	Price per lb.
Corn flour . .	0	100	$5\frac{1}{2}$d.
Arrowroot . .	1	99	6d. to 9d.
Tapioca . . .	2	98	5d.
Rice flour . .	6.5	93.5	2d.

If it were only patented as a food for children and invalids, and called by some Greek name, it might possibly command a ready sale.

Sufficient attention has not been called to the danger

of feeding children exclusively on those "starch foods" that contain little or no nitrogenous matter. Dr. Bartlett, in his evidence before the Adulteration Committee of the House of Commons, in 1874, stated that numerous instances of children reduced to skin and bone from being fed with corn flour had come under his notice.

Rice flour, which might well be used for food, has a prejudice against it, and in England is used principally for "sizing" Manchester goods. It is sought after, however, for mixing with wheaten flour for bread-making, both to bring up the colour and in times of a damp harvest as an "absorbent," to improve the rising properties of the bread flour. Granulated or "ground rice" is made by crushing rice small between smooth iron rollers. It is used only for making light puddings and confectionery.

Rice meal is used for cattle, poultry, and pig feeding, never for human food, because the taste is bitter and unpalatable. It is so little known, as compared with Indian meal, that although its food value, as shown below, is better, it can be generally bought at two-thirds the price—*i.e.*, when Indian meal is quoted at 6s., rice meal can be bought at 4s.

	Rice Meal.	Indian Meal.
Moisture	8.80	12.00
Oil and fatty matter	9.50	7.00
Albuminous compounds	12.75	11.00
Starch, cellulose, &c.	64.85	68.50
Ash	4.00	1.50

In some markets—Derbyshire, for instance—rice meal has all its own way; in Yorkshire it is almost unknown.

The British farmer has a prejudice against feeding his stock on food that his ancestors have not used before him. Indian meal has had a long fight for it. Rice meal is competing, and in good time its cheapness and food value will be recognised.

Lastly, the husk. Such husk as is quite clean and free from rice meal and rice is sold partly for Holland, where it is used for packing gin and hams. It is more elastic than sawdust, and does not so readily shift in the packing-cases with the motion of travelling. Part is ground into fine meal for the provender dealers, who use it for mixing with linseed cake, Indian meal, rice meal, and other feeding stuffs, and a large quantity is exported to the Continent yearly for the same purpose. The coarser ground strude, called the strude bran, is sold for polishing tin plates, the large amount of silica it contains making it valuable for this purpose. As ground strude contains only fifty per cent. of feeding matter, a small proportion added to rice meal soon brings down the food value. If farmers were to consult their interests, they would buy rice meal either direct from the maker, or, if from a dealer, on a given analysis guaranteed, then a pure article and money value could be depended upon.

IV.

PEARLS.

In one of the finest passages in the "Paradise Lost," Milton painted the throne on which Satan sat, "by merit raised to that bad eminence," as outshining the "wealth of Ormuz and of Ind," and described the gorgeous East as with richest hand showering on her kings "barbaric pearl and gold."

What might seem at the first glance somewhat out of keeping, on a more close examination only attests the exactitude of Milton's knowledge. For it might be asked why pearls are here alone associated with gold? Are there not rubies and emeralds, opals and diamonds, and sapphires, and the topaz, the beryl and the chalcedony, and the turquoise, and the onyx, and the jasper, and the carbuncle? These are all more gorgeous than the pearl; and if the marks of barbaric taste are, as is usually assumed, flash of colour and variety and radiance, then surely is the pearl the very last of gems to be so chosen out and celebrated.

Barbaric *pearl* and gold!

At first sight the words seem to be contradictory; in the subdued colour and modest purity of the pearl there is nothing of "barbaric gorgeousness." In most regions

of the East, however, and particularly in Persia, in ancient times the pearl was ranked the first of all gems;
and no end of legend and myth was associated with it.
Even in India, which furnishes a partial exception, as
putting first the diamond, the Hindoos endowed Vishnu
with the special honour of having created pearls; and
all their gods are so richly decorated with pearls as to
have awakened in the minds of many travellers no little
surprise and admiration.

Egyptians, Babylonians, and Assyrians, as well as
Persians, held them in the highest esteem, and the
ancient Mexicans were in no whit behind in their
appreciation and reverence. The palace of Montezuma,
we read, was studded with pearls and emeralds, and
the Aztec kings possessed specimens of pearls of the
utmost value, got, as is believed, from the pearl-fisheries
of Panama.

In the barbaric East, therefore (for India was even
in those days hardly barbaric), the pearl took precedence
of all other precious stones; and Milton was quite right
when he spoke of the gorgeous East, with richest hand
showering on her kings "barbaric pearl and gold."

The ancients do not seem to have had any clear
conception of the natural process by which pearls are
produced, and it is possible enough they would have
rejected it even had it been made known to them.
Greeks and Romans, so far as we can ascertain, were
in this no whit in advance of Egyptians, Persians, and
Babylonians. Even in the days of Pliny men's ideas
were vague enough on this subject, as on many others
which science has made plain. One can hardly restrain

a smile as one reads these words of Pliny, whom, moreover, one could hardly wish to have been deceived, such a pretty poem has he made of it.

"Pearls," says he, "are great or small, better or worse, according to the quantity and quality of the dew they received. For if the dew were pure and clear that went into them, then were the pearls fair and orient; if thick and troubled, then the pearls likewise were demure, foul, and dullish; whereby, no doubt, it is apparent and plain that they participate more of the air and dew than of the water and sea, for according as the morning is fair so are they clear; otherwise, if it be misty and cloudy they will be misty and thick in colour. Cloudy weather spoiled their colour, lightning stopped their growth, and thunder made the shell-fish miscarry altogether, and eject hollow husks called *Physemata* or bubbles."

To turn from the fancy and romance of the ancients to the sober facts of nature is only to find a truer romance.

The pearl is simply a secretion of the common substance carbonate of lime, which is drawn in by the oyster from the water, and employed, mixed with some fluid proper to itself, and along with some extremely thin, almost transparent membrane, in forming the lining of its shell.

What is called the mantle of the bivalve is the medium of this secretion. The peculiar nacreous lustre, the soft, shimmering, subdued gleam, is caused by these being laid on alternately in exceedingly thin layers in slow succession; these layers not being absolutely smooth, but having a gentle, almost unnoticeable series of waves or undulations, which are easily detected by scientific instruments, and are invariably present. This is so certain, says a good authority, Mr. Hugh Owen, that "a similar nacreous lustre has been produced on buttons by engraving a steel die with a diamond point in a regular series of undulating lines, and then striking the button as a coin would be struck."

The gem. is due either to some wound, which throws off osseous particles, or to some irritating substance, such as a grain of sand finding its way within the shell, against which the oyster fortifies itself by wrapping it round in layer after layer of the same substance as that with which it lines its shell. In the centre of every pearl, it is said by scientific men, there will be found in cutting it some such particle as this.

The creature thus translates the cause of its pain or discomfort into a beautiful object, which has given rise to many fine thoughts and images; and none, perhaps, is finer than that of Jean Paul Richter, the great German romance writer, when he says: "Afflictions and disappointments to the true character are only means to its beautifying and perfecting, as the oyster, when it is injured, closes the wound with a pearl."

The knowledge of this fact has led to no end of ingenuity in introducing particles of various kinds within the shell of the bivalve. The Chinese, perhaps, have outstripped all others in this clever device. They introduce minute images of their gods and grotesque figures of animals into the open shell of the Chinese mussel, which, after a certain time, are found coated over with the secretion we call mother-of-pearl. They are then withdrawn, and find ready sale, some of them being of considerable value. But though much has been made clear regarding the circumstances of production, there are points still unsettled. The bivalves abound; but they do not equally produce pearls in all localities. The most probable explanation is, that the chemical constituents of the water have much to do with it, and, of course, they vary indefinitely—not only in different waters, but in the same waters at different times.

There are several species of bivalves which produce pearls. From that named *Unio margaritiferus* we derive our supply in Britain; while the pearl mussel—*Meleagrina margaritifera*—is the source of the Oriental supply. Those derived from others are of little or no value, and vary in colour from pinky-purple to rose-colour, some being almost black. The British pearl-producing bivalve is found in some of the mountain streams of England and Wales, and more abundantly in some of the mountain streams of Scotland; but, seeing that out of every hundred bivalves opened there may be found only one pearl, and even that of little value, it may be guessed that pearl-fishing in our country can hardly be a very profitable calling; though it must be said that, owing to a passion for rose-coloured pearls which set in among the ladies of Paris a few years ago, some good has been done to the Scotch pearl-fisheries; for pearls of a rose-colour are more frequently found there than elsewhere.

The presence of a foot and mantle is one of the marked characteristics of pearl-producing Mollusca. The first is familiar to us all in the common garden snail, and to those who have seen and opened the fresh-water mussel (*Anadon cygnea*) the covering of flesh called the mantle is equally well known.

The function of the foot in the acephalous mollusc is not that of locomotion, but rather to enable the animal to retain a fixed position upon the rocks. This it effects by projecting and spinning long silky threads with the foot, and attaching them so firmly that the wind and waves have no power over them.

"The threads," says Dr. Johnstone, "are of perfect equality throughout, and are well cleaned by washing in soap and water, are then dried by being rubbed with the hands. It is then mixed with about one-third real silk, and is spun on the distaff and knit into gloves, caps, stockings, vests, &c., forming a stuff of a beautiful brownish colour."

This strong cord the animal has the power to discard at will and can refix itself without difficulty. This fact, which is well authenticated concerning the *Pinnadæ*, has thrown some light upon the occasional falling off of the pearl-fisheries. Some say that the genus *Margaritiferus*, or pearl-oyster, cannot move, but it has been demonstrated, not only that it possesses locomotive powers, but that these powers are absolutely essential to its digestive economy; for water too salt or too fresh is fatal to the delicate system of the species, and its power of shifting from place to place is essential to its preservation—not to speak of its health and reproduction.

It is only necessary to add that when withdrawn into the shell the foot lies between the folds of the mantle and appears a hard firm pad of flesh.

In the *Unionidæ* or Mussel family the intestine is so involved with this mass that there is much difficulty in tracing it. The common oyster is the only specimen of Mollusca that is dissected daily and without disgust ; but it is of no use for illustration here, being a true oyster, and has really no connection with the Pecten and Mussel, which is proved by the absence of foot and by the open mantle.

This latter, as we have seen, is the important point in any consideration concerning pearl-growth. The body is enveloped by this elastic fleshy membrane, which is furnished by a skin covered with moving hairs or *cilia*, and is also provided with tentacles. A close examination of the lip of a mussel-shell will explain the manner of its growth, as it is clear that the function of the mantle is to secrete calcareous matter for the hard protective covering, as has already been pointed put. The inner surface of all shells presents the glistening appearance with which we are all familiar as the mother-of-pearl. At its margin the mantle is attached to the shell, and secretes this prismatic layer in the manner already indicated ; and, as may be expected, the shell is thickest where the growth is the most rapid. The glistening brightness is caused by the refraction of the rays of light from the apparently smooth surface, but which, as we have seen, is really both rough and uneven, the delicate plates or lamellæ overlapping each other. Sometimes, in a dry specimen, the structureless membrane can be separated from the true shell, a fact of significant importance to those who maintain shell-growth to be from within outwards. The power of the *Unionidæ* and

Pectenidæ to ensure a soft lining to their home is a key to the formation of the pearl.

Many and varied are the methods which have been adopted for the securing of these precious gems.

One of the earliest Arab geographers in the ninth century describes the habits of the pearl-divers with which he was acquainted. They filled their ears with cotton and oil and compressed their nostrils with tortoise-shell before they dived : this practice, we believe, continues among the pearl-divers of the Persian Gulf even to the present day.

Sir J. Emerson Tennant, in his interesting description of the pearl-fisheries of Ceylon, gives some very instructive details. The diver inserts his foot in a sinking stone and inhales a full breath. He presses his nostrils with his left hand, raises his body as high as he can above the water to gain impetus in the descent, and the stone being at that moment liberated, he sinks rapidly to the bottom. As soon as this is reached, the stone is drawn up; and the diver, having thrown himself on his face, with all alacrity fills his basket. At a given signal this is drawn up by the cord which is attached to it, and held above by the men in the boat ; and the diver assists his ascent by springing on the rope as the basket rises.

The divers remain about fifty-five seconds under water; and accidents are rare. The noise and constant excitement of the water, during the fishing season, is found to be quite sufficient to protect the men from the sharks ; and it may be that additional confidence is given to the men by the fact of a shark-charmer being present in each boat !

The shells are taken out and thrown upon the shore, and as soon as the animals are dead the pearls are easily extracted. The thickest and finest shells are carefully selected from the mass, and are destined to be worked out for mother-of-pearl. The more worthless are left, and groups of the poorer people may be seen turning and turning them over in the hope of finding some stray pearl that may have been overlooked.

Pearls have had their own share in determining the history of the world.

There is no doubt that Julius Cæsar found his main inducement to visit Britain in the reports of great pearls to be found there. He is mentioned to have been seen weighing British pearls in his hand, and comparing them with others from the East, a short time before his expedition to our islands was undertaken. We know that he shared to the full the Roman love of pearls. On his return to Rome from these islands the breast-plate which he dedicated to the Venus Genetrix was formed from pearls taken from British waters.

We have thus conclusive proof of two things: (1) that Cæsar's main aim was not forgotten in the midst of the warlike and imperial ambitions which in the Romans always mixed with and modified any personal or narrower preference; and (2), that the ancient Britons knew the value of pearls and worked their waters for them, that they traded in them, and that they found their way to distant regions of the earth even at that early period. But pearl-fishing was for a long course of centuries in abeyance in our country.

The revival of the pearl-fishing in Scotland is of

comparatively recent date. In 1761 pearls were sent from Scotland to London to the value of £10,000, and these were mainly taken from the Tay and Isla. And year by year the trade languished until an Edinburgh jeweller of enterprise made the generous offer to purchase all that were brought to him. The highest price given for a single pearl has not, so far as we know, exceeded £60.

Endeavours have been made to imitate pearls, just as endeavours have been made to manufacture diamonds, but not with much success. Nor is this anything new. The Romans and other early nations of Europe endeavoured to unite and file pieces of shell into the form of spherical pearls; but no one of the least skill or judgment was likely to be deceived by them, though as ornaments they no doubt had their claims.

In 1680 Jacquin, a rosary-maker of Paris, filled hollow glass beads with the scales of a small river-fish (the bleak), putting them through some process of condensation, and since then the world has been at no loss to procure what superficially passes for beads and pearl-necklaces.

No city in the world, we read, was ever richer in precious pearls than Rome in the time of the Cæsars. Special mention is made of Lollia Pollena, wife of Caius Caligula. "I have seen her," says Pliny, "so bedecked with emeralds and pearls disposed in rows, ranks, and courses, one by another, round about the attire of her head, her cowl, her peruke of hair, her band grace and chaplet, hanging at her ears, round her neck as an ornament in a carcanet, upon her wrists as bracelets, and on her fingers in rings, that she glittered and shone like the sun as she went." The habit was so common of using pearls as a base to throw up the brilliance of other gems, that we may, perhaps, believe even in Caligula's slippers of pearls, with rubies and emeralds set upon them like flowers.

The Roman ladies had a special favour for pearls as ear-rings, and it was one of their consuming ambitions to possess exceptionally fine specimens for this purpose. They preferred the pear-shaped pearls, and often wore two or three of them strung together. They jingled gently as they moved about, fitting accompaniment, it may be said, to their graceful movements, and from this jingling they got their name, which was *crotalia*, or " rattles."

And the taste of the Roman ladies for pearls has perpetuated itself, though other of the ancient luxurious habits, which in their case accompanied it, have long died out. The women of Florence even now are not contented if they do not possess a necklet of pearls, and this generally forms the marriage portion of the middle-class women. It is thought, just as it was in ancient Rome, that this gives an air of respectability, and forms a sure protection from insult in the streets or elsewhere.

Pearls are only twice mentioned in the authorised version of the Old Testament, and both times the pearl is used as a symbol of wisdom.

Some critics have held that the Hebrew word did not exactly mean pearl, but since there can be no doubt that our Saviour referred to the true pearl when He spoke of the " pearl of great price," we may the more implicitly accept it, and gather from the use of the pearl as a figure by the Jewish writers that a perfect pearl has been rare in all ages, and considered of the greatest value.

As may be presumed, from what we have just said, the Romans classed first among pearls those which were pear-shaped, and gave to them the name of *unio*, or unique, a name now in our scientific terminology attached with fitness, as we have seen, to the species of mollusc from which some of the most perfect pearls are obtained.

"To be perfect," says Mr. Emmanuel in his valuable work on gems, "a pearl must be of perfectly pure white colour; it must be perfectly round or drop-shaped; it must be slightly transparent; it must be free from spots or blemish; and it must possess the lustre characteristic of the gem."

At the breaking up of the crown-treasury of France in 1791, a magnificent large spherical pearl, unbored, was sold for £8000; and two pear-shaped ones, which each weighed 214 grains, were valued at £12,000. Another famous pearl of history was that sold to Philip the Fourth of Spain in 1625. It is said that the Shah of Persia is the happy possessor of a pearl valued at £60,000—a goodly estate in small compass, light and portable—and the Imam of Muscat one for which he has been offered £30,000.

The second division in the Roman classification of pearls was "Margarites," which included pearls of any shape or colour, large and misshapen often, but often, too, of exceptional purity and beauty. The jewellers of the Cinque-Cento period, with the fertile ingenuity that distinguished them, gave a new value to these eccentric

G

specimens by mounting them in styles as eccentric. Mermaids and sea-monsters were favourite designs; and some illustrations of this treatment are to be seen in collections in this country, notably in the Devonshire Cabinet.

Unlike most gems, the pearl comes to us fresh, pure, lustrous, direct from the hand of nature. Other precious stones undergo much careful labour at the hands of the lapidary, and sometimes owe much to his art. Diamond-cutting is indeed a branch of art, and cameo-carving is a yet higher one. But the pearl owes nothing to man.

This perhaps has a good deal to do with the sentiments we cherish toward it. It touches us with the same sense of simplicity and truth as the mountain daisy or the wild rose. It is absolutely a gift of nature's own. When we turn from the brilliant, dazzling coronet of diamonds or emeralds to a necklace of pearls, there is a sense of relief, of soft refreshment. The eye rests on it with quiet, satisfied repose. It seems so truly to typify steady and abiding affection, which needs no accessory or adornment to make it more attractive.

But pearls, despite all this, are not free from the fluctuations of fashion and caprice which assail all such commodities.

We have seen how for some years the Scottish fisheries have been affected by the craving for rose-coloured pearls among the ladies of Paris. And different people in this, as in so many other things, display varying tastes and tendencies. The Chinese prefer those of a yellow tint—a dark gold-colour, as one describes it. This tint is peculiar to certain classes of Oriental pearls. Those found in Panama, California, and the South Pacific are more or less dark-looking.

Pearls are pre-eminently children of the light. Not only do they reflect it, but, like flowers, they lose their purity and delicacy of colour if light is for any lengthened period withdrawn from them. So say they who have had most experience of pearls ; and the fact adds a new association and poetic suggestiveness, as it were, affording another very beautiful hint of distinction between them and other gems of purely mineral origin. Those who possess fine pearls had better not forget this, and keep them too long immured in dark and secret corners, however safe. Pearls, we may say, were created to diffuse gentle pleasure, to delight the eye, as they shine simple and translucent.

We have all heard of that draught in which it was said that Cleopatra dissolved her famous pearl, and which she drank at that memorable supper. But science gives the lie to the possibility. No acid the human stomach could receive would be sufficient to dissolve a pearl, and even with the acids of the greatest strength the outer coatings are alone discoloured or destroyed, and this only after a considerable lapse of time. As has been suggested by a very good authority on gems—Mr. King—it is likely that Cleopatra swallowed the solid gem, or found some other means of eluding the vigilance of Antony and those who were with him. Some cynics would say that woman's wiles were quite equal to that enterprise or deception.

References to pearls by great writers, ancient and modern, are very plentiful, as the beauty and purity of the gem would lead one to expect.

We have referred to some of the expressions of Scripture; and we have seen how Pliny viewed the matter, giving in compact version the very unfounded theory of the Romans as to the origin and growth of the pearl. Now that science has taught us better, literature has only found in it, as is invariably the case, a wider field of illustration and imagery. The very associations inseparably linked with the name Margaret, which is only an adaptation of the Greek for pearl, might themselves be cited here. We think of one named Margaret as pure, guileless, untouched with the *finesse* of society, as unspotted with its vices. Something of this Goethe may have had in his mind when he named the heroine of "Faust" Gretchen or Margaret.

Wordsworth, too, makes one of the most touching episodes in the "Excursion" to circle round an ill-fated but noble Margaret. Tennyson, in what is, perhaps, the very finest of his elaborate cabinet of female portraits, painted when he was still a young man, has given us "rare, pale Margaret," and this is, perhaps, the finest of them all. Othello, in his last touching speech, speaks of himself as

> "One, whose hand,
> Like the base Indian, threw a pearl away,
> Richer than all his tribe."

To him Desdemona was Margaret—a pearl. He could not otherwise have so truly and concisely expressed himself.

Herrick is not to be outdone by any in his own line. In the midst of his quaint conceits about Julia he has this verse :—

" Some asked how Pearls did grow and where?
Then spoke I to my Girl
To part her lips, and showed them there
The quarelets of Pearl."

The old fable of pearls being generated by contact with rice, and actually revived not long ago, is only a monstrous imposture. Mr. Hugh Owen has thus disposed of it :—

" The so-called rice is a marine shell of the genus *Cyprœa*, the end or apex of each example carefully filed or ground off to represent the effect of having been fed upon by the pearls. The whole is a deliberate and barefaced imposture, and it is to be hoped that when, some generations hence, this miserable myth again crops up in the repetitive operations of history, some more powerful pen than mine may find employment in denouncing the shameless attempt to impose upon the credulity of the scientific world."

Hypocrisy was said by the witty Frenchman to be the tribute vice pays to virtue. Such imitations and impostures are the respect which Fraud pays to Nature's unsullied Beauty.

V.

AMBER.

THE chastest, and perhaps also most permanently attractive, of gems and ornaments are those that come most direct from the lap of nature and need least from the hands of lapidary or artisan. We have seen how this affects us in the case of pearls; it is almost equally so in the cases of coral and amber. The diamond needs much cutting and polishing ere it sparkles and glitters before us like a second sunlight; and when we look on a first-rate brilliant we perforce acknowledge the fine art of man as well as the wonder and the wealth of nature. The gem that has passed through many processes, and has thus lost much in size and weight, may be very valuable, but it is the emblem of artificial life and its resources, as much as of the amazing fertility of natural laws. We contemplate it with the feelings we would experience in looking on a fine picture rather than on a beautiful landscape; on a portrait rather than on the person it represents. And it is perhaps worthy of remark that the superstitions and dreams of men have been apt to choose out as subjects the purely natural gem rather than the semi-artificial one. This may be due to the fact that the love of charms and spells sustains its force only in a primitive and savage period, and has already faded and become faint when men have risen to some degree of scientific knowledge and artistic skill.

Be this as it may, we are now to deal with a substance which has, in this respect, been particularly favoured. Even the common use of amber as a mouthpiece to tobacco-pipes, &c., is due originally to its having been accepted as a charm; it was believed that the amber would act as a charm or protection against any evil influence that might be present in the tobacco; and among Turks and Arabs, even at this day, the belief is acknowledged. Utility and beauty here once more, though with somewhat of grotesque association, go hand in hand. There is a good deal, therefore, to interest us in amber; and perhaps our time will not be wholly wasted in alluding to it for a little while.

It is not an article of very great consideration, commercially speaking—it does not figure largely in exports and imports—but it is very beautiful; and it has a strange history, due partly to the mystery that long surrounded its origin, and partly to the religious superstitions that were connected with it. Known at an early stage to many peoples, it has not failed to impress their imaginations; and it would claim attention were it only for the recognition accorded to it by poets and romancers. "The fly in amber" has become a proverb. A common object, which in itself would not claim more than common regard, is transmuted into a gem by imprisonment in its shining substance, and becomes of the greatest value.

As to the early ideas of its origin, it may be said that the primitive naturalists all became poets in its study.

The prevailing idea among them was, that amber was a concretion of the tears of sea-birds ; and though later researches have harshly dissipated this fond fancy, the poets, pertinacious as they are on the side of the beautiful and fine sentiment, refuse to let it go. The Baron de la Motte Fouqué, in his exquisite romance of " Undine " —one of the classical productions of modern days—takes this view of it ; and Thomas Moore, in one of his finest efforts, anew consecrates, by his genius, the error. He sings :—

> " Farewell ! be it ours to embellish thy pillow
> With everything beauteous that grows in the deep ;
> Each flower of the rock and each gem of the billow
> Shall sweeten thy bed and illumine thy sleep.
>
> *Around thee shall glitter the loveliest amber*
> *That ever the sorrowing sea-bird wept ;*
> With many a shell in whose hollow-wreathed chamber
> The Peris of ocean by moonlight have slept."

Mrs. Barrett Browning also, in her fine sonnet titled " Comfort," seems to have had some reminiscence of this legendary belief about amber :—

> " Speak to me as to Mary at Thy feet !
> And if no precious gums my hands bestow,
> Let my tears drop like amber as I go
> In reach of Thy divinest voice complete
> In humanest affection—thus, in sooth,
> To lose the sense of losing. As a child
> Whose song-bird seeks the wood for evermore
> Is sung to in its stead by mother's mouth ;
> Till, sinking on her breast, love-reconciled,
> He sleeps the sounder that he wept before."

The Greeks, with their usual tendency to set every belief into anthropomorphic or parabolic form, have thus delicately rung the changes on the tear-idea. The daughters of the sun, they said, were changed into poplars on the

banks of the 'Eridanus, and their tears shed for the death
of their brother Phæthon were converted into amber.
The first mention of amber is found in Homer's "Odyssey"
(xv. 480). There the poet makes Eumæus say, in the
course of his recital of his story—

> "An artist to my father's palace came
> With gold and amber chains, elaborate frame.
> Each female eye the glittering links employ ;
> They turn, review, and cheapen every toy."

This is Pope's translation—hardly so strong and grand
as the original, of course, but the lines give the general
idea, and show that in early Greece, as to-day, the
women were curious and eager for new and beautiful
ornaments ; and the gold and amber chains must have
combined beauty and novelty, and delightfully called
forth, and so far satisfied, both senses in the Greek dames.

By the ancients amber was used at once as a medicine
and as a charm. It was feigned to mitigate, if not to
destroy, the power of evil spirits. And, with many
nations, it was customary to bury amber with the dead,
probably with the idea of its powers as a charm sustain-
ing themselves into the next world. At all events, small
articles and ornaments made of amber have been found
in the tumuli of the Celtic and Saxon periods.

At an early date the electric properties of amber were
discovered by the Greeks ; and in the sixth century
before Christ, Thales the philosopher turned the discovery to some practical account. Lengthened discus-
sions have taken place about the origin of the Greek
name, Electron—some deriving it from the verb *Eleo*, to
draw, accorded to it because of its attractive properties,

which Thales turned to account; but it would appear to have been called Electron long before this discovery of its attractive property, which suggests that it received the name on account of its shining aspect, from the great shiner and source of light, Elector, or the sun. This same term reappears, indeed, in the name of the star Electra, one of the Pleiades. However this may be, whenever we use the term electricity we pay a compliment to amber; for it is through the electrical qualities which amber was found to possess that we call that most subtle and serviceable of modern agents—swifter than Mercury and more reliable—by the name we do.

And now for the prose. It is undoubted that amber is the fossil resin of the *Pinus succinifer*—a species of pine now extinct, but large forests of which covered extensive tracts in certain districts during the Eocene period. A great portion of the sea-bottom of the Baltic is a submerged amber-pine forest; and on the shores the amber is washed up by the tide or hidden in the sand. The trees seem to have exuded this viscous fluid so liberally at certain seasons, that fossils of whole trees have been found so completely covered with it that the amber sheath literally formed a more gigantic model of the tree. This fact accounts in so far for the numbers of insects found imbedded in amber. The condition of many of these proves that they had alighted upon the tree when the amber was still liquid and got entangled in it, and sank and sank till entirely covered, just as we see insects now caught in honey or gum or treacle—in fact, what naturalists name "treacling" (spreading treacle or sweet gum on a tree to attract and to ensnare desired specimens) is only doing in a small way what nature with amber appears to have done in a wholesale way in days long gone by—days prehistoric it may be. Often the insects struggled so hard to escape that they mutilated themselves, leaving only a wing or a limb, as many specimens exist to prove.

We learn that as many as 800 different species of insects have been traced in Prussian amber alone ; and a good deal of light has been thrown on the flora of the amber-pine forests by examination of minute leaves and particles preserved in the amber. Many delicate mosses, ferns, liverworts, and fungi have been found buried in it ; and submitted to microscopical examination, scientific botanists have been able to determine their species.

Amber has also been found in England—on the coasts of Norfolk, Suffolk, and Essex on the north-east, and on the coast of Sussex on the south, and in the London clay at Kensington, but mostly in quantities quite inconsiderable. A mass weighing more than ten pounds is very rare, and a piece which turns the scale at two and a quarter pounds is worth about £9. Its composition chemically may be set down thus :—Carbon, 78.94 ; hydrogen, 10.53 ; oxygen, 10.53.

It would be strange in these days of hard competition —when paste so often does duty for precious stones, and manufactured diamonds are difficult to distinguish by ordinary eyes from the real ones—if sometimes substitutes for amber were not imposed on those unskilled in the matter. And we find that it is so. Copal and Animé resins, obtained from certain trees in India and America, are often sold for amber, especially when insects have been imbedded in them.   One important test there is, however, and we believe an infallible *one*, to those whose knowledge enables them to apply it.   The insects found in amber are invariably of *extinct* species, or of species peculiar to warmer climates ; those in copal are all referable to existing and to indigenous kinds.   The differences in the colours of different ambers, it may be well to add, are due to accidental chemical combinations.

A considerable number of people on the coasts of the Baltic are employed in the search for amber ; and though the find varies—just as it does with our own jet-seekers on the Yorkshire coasts—they succeed in making, on the whole, a comfortable subsistence.   The chief uses of amber are well known, and its presence in the more ornamental tobacco-pipes along with *meerschaum* is almost invariable.   We have already hinted at the superstitious notion to which this custom no doubt was due.

Samland, which lies between the Frische Haff and the Kurische Haff, about midway between Danzig and Memel, is the headquarters of the fishers of the Baltic, and the bulk of the amber-supply of the world has been obtained from the district of which this may be regarded as the centre.   The sand-dunes extend for miles around, and run in under the ocean-floor, and are composed of the veins of blue earth, in which the amber is found imbedded.   A little way out beyond the lighthouse, on what is called the Fox-point, is one of the great amber-reefs of Bernstein-Küsti, which is a great ridge of amber cropping up in the sea-bed, and washed and heaped up with sand and sea-weed by the ceaseless movement of the water.   This reef runs a good way inland, but underground. Amber can thus be mined as well as fished, but the valuable yellow deposit being nearer to the surface under the sea than it is on land, fishing is found to be more profitable than mining. In contrast with most other fishers, who delight in calms, and, as far as they can, eschew the storms, the Baltic amber-fishers are always active in time of tempest. Wave and wind do then more than half the work. The sea in fury loosens and throws aside the sand and boulders which have gathered over the reef, and sets them rolling in great masses towards the shore. Then the fishermen, armed with long hooked forks and hand-nets, wade almost up to the shoulders into the sea. While some poke at the masses of seaweed and tangle, driven towards them by the waves, and strain to pull as much of it as they can to the land, others try to gather into their nets the stray pieces of amber tossed about by the waves. As the masses of weed, &c., are landed they are passed on to women, who quickly loosen from them the fragments of amber that may have adhered to them. Only, however, the smaller pieces are thus cast up by the sea. The larger and more beautiful are almost invariably rolled about on the seabottom, and to recover them the amber-fishers must wait for the first clear day. Then they row out into the shallows, and when they see a fine bit of amber they raise it by means of their long-pronged forks and nets.

Sometimes, too, diving is employed. One reef in especial, a little to the north-east of Samland, is worked in this way. It is said to be the most valuable in existence, producing by far the finest amber. It is over 600 feet long and more than 400 feet broad, and consists of solid pieces of amber deposited by the currents that meet just there, and imbedded in the sand and sea-weed that accumulate about it. A little flotilla of boats are to be seen there on almost any day of the ten months when it is worked. Their process of work has thus been described by an eye-witness :—

" Each of the half-score boats at anchor here has six hands on board, besides the divers who are at work below. Two pair take charge alternately at the air-pumps, which must be kept going without an instant's stoppage; one holds the life-lines in his fingers, watching for the least pull, which is a signal to haul up, and the last is the overseer, who keeps his eye on everything. With stout crowbar and pronged iron the diver fishes about among the masses of weed and sand and stone that form the sea-bottom until he detects the presence of an amber-mass; or crawling about on hands and knees, he loosens from the sea-floor any blocks recent storms may have partially dislodged. Often these pieces require two or even three divers to move them; and gigantic slabs have now and again been found that resisted even the united strength of three pair of hands to disengage them from the masses of stone and weed encumbering them. The fishers remain down five hours a day; and though in autumn the sea is icy cold, so severe is the strain of working under water that they rise to the surface bathed in perspiration."

It will thus be easily believed that the amber-fishers are a strong, brave, resolute set of men. When the temperature is very low down they go into the depths with their heavy diving armour, and remain down for long periods. They are not Germans, we are told, but Samiates of the Kurish race, who have often dealt sturdy blows to Cossacks and Russians in frontier wars.

Water amber is by far the best, being clearer, brighter in colour, and more transparent than land amber. The best of the amber, we learn, goes to Constantinople and the East, where much store is laid by it for mouth-pieces; Italy receives most of the lighter-tinted specimens, and some of both sorts find their way to Germany and England; while the more dense and less well-coloured is mostly made up into beads and ornaments to barter to the natives of the South-sea Islands and Central Africa for other things—the product of their lands.

VI.

COMMON SALT.

ONE of the most remarkable errors of a great writer
was that of Dean Swift about salt. In his "Voyage to
the Houyhnhnms," after describing his efforts to find
food for himself, and his dependence upon herbs, milk,
and butter, he proceeds :—

"I was at first at a great loss for salt, but custom soon
reconciled me to the want of it ; and *I am* confident
that the frequent use of salt among us is a luxury, and
was introduced only as a provocative to drink, except
where it is necessary for preserving of flesh in long
voyages, or in places remote from great markets. For
we observe no animal to be fond of it but man, and as
to myself, when I left this country, it was a great while
before I could endure the taste of it in anything that
I ate."

Swift is sometimes guilty of gigantic jokes, even when
he is most sardonically in earnest ; but here he cannot
be regarded as humorous and playful, nor would he have
knowingly laid himself open to the risk of being charged
with ignorance of nature or of science. Here he certainly is in error. Salt is as needful to animals as to
man, and some of the most remarkable phenomena of

the animal creation are due to the need for it, and the powerful, if not irresistible, impulse to gratify the craving. Some diseases in animals, indeed, can only be cured by salt. The peculiar effect of feeding on salt-marshes in restoring sheep to good condition is well known, and the remarkable impulse which directs herds of animals from great distances at certain seasons to the "salt-licks," or earths impregnated with salt, is well known. The migration of the lemmings—which has astonished so many travellers in the colder regions—is probably due to this cause. Those who know about the proper treatment of horses and cows are well aware of the simple method by which the risk of deficiency of salt in the food is provided for. Lumps of rock-salt are put into the mangers or scattered over the pastures. It is often mixed with hay. Even bees and other insects will, with avidity, sip a solution of salt. Men will barter gold for it in countries where it is scarce, and for it husbands have been known to sell their wives and parents their children. In hot countries it is even more a necessity, as we shall see, than in colder ones. In India—that is, British India—the State takes advantage of this with a view to the exchequer, and heavily taxes salt, in some places not even allowing the poor peasants to drive their oxen to the "salt-licks," that they may not escape from the full payment of this severe tax. Salt-water lakes abound in Southern Africa, but Mungo Park relates that in the interior districts, where salt is exceedingly scarce, it was regarded as the greatest luxury. He tells us that he frequently met little naked children sucking lumps of rock-salt like sugar-candy. To say of a man in that

H

region that he eats salt with his dinner was to signify that he was a person of wealth and station. In Abyssinia —and no wonder—salt ranks as a precious metal, which it is, and there, as in other parts of Interior Africa, is used as money is used in other countries—it is a medium of exchange. Professor Max Müller, indeed, on this ground, traces the verb "sell" itself to the root *salt.** The Abyssinian carries small pieces of salt about with him, and the highest honour he can show to a friend or guest, is to present him with a piece, or to let him taste it. The necessity for salt is universal with all living creatures, and a good argument for design in nature might be based on the fact that what is so universally required to sustain healthy animal life is also universal, though very unequal in its distribution. Salt is found everywhere. Indeed, except air and water, nothing on this globe exists in such a quantity or is so universally distributed. Nature has stored it up in veins in the earth, has spread it, like hoar-frost, over vast plains, has dissolved it in swamps, in seas, and inland lakes; it is in solution in all springs. It is an important constituent in the blood of all creatures, a component of their bones, and of the flesh which covers them. It is hidden in trees, and the sap which stirs and trembles through every fibre in vegetation would become slower, at length sluggish, and cease altogether were it not for the salt that also seasons their life.

Chemically it is known as chloride of sodium—a name given to it because of its chemical constituents. It is a combination of two very simple bodies in certain propor-

---

* " Biographies of Words," p. 76.

tions. In 100 parts of salt there are 60.4 of chlorine and 39.6 parts of sodium.

It furnishes one out of many instances of the wonderful changes which come over substances when chemically combined, and which form the unceasing wonder and charm of chemistry, as the doorway to mysteries and to endless possibilities of discovery and invention. Here we have indeed a transformation as surprising as any fairy scene.

Chlorine is a yellow gas, and sodium is a metal of silvery lustre, which will burn in the open air, and burns spontaneously in water. Combined in the proportions given above they produce the white substance with which we are all so familiar that it ceases to be regarded with any special interest. It is only *common* salt. It is twice as heavy as water, in which it is soluble, 100 parts of water dissolving 37 of the salt. It dissolves much more quickly in sea-water than in fresh, owing to its affinity to the salts already there.

As regards solubility, it is but little affected by temperature; if you warm a piece of salt and throw it into sufficient water to dissolve it, it disappears almost instantly. The air has little or no effect on dissolving or moistening it; that the salt we use gets moist and melts in some circumstances is due to the fact that the salt of commerce is seldom quite pure, as a chemist would judge it. Minute quantities of magnesium chloride are, we are told, present in it, and this is one of the most easily damped or melted of all substances by the moisture of the air.

But this detracts nothing from the health-giving effect,

nay, is rather said to add to it, alike in the physical economy of man and in the animals and in nature. By absorbing moisture from the atmosphere it keeps the earth damp, and thus increases the nourishment of vegetation, besides destroying many kinds of insects, caterpillars, grubs, &c. The earth, the air, and the sea are thus one vast laboratory for the preparation of salt, in which incalculable stores of life and health and strength are being continually produced and preserved.

That remarkable genius and clever chemist, Dr. Angus Smith, whose mind delighted to dwell on the common things of life and nature, and to reveal their wonders, has some very fine passages about salt.

In his work on "Air and Rain" he finds himself under the necessity of directly connecting tempests and storms with the distribution of salt. He inquires, "How comes this salt to be present in soils far inland, hundreds of miles, it may be, from the sea?" And he supplies this answer: "One of the uses of storms is to supply the world with salt. The salt is brought by the travelling clouds, each vesicle charged with a precious burden, sent up by evaporation from the surface of the ocean." And he winds up by asking, "Are there not traces of a superintending Mind in this vast system of 'demand and supply'?"

He further suggests that these same travelling rain-drops, swiftly borne on the wings of the tempest, not only serve the purpose of great salt-carriers, but at the same time act, in some degree no doubt through the very presence of that precious antiseptic, salt, as power-ful scavengers in clearing the air of noxious gases, and also as subtle fertilisers, bringing down ammonia and nitric acid to the earth.

Small as they are individually, in their combination they form also a great earth-plough, by corrosion of the rocks, loosening the particles by processes most gradual, and thus by aggregation of fine loose particles forming fresh soils.

And not only this, they are great burrowers, and penetrate by the tiniest veins and fissures down to the dark underworld, there to continue their most salutary work. They dissolve the mineral constituents prisoned down below, and set certain of their elements loose for their needful and beneficent purposes above, and thus all our plant-food is presented to us and to the animals in the proper state for assimilation. "Pursuing their journey to the nearest river, they finally return to the ocean. No single drop, however, goes back empty. Each is laden with an invisible burden of salts, held in suspension and drawn from the rocks and surface-soil through which it has passed." In this way, in return for the salts supplied to the rising vapour, the ocean receives back those necessary for marine vegetation, and the all-essential lime for the shells of the mollusca, for the work of the coral-builders, the pearl-producing bivalves, and all the rest of this class.

So it may be said that the air circulates, the rain-clouds form and float, the storms sweep from sea to land, the tempest roars, and in a sense the sun itself kindly shines to carry on the salt-supply, to equalise distribution, and to purify the world, and make it habitable, healthy, and beautiful. We do not need to go far for

wonders equal to those of any fairy-tale. When we see
a rain-drop, or hear the wind blow, or see a cloud sailing the sky before the wind, or listen to the whisper of
the leaves in summer, we may think of that mysterious
system of circulation which ministers to the necessity
and well-being of everything that breathes and lives.

And in the seas themselves, though we are wont to
speak of *the* "salt sea," as if it were all uniform, there is
constant variability. Currents and streams are there
too, and there is continual flow and change and variation. All parts of the sea are not equally salt; the waters
at one spot are not always uniform; nor are all seas
of the same saltness, as the Dead Sea or Salt Sea of
Scripture is enough to tell us. Temperature and evaporation, which is constantly modified by temperature, are
the two great agents in this modification. Rains, too, and
streams constantly falling into it have their own influences.

Salt water and fresh mingle slowly. The fresh water
passes away from the shore, and in many cases proceeds
a considerable distance, directed as it were by the
ocean currents, before it wholly assimilates with and is
lost in the salt water that encompassed it. We know
this, for one thing, from the difference of colour between
the salt water and the currents of fresh water. Heavy
rains, too, will sometimes rest for a definite period,
floating oil-like on the top of the salt water, so that those
at sea have been able actually to secure fresh water from
the surface of the ocean by hollow vessels or by absorbing it in woollen cloths or sponges, and then drawing
it up.

The reason why some inland seas are more salt than

the great ocean is, that there evaporation proceeds more quickly than the supply of fresh water; this is the case with the Dead Sea. Others, again, receive supplies of fresh water more quickly than evaporation proceeds, and are more or less fresh. The Mediterranean Sea is much more salt than the Baltic, and for the same reason. The Black Sea is almost fresh, from the enormous quantities of fresh water poured into it continually and the slowness of evaporation there. It contains only 0.17 solid parts per 1000, while the English Channel, on the average, contains 35.23, and the Dead Sea so much as 245.80.

Salt, as may already have been inferred, is got in three forms, the processes through which it is put varying according to the source, and these we shall try very shortly to describe. There is (1) rock-salt, which is obtained from mines; it is found among stratified rocks, and has been formed from water mainly by evaporation. Then (2) there is the salt from the sea; and (3) there is the salt found scattered over the surface of the earth at certain parts in such a quantity as to render collection of it profitable.

1. The accepted theory about the formation of rock-salt is, that it is the result of evaporation on the beds of estuaries or rivers, when these have either dried up or have changed their course, other deposits of silt and earth forming over the bed of salt, and the rock being formed by natural pressure through gradual processes.

This is proved by the fact that fossils of zoophytes, univalves, and crustaceans, and other specimens of creatures still found living are to be discovered in it, which proves also that rock-salt beds, though gradually formed, do not require a very lengthened or indefinite period of geological time. Indeed, it is a comfort to know that salt is thus being formed day by day throughout the world in at least an equal ratio with the consumption of it, and, unlike our coal-seams, has no prospect of being exhausted even at the most distant period.

Scientific men tell us that the ocean itself has been the source of all rock-salt, and this fact only adds another to the many wonders of the subject, since evaporation is always so busy, and the salt, after all, does not settle on the sea-bottoms, so far as we know.

The salinity of sea-water has been ascertained to decrease with its depth; and from the forms of life found at great depths, and other circumstances, we know that the bed of the ocean is not salt. Salt is found in every aqueous formation. The most extensive deposits in the world are in Europe, extending for over 500 miles along the Carpathians, in some places with a width of about a hundred miles and a thickness of about 12,000 feet. The mines of Upper Austria, Hungary, the Tyrol, Salzburg, Transylvania, Wallachia, and others belong to this range.

The Vieliczska mines in Poland are the largest in the world. Although they have been worked since 1251, the resources of the mines have been hardly touched. Already there are from thirty to forty miles of gallery, and the extent of this, of course, is being increased every year. In our own country there is a vast bed of salt under the valley of Cheshire, stretching all the way from Malpas to Congleton. At Northwich there is a mine which has been worked since 1670. And one of the phenomena observed by travellers in that region who do not take any particular interest in salt or its chemistry is the irregular subsidence of the houses owing to the mining and brine-pumping. They nod and bend towards each other at some points in the most remarkable manner.

In Spain there are some extensive salt-mines; and at Cordonna there is a mountain of salt upwards of 500 feet high. In Nevada there are still more wonderful salt mountains, transparent almost as glass and almost as white as snow.

Rock-salt is worked at various depths and various heights.

The Vieliczska mines are some 860 feet below the level of the soil and 300 feet below the level of the sea, while in Arbonne, in Savoy, the salt is 7300 feet above the sea-level, actually among snow-peaks.

Rock-salt, too, is mined in various ways. Sometimes it is quarried by water, but this is in most cases found to be an expensive process, and the most common method is simply with pick, crowbar, and gunpowder.

Wherever water touches the rock-bed there are likely to be brine-springs, and sometimes brine-springs are artificially made by boring and introducing water. The brine is then pumped up or drawn off, and the salt in solution crystallised in the ordinary way.

Even after mines have been opened it has often been deemed advantageous to dig pits within the mine and flood them with water to dissolve the salt, so as to procure the brine without the labour of mining.

In England salt was derived from brine-springs long before the beds of rock-salt were disclosed and worked. William the Conqueror instituted an inquiry into the "salt-houses" in operation in the time of Edward the Confessor; and Henry the Third, when at war with the Welsh, caused their brine-springs to be destroyed, that they might be deprived of salt. The beds of rock-salt from which the springs originated were not discovered till 1670.

2. The next great source of salt-supply is the sea itself. The usual method of obtaining it is by estuaries or back-waters, or by artificially constructed places called "salt-gardens." At certain seasons the sea rushes with great force into these spaces, and then, when the tide falls or the storm is over, the mouth of the estuary, or "garden," is closed with sand or otherwise, leaving the backwater, which evaporates and leaves a saline deposit, in some cases really a bed of salt, or very strongly impregnated brine, which is either conveyed away or pumped into the receptacles necessary for its further purification.

3. Swamps. In some cases these are formed by sea-floods in low-lying places, where the sea-water is retained and evaporation leaves a deposit of salt; in other cases walls of mud are built, to keep a greater quantity of the water. In these cases the product is called "spontaneous salt."

Sometimes, in exceptional situations, the rain causes the salt which exists in too abundant measure to ooze out of the soil and to crystallise. This is called "efflor-esced salt." Sometimes, too, when the shore of a sea is formed of a particular loose kind of sand, which has a

retaining hold over the salt, the water percolates inland
for some distance, depositing salt as it goes. Wells are
sunk, and then these seaside districts yield a brine more
saline than the ocean, and this is then dealt with in the
ordinary way, and made to yield its quota of salt.

Generally speaking, the salt as procured from nature
is in too crude and impure a condition for use without
undergoing further elaboration. It is first dissolved,
evaporated, and then crystallised by ordinary processes,
of which we shall now proceed to give the simplest outline.

This after-process of purification may briefly be said
to have these results in view. Crude salt is sure to
contain a certain proportion of magnesium chloride,
which, as we have seen, is the element which causes
salt to melt in exposure to moisture of the air; and also
a proportion of magnesium sulphate, which in common
language is Epsom salts. The presence of this would,
in addition to other disadvantages, vitiate the taste; and
in smaller quantities calcium sodium is also found, which
must be withdrawn. But, owing to the chemical law
that as the bulk of water needful to dissolve them is
evaporated away the salts separate, the less soluble first
and so on, the salt manufacturer, with attention to grades
of temperature, finds this easy, and with his knowledge
and engines reduces it almost to a mechanical process.

The following is a very simple and general description
of the process followed at the Cheshire mines.

First, the blasting of the mine. A shot-hole is drilled
with an arrow-headed rod of iron some eight feet in
length. The hole is cleared of every particle of dust,
and then charged with several ounces of coarse powder,

some salt being laid on the top. A straw filled with fine powder is then placed in the shot-hole, and the charge is fired with a piece of cotton-wick.

In a second or two the charge explodes, and many tons of solid rock-salt are blown outwards to a short distance.

These fragments are then collected, placed in baskets, and pushed on rails to the mouth of the pit. They are then raised by steam-power.

Two qualities of salt result. One called Prussian rock, from its being largely exported to the shores of the Baltic; the other coarser, used chiefly for agricultural purposes. Much of it is sent to Australia, where the land in large areas in some quarters demands its application.

In Cheshire there are constant brine-springs in working, as well as rock-salt mining. To raise the brine various methods are adopted. Not very many years ago it was raised by human labour, men half-naked descending to the pit by stairs and drawing up the water in leathern buckets. Water-wheels, wind-mills, and horse-power took their place; and these, in their turn, have given place completely to steam.

The brine is pumped up through a series of iron tubes screwed together and called *trees*. It is then carried across the yard in a wooden trough fixed to the tops of the *trees*, and emptied into a vast cistern or reservoir. Here, while it remains unagitated, an iron-grey scum forms on the top, which is filled with bubbles. A quantity of rock-salt is kept in the reservoirs, to ensure the complete saturation of the brine.

This salt water is now ready for the process of manufacture into table-salt by means of artificial evaporation.

The brine is made to flow through pipes into the evaporating pans. These are large square or circular vessels made of wrought iron, and supported on brick furnaces, which extend far beneath the pans. Some of these pans are sixty feet long and forty feet wide, while others are considerably larger even than that. Over furnace and pan is a wooden shed to keep out all cold air.

The pans being filled with brine, the fires are lighted, and the work of evaporation begins. After a short lapse of time a man takes his place on a platform at the edge of the pan. His business is that of "raking." He throws out constantly into the midst of the boiling fluid a long iron rake, with which he draws to the surface of the fluid masses of a fine white substance which had settled at the bottom.

As soon as the brine begins to boil the salt rises to the surface in a kind of scum, and then, after a short time, it sinks slowly to the bottom, when it is drawn together and lifted out, with a large perforated "skimmer;" all the brine escaping through the holes as it is being lifted.

The salt is then placed in little wooden tubs, also bored with holes, set round in spaces by the side of the pan.

Having filled a certain number of these tubs, the man *haps* or smoothes the salt carefully over, and sets the batch on a kind of hurdle to be conveyed to the drying-room, a long low chamber highly heated by flues extending from the furnace. The spaces between the flues are called "ditches," really drains to carry off the water from the tubs. After a certain exposure here the salt becomes thoroughly solid. Then it is removed in the oblong blocks in which it is sold.

The production of the different kinds of salt is determined by the degree of heat to which the brine is exposed, and the time thus allowed for the process of detachment from other salts and for crystallisation. The process we have more particularly described above is that of "Lump Salt." What is called "Patent Butter Salt"—the finest of all—is made in circular pans, completely covered over; the salt, as it settles at the bottom, being "raked" by a mechanical process of leverage into what is called a "hopper," a kind of square tub, placed at the side of the pan.

"Common Salt" is made in pans which are never heated to the boiling point. This kind of salt is largely used for chemical and preserving purposes, being coarser and more open, from the length of time it has been allowed to settle or "feed" at the bottom of the pan.

"Rough Salt" is made from brine just warmed through and no more. The pans, in this case, are only cleared about once a week, and the salt, being very coarse in the grain, is much in demand for salting herrings and such things.

"Fishery Salt" is coarser still: it is only drawn once a fortnight or so, with grains sometimes as much as half-an-inch long. This is entirely used for salting fish. To aid in purifying the salt a pinch of soft soap or glue is generally thrown into the brine, and the pans are kept always full.

Thus the description of crystals of the salt obtained from the brine varies precisely according to the degree of heat used in the evaporating process. A temperature of 120 degrees will produce bay salt, whereas a temperature of 225 degrees is necessary for producing the finest table-salt, which, as we have seen, cannot be obtained in open pans. Within this range of temperature all the different forms of salt-crystals are deposited.

The workers have heavy, heating labour and long hours, and many must perform night-work, as the furnaces must be kept up and the pans never allowed to become exhausted. Most of the workers at the pans are Poles or Germans.

Each evaporating pan in some of the works at Droitwich was recently attended by four women, two on each side, who lifted the salts from the boiling brine, as it crystallised, and placed it in moulds. When the moisture was sufficiently drained away through the perforations in the moulds at the smaller end they were removed, and carried into the drying stores, which were always kept at a temperature of from 120 to 160 degrees.

The work of the women began at six in the morning. At that operation each woman was expected to fill seventy moulds, which are formed of stout boards, and to carry the solidified crystal blocks into the drying-store. At one o'clock they had to fill and remove sixty, and at half-past four an additional thirty. As these moulds with their contents weigh from forty to sixty pounds, and sometimes even more, the reader will understand something of the weights these poor women had to carry, and will join with us in the hope that more and more this kind of female labour will give place to lighter and more suitable.

That salt in its pure state does not melt under any circumstances of exposure to air is proved by many facts.

Salt in its rock form is one of the hardest minerals. It can be cut and carved into the most beautiful shapes. Indeed, in some parts of India there is a considerable industry in making ornamental articles from it—jars, platters, cups, and even knives have been made of it. In Poland it is carved into crucifixes, beads, inkstands, and many other articles, even billiard-balls. In the mines of Vieliczska, which, as we have seen, are very extensive and very celebrated, there is a statue of King John Sigismund in salt. For a considerable period this statue was at Warsaw, and showed no injury from the changes of climate. We read that in 1698 a chapel to St. Anthony was excavated in these mines; and all the furniture—the pulpit, the pews, the altars, doors, statues and ornamental work—was formed of the beautiful crystal rock-salt. The mangers, troughs, and stalls for the horses which work in the mine were also formed of it, so that in this case the animals could not possibly suffer from a neglect from which other domestic animals often suffer elsewhere.

Very often people make a great mistake when they use salt to melt snow at their doorways and fail to remove the liquid mixture, increasing thus the cold temperature of their houses in winter. When salt is mixed with snow the heat of the crystals becomes latent in passing from the solid to the melted state. The mixture is thus much colder than melted snow would be of itself. This, indeed, was the mixture, called "frigorific mixture," which Fahrenheit used in 1714 when he made his thermometer, as it was then the lowest temperature known—the zero, indeed, of the scale of the thermometer which is so well known by his name. Since then, however, a greater degree of coldness has been produced by the evaporation of ether and of ammonia, and by the liberation of compressed air.

The statute-books of the world, too, bear good witness to the necessity of salt as food.

Several countries in old days adopted as a punishment deprivation of salt. One of the old laws of Holland ordained as the severest punishment that can be conceived that certain malefactors should be fed on bread in which there was no salt. The effect, we learn, was horrible and painful in the extreme; and, of course, it was aggravated by the moist climate of the country. The wretched creatures sentenced to this penalty are said to have been literally devoured by worms engendered in their own stomachs; and medical men know that there is a tendency to a disease which issues in something of the same result in those who have an aversion, individual or inherited, to salt.

Not only is salt a great and necessary element in the blood, but it is a wonderful aid in exciting the gustatory nerves and stimulating the flow of saliva, and is a great assistance to digestion. In the stomach the salt is decomposed into what is called hydrochloric acid and a soluble sodium salt. The acid is essential to digestion, and the sodium salt is absorbed to sustain the alkali-

I

nity of the blood and to preserve the density of the fluids of the body.

Its antiseptic action, also, should be remembered—its power in preserving flesh from decomposition. Salt-miners and sailors are among the most healthy and robust classes of workers. The amount of salt needed by individuals varies, and it will vary by a slight degree with certain kinds of food, because some foods contain less salt, some more; but half-an-ounce a day may be set down as a safe allowance, always remembering that here there is more safety in excess than in defect, and that moderation may hardly, in this case, be the golden mean. Any excess the system easily carries off, whereas too little can only have injurious results. Rice and other farinaceous foods demand more salt than any other kinds of food, to prevent the appearance of certain diseases—gastrodynia amongst them, from which the poor Hindoos are wont to suffer, through an enforced economy in salt.

Salt, too, is an admirable aperient. Many persons in India take a glass of sea-water every morning. It has also been successfully used in this way in Jamaica and other West Indian islands. Dr. Priestley found that sprigs of plants and vegetables lived longer and flourished better in water containing two grains of salt to the ounce, but that they speedily died in water containing twelve grains to the ounce. This is quite in keeping with the experience of farmers. If there is a deficiency of salt in the land on which, more especially, serials are grown, then it must be sown in the field.

The place of salt in industry would, however, need a

long essay to itself. It is essential in the production of certain glazes for pottery; for improving the whiteness and clearness of glass; for giving hardness to soap; for preventing calcination on the surface of certain metals by protecting them from the air; for improving certain colours; for assays, and for certain processes in photography.

Salt is often referred to in Scripture, and there at first it is used as a type of barrenness and desolation due to the bare and utterly sterile aspect of the salt-plains, on which the early writers would look with no clear scientific knowledge to modify their views. It is very odd indeed, and instructive too, to read in Judges ix. 45, that, when Abimelech destroyed the city of Shechem and completely razed the place, he "fought against the city all that day; and he took the city, and slew the people that was therein, and beat down the city, and *sowed it with salt.*"

But more knowledge and attention to the properties of salt in course of time modified (as was most natural it should) the whole conception of it among the Jews, and made it the emblem of health and purity, instead of that of desolation and barrenness and death.

Great stress was laid upon salt in the offerings under the Levitical Law : " Every oblation of thy meat-offering shalt thou season with salt; neither shalt thou suffer the salt of the Covenant of thy God to be wanting from thy meat-offering; with all thine offerings shalt thou offer salt."

The meaning of our word salt, which is Gothic, has been defined as that which " occasions all tastes ; " and this was the view which the later Old Testament writers took of it. With them it stood for the symbol of wisdom, giving savour to a man's character. St. Paul, writing to the Colossians, urges that their speech should always be "seasoned with salt;" and our Saviour Himself called His apostles "the salt of the earth."

Livy paid a fine compliment to Greece when he called it "Sal gentium," from whence scholars say that the common phrase "Attic salt," or the wisdom and wit that seasons speech, was derived. Shakespeare mentions salt some thirty-nine times; sometimes in the ordinary sense, sometimes figuratively. It is very peculiar to notice that he regarded salt as essential to tears, and seems to have had an idea that the deeper the grief the salter the tear-drops. He also knew that salt formed an important part in the economy of the human body, for more than once he speaks of a "salt rheum which offends me."

Very probably it was this idea of the saltness of tears which gave rise to some of the superstitions connected with salt, which are very numerous.

It is thought unlucky to help any one to salt at table, and the superstition has given rise to the proverb, "Helped to salt, helped to sorrow." To spill salt also is held to be unfortunate, and when threatened with ill-luck it was a custom in old times to throw salt over the left shoulder. Houses were salted for luck, and salt was invariably put beside a corpse as well as the lighted candles. No wake in Ireland at this day would be considered right without the salt in the plates beside the dead; and in Scotland long after the era of the Reformation the Church found it very difficult to cast out these practices.

Salt in early times was symbolical of favour and good-will, and covenants of friendship were ratified by this gift. In the Old Testament, even, we have the Covenant of Salt. Among Jews and Greeks and Romans, as well as among less civilised tribes, salt was used in their sacrifices as emblematic of fidelity, and for some reason or other it also came to be regarded as a charm against witchcraft and evil influence or fascination. It was all-potent as a protection for children among Roman Catholics before the administration of the rite of baptism. This practice is referred to in many of the old ballads and romances. In a ballad called "The King's Daughter" a child is born, but in circumstances which do not admit of baptism being administered. The mother privately puts the baby into a casket, and, like the mother of Moses, sends it afloat, and as a protection places beside it a quantity of salt and candles. One verse of the ballad is :—

> " The bairnie she swyled (swathed) in line sae fine,
> In a gilded casket she laid it syne (then) ;
> Mickle saut (salt) and licht (light) she laid therein,
> Cause yet in God's house it hadna been."

The reason that lies at the root of these strange customs is, that the evil spirits were held to be kept away by the salt, not being able to come near what Christ had chosen as the symbol of the savour of the earth.

Another instance of the use of salt as a superstitious aid to the undoing of evil influences may be cited from Mr. C. G. Leland's " Toad Lore :"—

"I have been informed by gypsies that toads do really form unaccountable predilections for persons and places. The following is accurately related as it was told me in Rommany fourteen years ago, in Epping Forest, by a girl: 'You know, sir, that people who live out of doors all the time, as we do, see and know a great deal about such creatures. One day we went to a farm-house, and found the wife almost dying because she thought she was bewitched by a woman who came every day in the form of a great toad to her door and looked in. And, sure enough, while she was talking the toad came, and the woman was taken in such a way with fright that I thought she'd have died. But I had a laugh to myself, for I knew that toads have such ways, and can not only be tamed, but will almost tame themselves. So we gypsies talked together in Rommany, and then said we could remove the spell if she would get us a pair of shears and a *cup of salt.* Then we caught the toad, and tied the shears so as to make a cross—you see!—and with it threw the toad into the fire and *poured the salt on it.* So the witchcraft was ended, and the lady gave us a good meal and ten shillings.' A Rommany poem has been written on this subject, which is so good that we must give it here : *—

"THE WITCH.

"We went one day to a farmer's house,
  His wife was so weak she could scare arouse ;
  But when she saw we were Rommany,
  She spoke to us very civilly,
  And said with many a gasp and twitch :
  'I'm dying—and all of a wicked witch.

---

* "English Gypsey Songs." Trübner & Co., 1875.

Look there ! look there !   It is coming now ;
The evil thing is dancing, I vow !
My God ! oh, help me !'—and peeping in
At the open door, with a wicked grin,
Came a great grey toad, with a hop and a hitch :
'See there !' cried the woman—'see, there's my witch !

Every day and hour it is coming here—
The devilish creature is always near ;
If I throw it away, the first thing I see,
It is jumping again, and staring at me ;
All night I hear it hiss by the ditch,
And all night long I dream of the witch.'

Then we spoke together in Romniany,
And told her at last how the thing must be :
'If you have shears, just bring them here,
And with them a cup of salt, my dear,
And as sure as we're poor and you are rich,
The gypsies will soon take care of the witch.'

Then the lady gave us all a treat,
Ale and bacon and plenty to eat,
And a ten-shilling-piece as we went away—
Since people who work must get their pay ;
And it's good for all, be they poor or rich,
If gypsies come when they're plagued with a witch."

Salt is a symbol of hospitality all over the East.   To
have eaten of a man's salt means that he is your friend,
and to be false to your salt is to descend to the level of
a betrayer and a traitor.   Among the Arabs, perhaps, this
sentiment is carried to the highest pitch.

We have spoken of the taxes on salt.   The more
fully we come to realise the absolute necessity of salt to
life, the more grievous does this taxation appear.   But
this is no new grievance.   History has its own tale to
tell on this score, by no means *creditable to kings* and
governments in the past any more than in the present.
Salt was taxed in ancient Rome.   In France the taxes

on salt had a good deal to do with the discontent that finally issued in the Revolution. A code of salt-laws called *Gabelle* were so severe that nearly five thousand people were every year sent to prison for offences against it. At present the duty on salt in France is 100 francs a ton. In England a salt-tax was imposed in the reign of William the Third, and there were continual affrays with smugglers on account of it. The tax became very obnoxious, and loud agitations were raised against it. It was finally abolished in 1825. Other nations have hardly yet been so lucky. In Prussia its sale is still a Government monopoly. In Hungary it is still heavily taxed. But India is perhaps the saddest case of all as regards the taxes on salt. It is a Government monopoly in the Madras Presidency, and it is subject to a heavy excise in the Bengal and Bombay Presidencies. In Madras, it is said, there is a good deal of salt smuggling, and no wonder! Hundreds of natives are annually convicted for taking salt that has paid no duty, and where it is impracticable to watch and protect a natural salt-supply, it is destroyed because it is a "menace to the revenue."

In some parts of India salt is thus almost as high as is the price of oatmeal in Scotland. The total cost of a ton of salt as delivered at the depôt is only 17s. 6d. The price which the traders pay, including the duty, is £8, 5s. in silver. The figures are eloquent of the sufferings which must be imposed on the poor people by this import, and surely true motives of statesmanship as well as motives of philanthropy should lead to some reform in this respect very soon.

VII.

BURTON ALE AND DUBLIN STOUT.

BURTON-ON-TRENT is a town by itself. It seems to exist for ale as well as to live by ale, and has actually the look of one great brewery, which, like some mighty monster, has put forth arms and settled new centres at remote points. Barrels full, barrels empty, meet the eye at every turn ; barrels piled up in pyramids or ranged in gigantic rows, barrels being rolled from point to point and laden on carts or waggons or railway-trucks. Wonder overtakes one, as one walks about, as to where boundaries begin and end ; for none seem to be definitively marked by the ordinary means. The railways traverse the streets on the same level. Gates fly open at crossings, and there is no " Open sesame " for the foot-passengers till the barrel-laden trains have passed, and sometimes they take a good long time. Foot-passengers—more especially strangers in the town — are apparently not of much account ; and if they do not know the ways of the place it is all the worse for them. Here, *pace* Sir Wilfrid Lawson, Beer truly is king. It is only after the exercise of a considerable amount of thought and oft-repeated inquiries that one gets to realise the Bass's works end here, and Allsopp's begin there, and that Ind, Coope, & Co.'s are yonder; and that all this activity, directed to one object, is the result of rival establishments, which thus far, at all events, act harmoniously. You cannot escape from the flavour of malt; the scent of hops pursues you. As the result of some general questions, we learn that each brewery—at all events each of the larger breweries—has its own private railway (with several engines to work their traffic), the longest being five or six miles long—a circumstance which accounts for the interruptions to pedestrian progress we have noted, and for the somewhat confusing network aspect of the town.

The recent transformation of several immense brewing firms from private enterprises to Limited Liability Companies, in which lesser affairs have not been slow to follow all over the country, has interested a much larger public than before in both the process of brewing and its results; and, in spite of depressed trade in so many branches of industry, it would seem, from reliable sources, as if the malt and hops could hold their own; though true it is, and pity 'tis 'tis true, say the farmers, the brewing will succeed so long as barley and hops, for one reason or another, keep at prices so low as they have recently done; for they seriously urge that though they provide the raw material at a loss, the brewers do not lower the price of beer in any appreciable degree, or, at all events, you do not get any benefit of it, but otherwise, when you buy and pay for your glass of beer at the public-house counter, but most often the very reverse. Thus the brewers, and possibly the publicans also, go on coining money.

However that may be, we believe that a large number of readers will be glad to have a popular description of processes, and even teetotalers may *read* it without self-accusation or remorse; for to follow processes of this kind, and understand them, is merely a slight lesson in chemistry as applied to the industrial arts. It is in this light, at all events, that we would have them to glance over these pages, which in no sense seek to encourage the drink traffic in any form, but only to diffuse useful information. In a previous volume * we wrote of hops in some detail, and told all about their culture, though, unfortunately, we could not, any more than Miss Ormerod, disclose the whole secret of the destructive hop aphis, which we fear has some secrets of its own as to generation, and of change of abode not yet fully traced out, and the present chapter must in all good faith be accepted as only a natural sequence or a legitimate continuation of that essay.

The reader, then, must accompany us first of all to Burton, to which we have just introduced him in a general way, and make his observations. It has been said by Emerson that an institution is only the shadow of a great man. Burton-on-Trent is but the shadow of the early Basses and Allsopps. There are, in all, about twenty breweries in Burton. Messrs. Bass have three, and Messrs. Allsopp have an equal number—the latter being, as I learned, the largest.

The centenary of Bass's firm was celebrated in 1877, but Allsopp's goes back for more than 150 years. In an old map of Burton-on-Trent, engraved in 1720, there is a small brewery which then belonged to Mr. Benjamin Wilson, who was really the founder of what has since

* "Industrial Curiosities." T. Fisher Unwin.

become the well-known firm of Samuel Allsopp and Sons. Benjamin Wilson had a daughter, who became the wife of Mr. James Allsopp, and her son Samuel was the father of Mr. Henry Allsopp, who was shortly since raised to the peerage under the title of Lord Hindlip. One of the sons of Benjamin Wilson, having no children, took his nephew Samuel into the business, a movement which was looked upon with great disfavour by his father, who was anxious that he should take orders. When Benjamin Wilson the younger died, the business passed into the hands exclusively of Samuel Allsopp, who carried it on under the name of Wilson & Allsopp until 1822, when the name was changed to its present style.

It is to Mr. Henry Allsopp, or Lord Hindlip, that the credit is due for building up a concern which to-day is considered good value at £3,300,000. Mr. R. Parker, of the London office, who is a Burton man, can recollect the time, some five-and-forty years ago, when the barrels were carried away by hand-trucks, so limited was the scale of operations. Now the output taxes the capacity of railway-trucks, locomotives, and sidings, all arranged to secure facility and rapidity of transport. We have noted the peculiarity of the private railway lines running along the streets, connecting the breweries with the main lines, and there was a stiff battle about these; and beer and pedestrian comfort fought it out, and beer won. This system of private railways is quite unique in England; but had it not been for these connections, the Burton trade would never have attained its present dimensions.

As far as we are concerned, all the breweries are very much alike, so we do not propose to note nice differences or distinctions in process. On applying at Messrs. Bass's office we are furnished with an "order to view," and betake ourselves to the large brewery early in the morning.

The brewer, of course, is the great man in a brewery, and his work is the staple commodity of the whole. All that precedes him tends to him and his work, and all that follows him must of necessity tend backward to the same point. For him the malt is ground, and the hops stored, and the casks manufactured, and horses and canal boats, and telegraphs and pens set agoing. Immense stores of malt and hops—the latter in fire-proof buildings—are at his command, and are sent from the storehouses to the brewery by long wooden pipes with a sufficient incline to keep the material for the conduction of which they are constructed in constant motion. Casks trundle down to the vaults beneath his feet, and trundle back again charged with pale ale. Verily, therefore, the brewer of such a brewery must be a mighty man! Merely to come into contact with him must be informing and suggestive.

As I entered the brewery proper my conductor reminded me that only two articles besides water are used in the manufacture of ale in this brewery. But it may be said parenthetically that readers must not fancy this applies to all brewing. By no manner of means. One of the great complaints the barley-growing community have to urge is that nowadays there is no production which is more hopelessly given over to adultera-

tion in the very manufacture than beer. It is only a
degree better than butterine palmed off as butter, if,
indeed, it is at all better. They say that brewers now,
all brewers except the very highest class, use sugar and
other things instead of malt and hops, or to supplement
them; that no end of acids and other chemicals are in
use as substitutes for the genuine article, and that most
often when a man buys his glass at a public-house bar
he pays for what in a very large proportion is in no
sense beer at all, but a miserable concoction of chemical
devices and makeshifts, too often of a most deleterious
character. And not only this. The publicans have a
bit of "duty," what they call "cellar-work," which is
simply making up the beer, to which they add not only
water, but various other compounds for purposes of
clarifying, &c., to suit the taste of their customers or
their own profit, and this in spite of all adulteration
Acts; so that poor folks—and it is no wonder—come to
form queer tastes in the matter of their drink in a vast
number of cases.

Good, sound home-brewed beer will feed a man, but
it will take a very large quantity to make him mad
drunk. They say your adulterated public-house beer
has little or no feeding or nutritious elements; it flies
to the head and makes a man for the time being a
maniac, likely to do mischief. They would, if they
had the power, make the use of all such substitutes for
malt and hops illegal; and if they had chanced to see
in a comic paper of some years ago the following funny
definition of Liberalism they would have said that Parlia-
mentary toleration, in spite of adulteration Acts, had

come near to realising it:—"Liberalsh, Liberalsh!" replied a tipsy man; "you say Liberalsh: now what I call Liberalsh is to make things sho ash a man could get jolly drunk for, shay, twopence."

They would have a heavy tax put upon all materials used in the brewing of beer, except malt and hops; or else a very strict Act of Parliament to stop it. Of course, they are interested parties; but certainly there is reason in what is urged by them; and it may be added that it were well for the country generally, and the cause of morality and social progress, if all brewers, either by free choice or legal compulsion, followed the good example of Messrs. Bass and Messrs. Allsopp in this respect. But even they have not escaped inconvenience and trouble from the too common practice of brewers. Some thirty years ago Mr. Henry Allsopp had to meet great difficulties, when it was reported that several noxious materials were used in the manufacture of Allsopp's pale ale. This lying report had to be crushed, and Mr. Henry Allsopp announced through the public press, and in every way possible, that the brewery was open to the inspection of any one who wished to satisfy himself as to the way in which the beer was manufactured. Even to-day this custom is maintained.

And then there is the consideration how, in this matter of beer and a hundred others, the evil works downward, intensifying itself as it descends. The poor man who most needs what is nutritious and strengthening is the least likely to get it; he cannot order a cask, because he lives from hand to mouth, nor a dozen of Bass, for the same reason; he must take his half-pint where he can get it, and when he chances to have the money; and corrupt tastes, as we have said, are thus formed, and beer with acid and salt very powerful in it comes to be relished till the desire grows with what it feeds on, and thirst is generated by what should quench it. The first duty of a government is to take care of the property and the lives of its citizens—health is surely a valuable property of a people, and cannot be disconnected from life; and while parties wrangle and every question is transformed into a party-question, vital interests are neglected, and what might be done to ensure at least decently unadulterated food and drink is left undone that second-rate brewers and publicans may enrich themselves.

Malt and hops are the principals with Bass and Allsopp; all the rest is resolved into work and water. The first process is to grind the malt; the second to mix it with water, and extract from it the saccharine and other juices—to "mash" it, that is, in the "mash kieves." The washing-room, where the saccharine matter is extracted from the malt, and where processes of great delicacy are brought into play to secure the desired clearness, is an immense place, suggesting some odd reflections.

During the process of malting the barley is first made to germinate, and then to check the germination the grain is dried on kilns. It is next placed in sacks and conveyed in trucks, drawn by specially designed loco-motives. Hydraulic hoists take the sacks at almost lightning speed to the top floors, where they are emptied into hoppers clean and bright as tea urns with a capacity of a hundred quarters. From the hoppers the grain passes over screens, which eliminate all foreign substances, to the mills where it is crushed. It is then conveyed by Archimedean screws to another hopper from which the mash-tuns are fed.

Great skill is essential to the successful treatment of the material at this stage. Water of a certain temperature is mixed with the prepared grain, the resulting compound being termed wort, which is run into great copper caldrons, where the hops are added, and the whole boiled together for some considerable time. The liquid then passes through a perforated vessel which retains the hops, and it is next pumped into the coolers, which are large wooden pans erected at the top of the brewery. Atmospheric influences act upon the wort, and after it has attained a certain degree of coolness it is passed through refrigerators. Yeast is then added for the purpose of starting and perfecting the fermentation, which is indispensable for the after soundness and keeping quality of the beer. From the fermenting vessels the beer is passed into casks in which the fermentation of the beer is completed. Having been kept until it is bright, the beer is allowed to flow into large square wooden vessels termed "racking squares," in order that the clarification process may be continued.

When the fermentation and cleansing are finished the manufacture is complete, and the liquor is pumped into vats, where it remains for some time to " acquire age and tone," and then all that remains is to pump it to the vaults below and direct into the casks for use. There are close upon 100 vats in all in the brewery,

K

and the larger ones hold as much as 1782 hogsheads, of 52 imperial gallons each. Passing along the tops of them is like going along the roof of a house, and, of course, falling into one of them would be like falling into the sea, so far as unassisted chance of escape was concerned. The heads, however, are made very secure, and are covered with fine sand—I suppose to keep the liquid from the possibility of exposure to the air. The vats are all connected with pipes, and those pipes, carried on to the cellar, and direct into the casks, prevent the necessity of any hand-filling, or indeed of any meddling in any way dependent on the cleanliness of workmen. All is done by pipes and pumps. The liquor goes into the vats by pumps, and out of them by the same process.

This, in general terms, is the process of manufacture of Bass's or Allsopp's ale. It would be easy to extend the description to a much greater length; to tell of engines, coal-stores, "lifts," of the size of the vaults, and a host of other things. These, however, are pretty much the same, go where we may among large manufactories, for brewing or anything. They have all good engines (it would not pay to have bad ones), all hydraulic power, and (in the case of breweries) all large vaults, dismal to look at, but exceedingly useful, as many other dismal things are.

I need scarcely say that brewing is chiefly done in winter; the brewing of stock ales at Burton is from October to March, only light ordinary ales being brewed at other times of the year; but still the temperature is regulated by means of cold water in pipes, as before described. The ale can then be run off direct to the casks, 30,000 of them being there in the vaults ready for filling when required.

This, then, is the process of brewing; but the scale on which it is done here is marvellous, and the stores maintained for the firms in London and elsewhere are little less so. The storage accommodation at Burton, however, is comparatively insignificant (amounting only to about 65,000 barrels), as compared with the immense stores of the firm at Camden Town, where in one building as many as 60,000 barrels can be placed. The agencies throughout the country number over fifty, and the firm employs more than fifteen hundred workmen, in addition to clerks and the usual office staff. Some fifty dray-horses are employed in London in daily supplying the wants of the customers, and even that number is not sufficient for the work in busy seasons.

The cask-washing alone in any one of the three breweries before the reader is in itself like a large branch of industry; the cooperage is much more important; the storage of casks, in the form of immense pyramids, cover in each case, with the storage of staves belonging to the department, an amount of ground that would make a respectable street. The offices of both the Burton firms are on the same scale as the breweries, and are fitted up with taste, and on a system suited to the purpose required. Whatever can be done by machinery is so done throughout the works of both firms. The engines are there to lift or carry. In 1865 I find the gross returns of the firm of Messrs. Bass for the year stated at a million and a half—a million and a half returned for ale to this one of the twenty breweries of Burton-on-Trent! Since then, as everybody knows, the business has vastly increased. The quantity of coal used in the brewing season is stated at upwards of 160 tons per day; the quantity of malt made on the premises during the season is stated at 6750 quarters per week. I shall not trouble the reader with any more figures; for, after all, they only convey a poor impression to most minds of the facts they are intended to represent. But a town devoted to bitter beer—not to the drinking but the making of it—is a feature of English life worth looking at, if not for its novelty—for brewing is an old feature of Burton-on-Trent—at least for its exceptional character among staple manufacture. A town devoted to cotton, or iron-smelting, or mining, or pottery, or fashion, or fishing, or shipbuilding may find its like elsewhere, but where could be found the like of Burton-on-Trent? Whether it owes its distinction to its spring water, which is said to be good, or, as is more likely, to the fact that some skilful brewer chanced to select it for his residence in the old times and gave it a name, there is no question of its distinction at present as a town of brewers; and apart from brewing there would be little left of the town.

Even in old times, however, Burton had advantages that were by no means shared by the country at large. By its river and canal it had connection even then with the Mersey on the one coast, and the Humber on the other; and though its real rise to its present position as a great brewery dates from the railway period, it was a brewery by no means insignificant formerly, and

it was of note as such in times far away, it is said—
even into the dim ages of English history. If, therefore, as some say, it is the great thing for a man to
turn his attention to some one object, and bring all his
powers to bear on it ; and if, as is also said, a town is
merely an individual multiplied, then Burton is wise in
its generation, as it was wise also in the generations
gone by. It has certainly turned its attention primarily to
one trade, and that is a trade whose handiwork is in
demand. How many travellers it has constantly employed seeking orders for Burton ale it would be hard to
guess, but the little account handed to me states that, in
the year previous to its publication, Messrs. Bass shipped
for India and other foreign markets 65,052 casks ; and
these, of course, represented but one branch of the business done. One may take it, therefore, for certain that
Burton, as a whole, is great in commercial rooms throughout the United Kingdom, and far beyond it; that its
name is respected by waiters and chamber-maids, as well
as by railway managers and shipping agents ; and, in
short, that in high places and low ones it has won for
itself an immortal memory, of a kind, by means of its
beer.

If any persons are securely adding acre to acre and
building to building, the Burton brewers are doing so.
The business they did last year they try to increase, and
probably do increase, this. Depression, which is ruining
agriculture, wrecking the iron industry, and paralysing
dependent branches of trade, like the angel that smote
the Assyrian host, passes by the brewers and brewing.
Burton itself is growing rapidly. The description of it in

even recent gazeteers is " a town of 12,000 inhabitants,
with one principal street in a line with the river, and one
at right angles with that." A stranger would have some
difficulty in recognising in this description the same town
as it is to-day, with its new breweries of bright-red brick,
and its houses extending in all directions in that pretty
and picturesque valley on the north bank of the Trent.
The railways have, to a great extent, made the change,
as they have made many other changes. They have
done a good deal towards putting up the tall chimneys,
and the large buildings, and costly machinery; for, with
all the excellency of the canal system, and the Trent
communication with the Ouse and the Humber, neither
the one nor the other had the advantage of throwing out
arms in all directions as they can now be thrown by the
railways.

Into such a brewery it cannot have been altogether
useless to look, be our views of brewing what they may;
and if any one should deem the súbject so thoroughly
unfashionable as to reflect fashionable discredit on even
the reading of it, why, let the plan laid down at the beginning of the paper be rigidly adhered to, and all will be
well. But apart from brewing and brewers—apart altogether from the subject of the paper—young men starting
in life may learn herefrom one lesson, which cannot be
too pointedly applied. They may learn that strong efforts
brought to bear on one point are sure to succeed, grant-
ing even moderately favourable conditions under which
to do the work. Some families have thrown their efforts
into brewing, and some into money-lending and then
banking, bending great faculties for work to one end.

This is worth remembering and pondering over; only do not let us conclude that any end unconnected with benefit to those around us can ever be noble or great—can ever hallow a man's life or keep his memory green. It is necessary to say this much lest the story of great mercantile success should be misapplied.

Now, if our readers are pleased with our company, we shall venture, by the magic of the pen, if in no more realistic sense, to transport them across the Irish Sea and set them down in Dublin city, that together we may study another phenomenon of brewing enterprise. From Pale Ale we pass to Dublin Stout; and to have a temporary initiation into its mysteries, we make our way to the brewery—the famous brewery—of the Messrs. Guinness, whose out-turn is, perhaps, the largest in the three kingdoms in their particular commodity. Why Dublin should have become so intimately associated with stout is one of those things which, as Lord Dundreary was wont to say, "no fellah can understand," since certainly the Irish character does not suggest that stout—the comfortable and fattening and content-making beverage *par excellence*—is one of its delights and soothing enjoyments. The key to the mystery of Dublin's connection with stout is just as hard to get at as to understand why London porters have always had the pre-eminence, or why Burton has surpassed all other places for the production of pale ale. Doubtless the water has something to do with it. At all events, though the Liffey flows on with the same mellifluous murmur as met the ears of Dan O'Connell or of the poet Thomas Moore, Messrs. Guinness do not get their supply from that source, but by sinking wells. For such an enterprise as theirs pure spring water must be had from an independent source, with which the caprices of persons or corporations could not interfere.

This supply was here secured by means of a well 120 feet deep, sheeted with metal from top to bottom, and altogether made very valuable at much cost. Malt, hops, coals, wood for staves, &c., are stored within the brewery walls, where six hundred men in all are at work—about a hundred of them as coopers, millwrights, and carpenters, and the others in brewing, washing, carting, &c. Seventy horses also are regularly employed on the premises or in connection with them, and a number of canal-boats, the property of Sir B. Guinness, are in daily use carrying away the stout for exportation. Immediately inside the first gate there are large and elegant offices, divided into departments for " correspondence," " cash," and " booking," which altogether keep a respectable little regiment of clerks attending to the duties of the pen. Attached to the business offices are a telegraph office and a printing office, of course for the sole use of the brewery, and affording indications in themselves of the magnitude of the work to which they belong. These are a few of the facts that we see at the threshold of the big brewery.

It may be useful to say here that in all fundamental particulars the manufacture of ale and porter is the same, the difference being in mere matters of detail, such as the darkening of the porter by means of black (or " patent ") malt, while the great object in the making of Burton ale is to secure clearness. Of course cleanliness is as much needed in the one case as the other, and is secured in a thoroughly satisfactory way by a host of little contrivances, which one sees but can hardly take any note of. Here, as in the case of the pale ale brewing, the saccharine matter is extracted from the malt in a monster washing-room. The coppers into which the liquid then passes hold over 100 barrels each, and here again the same process is gone through as in the case of pale ale. The hops then pass into a strainer, and the liquor into coolers ; the former are also put under hydraulic pressure, and when all is taken from them that is wanted they are sold for manure. The liquor passes from the coolers into " fermenting rounds," or tubs, holding 110 barrels each. There are ninety of these, and 140 smaller ones, in this brewery. When the fermentation has reached a certain stage the liquor is run off into an immense number of what are called " minor casks," that is, casks that are joined together, and here the process is completed.

A little farther on are the stave and cask stores, with their casks and staves piled up as high as the brewery, and covering an immense space of ground. Near to these is the cooperage, a large yard where a hundred men can conveniently work together, with cask-making machinery and all else that they require for turning out good work expeditiously. The casks are washed also by machinery, in the open air, the water being pumped into them by a self-acting pump, after which a machine with a double motion does the cleansing. Then they are dried with hot air, which is pumped into them almost red hot. This process finished, they are ready for use,

and are put on a railway with a gentile incline, and left
to trundle their way—a very long way—down to the
vaults, where they can be filled, at a proper temperature,
in the hottest weather.   When they are filled they again
trundle them away to, and upon, a large wheel, the bottom of which is in the vault and the top above the
ground; and there they are lifted, with a revolution of
the wheel, to the height of a cart or railway-truck (a
private railway runs into the brewery), and packed for
transmission to their destination, that the process of
emptying may begin on the ordinary principles.

The big brewery of Dublin has reaped great benefits
from the development of steam-ships and the railway
system, though in a way less direct than Burton.   The
Liffey was always there, and the canals grew up to aid it,
as a grand artery of commerce; but there was also at the
end of these the beautiful bay of Dublin, with a claim, in
the very aspect of it, to world-wide commerce, where the
capital of Ireland could produce an article in demand,
as it produced one in Guinness's stout.   Communication
by sea was in favour with mercantile people when communication by land was, in some cases, all but impossible, and in most cases very inconvenient; so that, from
one cause and another, the family of Guinness, even in the
old times, had at least as good access to English towns as
many English brewers had, and was in all respects ready
for the coming of steam and the revolutions it effected
in every branch and kind of trade.   Dublin was soon
brought to a distance of a six hours' run (for heavy carriage) to Holyhead, and Holyhead to a distance of twelve
hours' run (for heavy carriage) to London.   Steam-pumps,

cranes, and all else followed. The old buildings would no longer answer the purpose, as in old times. There must be new wells, storehouses, vats, tubs, coppers, and all other articles connected with brewing. And so the trade went on till the brewery became like a little city in itself, apparently formed for an isolated existence, but really sending out its influence to all parts of the United Kingdom, to the Continent of Europe, to the other side of the Atlantic, and one knows not where besides.

VIII.

PETROLEUM.

PHILOSOPHERS tell us that the shock of an earthquake in the remotest regions is felt in faint vibrations along our own shores. This is but another illustration of the Laureate's fine lines with which he ends that exquisite apostrophe in the " Morte d' Arthur "—

> " The whole round earth is every way
> Bound by gold chains about the feet of God."

Perhaps the philosophers, at all events many of them, would rather say "about the feet of Law." Any way the quotation is suggestive, and serves to bring vividly before the imagination the fact that changes or discoveries in the most remote regions of the world come sooner or later to make themselves felt at their antipodes.

Recently we have had an instance of this in the revolution effected by the discovery of great oil-wells in different parts of the globe. Old industries have been ruined, new industries have risen, and the whole system of lighting and heating throughout the civilised world is likely to be changed. The old-fashioned candle, which through centuries held its place, is now likely to be less and less in demand; gas can be dispensed with, as well as the poisons which it conveys into the air, the more quickly the less pure it is, as is unfortunately most the case in the larger towns, where fresh air in houses is, at any rate, most rare. At all events, cheap and, on the whole, safe lighting is a great boon to the masses of the people ; and considering the interests at stake, it cannot but be interesting and serve a good purpose to give some information about the sources of the supply of what promises more and more to become the illuminant of the common people, at all events, till the day when electricity can be supplied more cheaply and turned off and on at single jets as easily as coal-gas or an oil lamp.

We shall first take a glance at the various points from which the supply of oil is drawn, and then inquire into its origin, and present some facts and figures with regard to the methods of boring and conveyance by which the supply is regulated and the demand duly met. The most fertile of the oil-fields yet discovered and in working lie around the Caspian Sea, or in districts more or less contiguous to it, so that to Russia and Russian men of enterprise has fallen these great sources of wealth and well-being. We shall take our start from what may really be considered, at present, the headquarters of the Petroleum traffic.

Imagine a vast bay surrounded by yellowish hills, stony, and bare of all vegetation. To your left, towards the west, the grey houses of Baku form an amphitheatre ; in face of you a vast fire seems to rise almost to the length of a mile—this is the *Black Town*, where the petroleum-works throw up towards the blue heaven vast torrents of smoke ; finally, to your right, extend the

flat coasts, uncultivated, desolate, of this peninsula of
Apcheron, where the subterranean fires spout forth in
great numbers of volcanoes of inflammable gas and mud.
Baku is, indeed, a town of petroleum, a happy resort, it
may be, for the industrials, but certainly not for the
lover of nature. When we arrived, says a recent traveller,
we held our noses with both our hands; when we left, it
was not without a certain horror. All the coasts that
you see from Baku rise and fall alternately under the
action of subterranean forces. The whole Caspian Sea,
indeed, shares in these movements of vertical oscillation,
which have overturned the Asiatic continent, destroying
the traces of old civilisations, drying up enormous
stretches of sea, and promoting the formation of inacces-
sible deserts, of steppes eternally sterile. Sea becomes
land, land is transformed into sea, in this region with
a suddenness which brings vividly to mind Lord Tennyson's fine lines in "In Memoriam":—

> " There rolls the deep where grew the tree ;
>   O earth, what changes hast thou seen !
>   There, where the long street roars, hath been
>   The stillness of the Central Sea ! "

One traveller says : " We visited one of these steppes,
and the line followed by our packet in the voyage from
Baku to Krasnovodsk was, at an epoch comparatively
recent, used by foot-passengers ; and, after having served
as route for many migrations from Asia to Europe, it is
now buried under the water, forming to-day a shoal between the two capes which occupy at the north and
south the basin of the Caspian."

As a necessary consequence on the Caspian harbours

springing up suddenly, the traffic shifts from place to place. Krasnovodsk and Mikhaïlovsk, on the opposite side from Baku, were, at dates not very remote, two stirring harbours; now they have yielded to a competitor better situated, alike in an economical and maritime point of view. This is named Ouzoun-Ada, the construction of which took only three months. The double word Ouzoun-Ada signifies literally Long-Isle. It is really in one of the numerous islets which stud the coast of Asia to the south of the Bay of Krasnovodsk.

But Baku is not without its amenities. It has some fine streets and squares—houses solid, substantial, with the flat roofs of the East, and here and there beautiful fountains, statues, and monuments. One of the finest bits is that which includes the Garden Michael and the House of the Governor, with a glimpse in the distance of the Tower of the Young Daughter.

The quays of Baku are very lively. Varied races are to be seen there, sometimes imposing figures in their diverse costumes. Crowds of Tartar women at certain times may be seen sitting by the sea in front of the great promenade—a striking spectacle to the European eye.

The cause of all the shiftings we have noted in this region is really the presence of that valuable oil, petroleum, which all round the shores of the Caspian, and even in mid-sea, rises up in great fountains, uncontrollable. Paraffin is manufactured at some cost and with considerable skill from bituminous shales in several of the Carboniferous districts of England, Wales, and Scotland, giving employment to many thousands of men,

On an average, we are told that about 1,250,000 tons of shale-coal are thus annually disposed of in Scotland, yielding about 70,000,000 gallons of crude oil. But on the Caspian petroleum flows up ready-made, a pure oil, needing but little further labour. All that is needed here is to bore at almost any point, to a depth of a few hundred feet (500 feet at the outside), and the valuable lighting-liquid will pour forth in such quantities that millions of gallons are annually wasted for want of any means of restraining the enormous outflow. In America, at the most successful points, borings of some 2000 feet or more are required. These Russian oil-fountains are so literally inexhaustible that competition on the part of home manufacturers is not likely to be found profitable, as now barrels are dispensed with, and it is transported in great iron tanks, first by rail across Europe to the Baltic, and then by German tank-steamers to London, where it can be sold at almost a nominal price—a vast benefit to the masses of poor people in our towns, but a severe blow to all such oil-industries at home.

Other vast districts in Russian territory are equally rich. "In some places," we are told, "there are great terraces resembling asphalt, and smelling strongly of petroleum. Natural gas bubbles up through pools and lakes, which are covered with rainbow-coloured scum, and thick oil oozes from rock crevices." The only likely future competitor with Russia in this petroleum is Burmah, where vast resources in this regard are undeveloped, if not untouched; but it is said to produce a heavier oil, with less of waste; and thus it may be that,

PETROLEUM WORKS AT BAKU.

[To face page 161.]

in the years to come, Burmah may become a great source of light and heat, and the long-deferred reward of our struggles there come to us in this unexpected if welcome form.

One product of petroleum which up till now has been almost entirely wasted is benzine, because there were no means of burning it with any degree of comfort. Now, however, an ingenious lamp for this purpose has been invented by a firm of engineers in Moscow. It is so constructed as to look like a candlestick; the candles being really hollow tubes of white porcelain, a wick passing through the oil and drawing the spirit towards the top of the tube, where two holes are so contrived as to ensure the escape of the gas. This style of candle, we learn, is becoming popular in Russia.

Other products of the petroleum refuse are certain kinds of fuel and a variety of aniline dyes. Baku is all astir with activity, and keen to secure means of utilising its treasures. With the best machinery and scientific appliances at command, the waste of oil at present is enormous and almost incredible. The engineer, as we have said, needs to bore only a few hundred feet, and up comes such a fountain that, geyser-like, it bursts all bounds, and in some cases has been known to bury factories and houses, the adventurous borer being then sued for doing damage to his neighbours' property. "In 1883 the great Droojba well was sunk at a cost of £1500, and for the first forty-three days it yielded an average of 3400 tons a day: 115 days elapsed before its owner contrived to check the flow and bring it under control. In that time, according to the correct estimate,

L

55,000,000 gallons were wasted." What is now clearly
wasted, or flows into the sea at least, trebles the amount
of the whole product of the Scotch industry. The
whole amount of crude shale-oil produced in Scotland
is about 70,000,000 gallons per annum ; and these figures
suffice to show how unequal is the contest.

Baku is so absolutely the Caspian town of petroleum
that it would have been a sad defect if, in passing, we
had failed to gather and to give our readers some facts
relating to this product and industry, which may yet
so affect the whole light and heat giving supply of the
world. Our coal-measures may be looked at with less
anxiety when this product and its waste can come in to
stave off exhaustion.

Nor, as we have said, is there much fear of the supply
failing. Of all the vast oil-yielding area of the Apcheron
Peninsula, extending at least to some sixteen hundred
square miles (not including the oil-springs in some of the
islands of the Caspian Sea, which at present discharge
vast quantities of oil into the waters), only some six square
miles have yet been worked. Other oil-bearing districts
farther distant have as yet only been tapped—if even so
much as this. One near Krasnovodsk is especially prolific;
there is another at Neft (Naphtha Hill), and still another
of vast magnitude, of about two hundred and fifty-six
square miles, all along the valley of the Koubau River.
Nor does this exhaust the springs which exist within the
Russian Empire. There is one near Tiflis ; another on
the Sea of Azoff, between Archangel and Khokhand ;
all along the Volga and the Toka Rivers, we learn, there
are vast supplies that only need to be worked, as well as

various springs scattered over the vast regions of Tur-kestan. There are also springs in the Vosges, at or near Hochwald. When bored to a certain depth a substance like black tar comes up so spontaneously, so powerfully, that in some cases the borings have been burst, and the black tar-like substance, overflowing beyond all control, transformed a large meadow into a black-tar lake. There are now some eight borings, and the supply of oil here too promises to be inexhaustible. This, however, needs considerable working and purification, for which purpose several factories have been erected with new and power-ful machinery, and it is found after purification and distillation that fully thirty per cent. of the black-tar is pure oil.

Dr. Lyon Playfair, one of the first chemists of our day, has paid special attention to petroleum, and, indeed, the suggestion that it might be distilled from bituminous shales was due to him, as well as the idea that from cer-tain particles in crude petroleum pure solid paraffin could be procured. He wrote, a few years ago, a valuable article on the subject in *Good Words*, from which we shall quote a passage here :—

" Petroleum has been known in some parts of the earth, where it occurs native, from the earliest periods of human history. The sacred fires of the sun-worshippers were fed by the gases which issue from it. The asphalt left by its evaporation was the basis of the mortar with which Nineveh and Babylon were built. It seems to be frequently referred to in the Bible, though biblical chemistry is much obscured by bad translation. As an instance of this, carbonate of soda, when referred to, is translated *nitre*, and is made to do things impossible to that substance. Thus Solomon tells us that as vinegar upon nitre, so is he that singeth songs to a heavy heart. This has no meaning, for vinegar does nothing to nitre ; but it causes a lively and unpleasant commotion when poured upon soda (νατρον). So, also, when Jeremiah speaks of washing with nitre and soap there is no meaning ; though soda and soap are used constantly in this relation. It is thus that petroleum in the Bible is concealed under the general word 'salt.' That word is both generic and specific in all countries. In the later limited sense it is sea or kitchen salt. In the more general sense it includes a vast number of substances, of which Epsom salt and Glauber salt are familiar examples. The connection of salt with petroleum, in biblical language, begins early in Genesis, when the Dead Sea, or Lake of Sodom, is called the Salt Sea. That sea abounds in petroleum springs, and has asphalt on its ancient shores. Accordingly it has also been called the Lake *Asphaltites*. Many things become comprehensible if we take the generic term salt, and apply it to petroleum and its residue, asphalt. Lot's wife, if converted into a pillar of common salt, would have been washed away by the first shower of rain ; but a pillar of asphalt, even as a memorial of her, would have been an enduring monument, and might have been seen by Josephus and his contemporary, Clement of Rome, both of whom declare that they saw it. So also when we are told by Mark that 'every one shall be salted with fire, and every sacrifice shall be salted with salt,' I see a meaning only when I recollect that, in regions containing petroleum, sacrificial fires were fed with this fuel to aid the burning. In like manner, when Matthew likens the blessed, first to salt, and immediately afterwards to a lighted torch (for candles, as translated, were then unknown), I see the connection in his mind. He had just said that salt which had lost its savour was only fit to be trodden under foot of men. Now salt never does lose its savour, and is never fit to be trodden under foot. But petroleum does lose its essence by exposure, and out of the residue the ancients used to make asphalt pavements, as they do at the present day. I only give some reasons for my belief that the salt of the Bible, in its generic sense, was often applied to petroleum ; but I admit, at the same time, that readers ought not to attach much importance to my opinions on any subject of biblical criticism.

" Petroleum occurs as a greenish or dark-coloured fluid in many countries. In small quantities it occasionally occurs in England. I found a well of it in Derbyshire many years ago, and induced the late Mr. Young to establish a manufactory of burning oil, and ultimately of paraffin candles. This suggestion led gradually, in his energetic hands, to the great petroleum industry which has carried cheap light into the houses of the poor. The small supply of native petroleum of Derbyshire soon became exhausted, but the discovery that it could be distilled out in Boghead coal and bituminous shales gave a great impulse to its manufacture. In 1859 America began to introduce native petroleum from Pennsylvanian wells. During that year eighty thousand barrels were supplied to commerce, and that quantity was thought to be immense, though it was insignificant with the present

supply, which reached thirty-seven million barrels in
1882. Other copious supplies of native petroleum have
been found in India, Burmah, and the Caucasian lands
about the Caspian Sea. The last source of supply is of
extraordinary magnitude. I may mention, however, that
at Surakhani, on the western shore of the Caspian, sacred
fires have been burning probably longer than recorded
history. The priests allege that the fires in their temple,
fed by gas issuing from the petroleum below, have
burned without cessation since four hundred years
before Christ."

Dr. Lyon Playfair holds that as no trace of organic
remains can be found in petroleum as it is found in
coal, and as petroleum is present in strata which know
little or nothing of such structures, it cannot be of
organic origin, notwithstanding that petroleum is artificially distilled from coal and bituminous shales at a red
heat. He inclines to the belief that petroleum is a mixture of hydrocarbons, continually being manufactured in
the deeper parts of the earth, which oozes up through
cracks and fissures, and being lighter than water, makes
that body a means, a kind of lever, in lifting itself up
to the surface of the earth. "Neptunists," * he says,
"could not explain the formation of petroleum by
aqueous *action ;* for it is so light that it would float on the
top of water, and would not be buried by deposit. Vulcanists of the old school would be equally perplexed,
because petroleum is so volatile that heat would convert

---

* Neptunists were an old school of scientific theorists who held that
the origin of all things could be traced to water ; Vulcanists, those who
asserted that all things owed their origin to fire. These schools for long
fought a keen and fiery battle.

it into vapour, and it would be dissipated. Indeed, I recollect an instance of this kind in a quarry near Dysart, in Fifeshire, where every fragment of stone freshly broken smelt of petroleum."

The degree in which the petroleum oils undergo refinement determines their class and gives them their distinctive name. Kerosine is the name given to the best, as it is clearer, burns brighter, and has less smell than that called, somewhat incorrectly, "paraffin." Paraffin, strictly, is a resultant from the refuse of petroleum obtained by distillation. It was got at first, after the oil had been procured, from shale, and is now in much the same way procured from petroleum. Crude petroleum is distilled, and the gasoline, benzoline, &c., are carefully treated and refrigerated, being extremely volatile; the distillate, which is known so well as kerosine, or burning oil, then comes off, and after that the heavier, darker oils, used chiefly for lubricating purposes. "Paraffin," which is really a solid, wax-like substance, is obtained from the remainder or refuse, which is then cooled, and the paraffin, so to speak, crystallises out in a white wax-like substance. It is much used nowadays for candles, and for other purposes in the arts. "Paraffin" tells something of its character in its name; it means "no affinity," and the substance has no affinity to anything.

Necessity stimulates invention. No sooner were the petroleum-works on the Caspian set in motion than great difficulty was experienced in finding vessels in which to convey it. Wood is very scarce in that region, so that the American plan of wooden casks involved great trouble and expense, even if it had not been very cumbrous and much exposed to the risk of bursting and oozing out.

The processes of refining, which are comparatively light and merely mechanical compared with the process of crushing and extracting the oil from shale, as was done for years in Scotland on a large scale by the Messrs. Young, is carried on by the Messrs. Noebel at Baku. Of the external aspect of their factories our illustration will give some slight idea, though only a vague suggestion of their extent.

Ludwig Noebel, the Baku oil-king, who died the other day, found himself equal to the task of devising a means of meeting the difficulty. He hit on the plan of pumping the oil through pipes to steamers fitted up with oil-tanks. The Americans, quick-witted, forecasting and ingenious though they are, refused to believe in the practicability of this scheme, and as they had plenty of wood, remained content with barrels. They have thus, we fear, lost their chance of commanding the markets of the world with their oil.

Experience has endorsed Noebel's plan. It is found safer to convey oil in tanks than in barrels. The strong construction which the introduction of tanks and bulk-heads into steamers so directly favours renders them far more seaworthy than other vessels; and, besides, the risks of explosion are greatly reduced, the one that occurred in the *Petrina* having taken place, oddly enough, through a piece of carelessness, when she was empty. There are now over thirty tank-steamers conveying oil from Russia; and though some of them were built by English firms, they all belong to Russian merchants or

Russian companies, so that the carrying trade as well as the production of the oil is entirely in Russian hands. As we write, we learn that some six more tank-steamers are being built on the Clyde for the Russian traders. Several of these tank-steamers are now running to London, each carrying about a million gallons of oil on board.

Another possibility is, that from the petroleum refuse —at all events from the refuse of the black-tar fountains —may be derived those more recent substances, which, like the fairy of fable, have come forth at the touch of the magician's wand of chemistry. The waste products of petroleum have been found to be the most valuable of all. Volatile benzole and solids known as naphthaline and anthracene are the chief. From the benzole can be made, says Sir Lyon Playfair, those beautiful aniline colours known as mauve and magenta, while out of the solid naphthaline and anthracene can be prepared alizarin, the red colour of madder, and also indigo, the staple blue dye. As we have seen in dealing with Quinine, one of the latest triumphs of chemistry is the discovery of specific antifebrines in these wastes. The coal-tar antifebrines are indeed likely, as we have seen, in some measure to displace quinine and the alkaloids of the chinchona-trees from their undisputed place as specifics in certain forms of fever. The possibilities of science in revealing remedial agents seem literally unlimited.

IX.

THE ELECTRIC TELEGRAPHS.

SOME time ago, when it was reported that a proposal was on foot to transform the Falls of Niagara into a great force for producing electricity, there were incredulous persons who laughed outright at the idea and chuckled over it as a fine joke. That was an illustration of the way in which mere magnitude often overwhelms men's minds. Niagara differs not from other waterfalls, save that it is bigger; and the same form of force has been turned to practical account in view of the same end. Some time since we read that two enterprising gentlemen had produced light in their houses by converting into that form the energy of a neighbouring waterfall,—the one was Sir William [now Lord] Armstrong, at his place near Newcastle, and the other was an intelligent and pushing hotel-proprietor in Switzerland. Water may thus practically be converted into light or heat, and the force which thus mysteriously transforms itself, in a more wonderful manner than the genii of any fairy-tale, may annihilate distance. The electric current will travel by many paths to many ends; and after all, we but imitate nature in the effort we make to gain perfection in our mastery of each of them. It has been well said by one of the greatest authorities on every point respecting electricity, that "the utilisation of the illimitable wasted energy on the earth's surface offers a fine field for the ingenuity of the electrician. The tides of the ocean, the motion of the atmosphere, the rapids of a river, the innumerable waterfalls that are found in every mountainous or hilly country, could be compelled to give up, in the form of electric currents, that energy which gives them existence, and which could thus be employed for providing power, generating heat, or supplying light, away altogether from their source of conversion.

"Wherever, in truth, wires can be stretched," says Dr. George Wilson, "whether suspended in the air, or buried in the earth, or sunk in the sea, there our wonder-working apparatus may be erected. A few square inches of zinc and copper will produce for us a force which, on the other side of a continent or an ocean, will speak for us, write for us, print for us, keep time for us, watch stars for us, and move all kinds of machinery. No distance will stop its march, for where the force of one battery is spent it can be made to call into action another, or *relay* battery, which will carry on the message, so that if the wires were laid it might sweep round the globe. Such a network of wires, we may hope, will one day connect the ends of the earth, and, like the great nerves of the human body, unite in living sympathy all the far-scattered children of men."

We think of Emerson's words: "Nature is a great storehouse of forces, and he is the benefactor of his species who shows how the seeming worthless tatters in her rag-shop are not waste, but, properly used up, are

of unspeakable value and power." Think of the centuries, the long millenniums, that have swept over mankind while all this world of serviceable force was practically unknown. The patriarchs, with their nomadic
faculties of observation and of meditation, no doubt
looked with pious awe, as Mr. Carlyle would have said,
at the lightnings that played in lurid zig-zags above them
in that Eastern sky, and wondered whence they came;
but the writer of the Book of Job regarded it as the last
possibility of man to tame and to use them for his own
purposes; for he asked, "Canst thou *send* lightnings,
that they may *go* and *say* unto *thee*, Here we are?"

Yet modern science has tamed the lightnings, and the
whole *rationale* of electrical science may be described
as a binding or insulating of a mysterious element which
no man can describe, and for which no one can fully
account. The greatest scientific man is as baffled about
it as is the simplest peasant. We know the fact of its
existence; and we know certain effects produced by it
under certain conditions; but that is all. We live surrounded on every hand by its tokens; we are the slaves
of its capricious or sudden outbursts; we are its masters,
to use and to apply it; and yet in itself it is a mysterious
veiled presence which may not be spoken with face to
face.

The practical problem with Mrs. Dods was "to find
your hare." *The* practical problem in electricity is, if
not to find your force, to keep your current. It ceaselessly aims at flying from you, losing itself in the air, in
the earth, becoming diffused, dissipated. The ancient
Greeks, by rubbing amber or *electron* (which has left its

record very clear to all time in the word electricity), got a kind of current; but they could not catch it properly and tie it to a wire as we now do; and the aim of scientific men has been, and still is, the search for the most effectual means of tying the current to the wire or finding the most efficient insulators. And as it is throughout the whole of nature, so it is here. As the old divine eloquently said, " All things are set over against each other, and there is nothing single or separate." When you have once chained your current well enough, by an inevitable law it generates another. One of the greatest discoveries of Faraday—that most patient, imaginative, and self-denying of investigators—was that, if a current of electricity passes from a battery along one wire, it develops a current along another and passive wire stretched near it. When Faraday's wonderful discovery of the generation of a current of electricity in a passive wire stretched near a charged one had led to the discovery of *relays*, new possibilities for telegraphy seemed to be opened on all sides; and these do not yet appear to have been practically laid hold of even remotely. But to enable the reader to realise even faintly the high point at which telegraphy has now reached, we must take a hurried glance at the development of the system from the beginning. The assertion is certainly fully justified, that the first great step in practical telegraphy was made when the true function of a wire in maintaining a current and producing a signal at the end was clearly grasped. Oddly enough, the first realisation of this seems to have fallen to a Scotchman. In the *Scots Magazine* for 1753 we find record of an "expeditious method of conveying intelligence" described under the initials, C. M. There is some doubt now as to who this C. M. was. Sir David Brewster says that he was a Greenock man named Charles Morrison; others give his name as Charles Marshall. Be that as it may, C. M. had caught a vision of the great goal. He aimed at the complete insulation of the conducting wire and producing a signal at the end of the wire which should be visible and intelligible. He did not attain to the next step of producing many signals by one wire; he used a separate wire for each letter of the alphabet. But the principle in his case was clear—he *telegraphed*.

The little that is known of him may be given in the words of an elderly Scotch lady, who remembered a "very clever man of obscure position who could make lichtnin' write and speak, and who could licht a room wi' coal-reek." It was a considerable time before the idea clearly dawned on electricians that one wire and needle could be made to represent several letters of the alphabet. When, by slow degrees, the wires and needles had been reduced to the lucky number five, we may say that a great step in the needle-form of telegraphy had been inaugurated. It was by means of one of these five-needle instruments that the capture of the notorious Tawell, the Quaker murderer, was effected, and a quaint incident is told in connection with it which fixes it the more firmly in the memory. In spite of its five needles the instrument could not make the letter "q," and but for the ingenuity of the telegraphist, who spelt the word "Quaker," "Kwaker," the murderer would in all probability have escaped. But five-needle instruments, useful as they proved in those days, are now looked upon by practical telegraphists as odd specimens of antiquity.

It took nearly a whole century from the date of C. M.'s somewhat rude invention to make the next fruitful and definite step. Then it was that Messrs. Cooke and Wheatstone introduced what is known as the "double-needle" telegraph. On the night of June 25, 1837, it was subjected to trial by wires stretched from Euston Square to Camden Town. At the one end stood Mr. Cooke, at the other Professor Wheatstone. "Never," says one of the inventors, "never did I feel such a tumultuous sensation before as when, all alone in the still room, I heard the needles click; and as I spelled the words I felt all the magnitude of the invention, now proved to be practical beyond all cavil or dispute." The double-needle telegraph held its own with considerable distinction for many years, and even now at many of the smaller post-offices, and on most railways, its "lineal descendant" is to be found in the handy "single-needle" instrument, which is, electrically and mechanically, just a double-needle cut in two.

The next great step in telegraphy was due to America, which, in these later years, has almost practically monopolised the inventive faculty in this department of science. The name of Morse has become so associated with his form of instrument, that the one is lost in the other. The principle was electro-magnetic. What may be called the "keeper" of the magnet is an armature or horizontal lever carrying a piece of pointed metal or "style," which embosses a mark upon a band of paper carried forward by wheel-work. The system of dots and dashes identified with the name of Morse, or a mere modification of its working, is that now generally in use throughout the world. If Morse, who had abandoned a promising career as an artist for the love of electrical experiment, did not realise the last possibility of his own ingenious invention, he may be said to have laid down the principles of all further development. It has been well said :—

"The great defect in the original 'Morse' instrument, or, as it is commonly called, the 'embosser,' is the difficulty of reading, unless under certain conditions of light and shade, the embossed marks on the strip of paper, as well as the unpermanent character of the record. This may, however, be said to have been a mere difficulty of detail, overcome by the introduction of the ink-writer—in connection with which it is proper to mention the name of Messrs. Siemens, of London and Berlin. The manipulation and electrical action of this instrument are in all respects the same as those of the 'Morse;' in fact, it is, to all intents and purposes, a 'Morse,' with the important addition of the ink-writing principle. The lever attached to the armature, which in the 'embosser' holds a style for the indentation of the strip of paper, has in the case of the ink-writer a small disc attached to it. This disc rests in a well or trough filled with specially prepared telegraphic ink, and each time the armature is drawn towards the electro-magnet the disc is raised by means of the lever arrangement, and being thus brought into contact with the paper as it is unwound from the instrument, resembling the manner in which the paper is unwound in the new 'Walter' printing-machine, beautifully distinct marks or signs are made, in place of the somewhat faint indentations produced by the original instrument. These ink-writing instruments are of two kinds, telegraphically described as double and single current ink-writers ; the former being used for long distances, where the signalling is more laboured and difficult, and the latter for short distances, and generally throughout the metropolis."

The name of Wheatstone soon recurs in the annals of telegraphic invention in connection with his automatic system, of which the distinguishing feature is, that the messages are prepared beforehand by being punched out on a strip of paper, somewhat after the manner of the pattern of a Jacquard loom. This done, the slip is simply passed through a machine called the "trans-mitter" or "sender," by means of turning a handle for the purpose, when, owing to the electric current being broken or maintained, according to the different perfora-tions in the paper, the message is recorded at the distant station in exactly the same form as by the ordinary Morse instrument. The transmitting process (that is, after the preliminary punching has been accomplished) is of so entirely mechanical a nature, that steam or other power might be applied to the working of the machine, and messages may be sent *ad infinitum* at a speed some-thing like four times as great as that attained under the "hand" system.

Of all the modern inventions in telegraphy, this is at once the most wonderful, the most interesting, and the most useful. By its means the capacity or carrying-power of a wire can be increased fourfold, with, of

M

course, a corresponding increase of staff at both ends; it is tolerably certain that the Post-Office could not have coped with the immense increase of traffic which has taken place since its acquisition of the telegraphs but for the largely extended use which is now made of this description of apparatus, pending the erection of new wires. This invention was only in what might be termed its experimental stage when the Post-Office took over the telegraphs—not more than two or three sets of apparatus of this kind being in use by all the companies put together. Now, however, there are some scores at work in the great Central Telegraph Office, and every provincial town of any importance has one or more of these fast-speed appliances.

And Morse, although the principle of his original instrument has been improved upon and adapted, still contrives to maintain his prestige and to perpetuate his fame, by what is called the " Morse sounder," which has been designated the "telephone of symbolic telegraphy ;" being at once cheaper to make, to work, and to maintain than the printing-machine of the early days of Post-Office telegraphy. And speaking of sound-telegraphs recalls the " Bell" instrument of Sir Charles Bright, which may be said to have accompanied the double-needle instrument into honourable retirement. In this interesting form of telegraph two bells of different pitch were fixed on a frame sufficiently apart to admit the head of the operator, who, with a bell close up to each ear, interpreted the sounds as they were given out with almost lightning rapidity.

" The Morse sounder is practically the Morse instrument. But inasmuch as the principal part of a recording instrument is that connected with the unwinding and marking the paper, the sounder may be said to be the mere skeleton of the printer. The clockwork is altogether dispensed with, and the apparatus may be said to resolve itself into a pair of coils and an armature, the stroke of which, as it is attracted by the electric current, creates the sound from which the signals are interpreted. In fact, it is little more than an electro-magnet, which may almost be carried in the waistcoat-pocket, while the Morse recorder, or printer, can hardly be accommodated in a smaller space than eighteen inches square. *Difference* of sound in the bell instrument has been substituted by *duration* of sound in the Morse sounder; and just as a stroke on the left-hand bell indicated the 'dot' of the Morse alphabet, or the letter 'E,' so a momentary click of the armature is similarly interpreted on the sounder, while a more decided click would represent the 'dash' of the Morse alphabet, or the letter 'T.'"

The Post-Office erred on the side of caution in regard to duplicate, adopting the view so strongly held by the leading telegraph companies, that some kind of record or other was necessary to the accurate transmission and decipherment of the messages. But lately experience has told in favour of "sound-reading."

Another interesting and ingenious form of telegraphy is to be seen in the "Hughes" type-printing instrument, which delivers its message in bold Roman characters, and which, although discarded by the Post-Office, is extensively used by the Submarine Telegraph Company and on the Continent.

It would be entirely beyond our scope to enter into any elaborate account of the telegraph galleries at the central office in London. Here we see most of the more recent instruments in active work — "Direct writers," which can deliver with ease forty messages an hour, duplex and quadruplex instruments, and single needles for shorter distances. The rapidity with which the ribbon-like bands of printed messages which faithfully preserve record are thrown out is truly astonishing. While we listen to the hurried click-click, which would to a stranger soon become altogether confusing, our attention is directed to some "Sound" instruments which demand the greatest nicety and tact in their treatment.

Here, too, we see all round the sides of the great gallery the receiving and despatching boxes of the pneumatic tube system, through which, as we have seen, messages are blown with the speed of lightning. What would perhaps prove as interesting to the general visitor, who cannot profess to grasp all the details about electrical systems, currents, needles, and insulators, is the composite character of the staff here, and the air of energy, industry, and enthusiasm which everywhere prevails. Great prominence is given to female labour. There are over 900 female clerks in this department of the public service, and, judging from appearances, they could hardly be more happily employed. "The whole world," said Mr. Scudamore, "is the country of the telegraphist. Sitting at one end of a wire, no matter what its length, he converses as easily with the clerk at the other end as if he were in the same room with him. Strange as it may seem, he knows by the way in which the clerk at the other end of the wire does his work whether he is passionate or sulky, cheerful or dull, sanguine or phlegmatic, ill-natured or good-natured. He soon forms an acquaintance with him, chats with him in the intervals of work, and becomes as much his companion as if he were working face to face with him."

And there is a story told by Mr. Scudamore of a clerk in London who formed an attachment for, and finally married, a clerk in Berlin with whom he worked; a relation which, we understand, has since then been repeated with varying attendant circumstances.

It is, indeed, not a little surprising to find that electricity, under some circumstances, may be superseded by air. To create a vacuum in a pipe or tube is merely a mechanical process, accomplished in an instant by a powerful steam-engine; and for short distances, especially within great cities, it has been found a greater saving of time to use such tubes for the despatch of the actual written message than to re-telegraph them from a general centre. The pneumatic tubes in London extend to some twenty-one miles; and the following very admirable description of the system has been written by one who has given much study to the subject :—

"Twenty miles of pneumatic tubes are terminated in graceful curves at what is called the 'tube-board,' which runs along the entire length of the central gallery, and at each of the thirty tubes thus represented is stationed a smart boy-attendant. Each tube is fitted with an elaborate and costly brass apparatus for regulating the pressure and vacuum to be applied to it, and with an electric bell for signalling purposes. The 'carrier,' in which the messages are enclosed for transmission, is a round tube-like box made of gutta-percha, and covered with several coatings of felt, so as to make it nicely fit the pipe through which it has to travel. The messages are rolled up tightly and placed inside the carrier, either singly or in half-dozens, as the pressure of business requires. The carrier is inserted in the mouth of the tube, pressure is turned on by the attendant, and away it goes, round the curve which takes it up nearly to the roof of the gallery, down through the flooring to the level of Newgate Street, until, speeding its way along busy thoroughfare and quiet court or alley, it reaches its point of destination, where it will probably ascend to the top of the building in which the office is situated, apparently for no other purpose than to descend again into the basement and project itself under the very nose of the messenger-boy whose duty it is to 'uncork' the messages and run with them to their final destination. The operation takes longer to describe than most carriers occupy in travelling from St. Martin's-le-Grand to their destination ; and we need scarcely point out that by simply reversing the process—*i.e.*, by exhausting instead of charging the tubes—carriers are drawn or sucked inwards as easily and quickly as they are blown or puffed outwards."

It was rather surprising to learn that practical telegraphists then thought that the increase of cheap telegraphy between various parts of London is more likely to lie in the extension of the tubes than otherwise. "Pneumatic telegrams" which could be sent closed as a letter and delivered as they are received would certainly be found of great value, lending themselves to a large class of correspondents who do not care to commit their secrets to telegraph clerks, however skilfully contracted and disguised, or transferred to imperfect cipher.   So long ago as the sitting of the Commission on Telegraphs in 1876 we find that this topic was made prominent.   Mr. R. W. Johnston, on being asked the question : " Have you at all considered any form by which telegrams might be sent to the public without any loss of facilities, and in a cheaper mode to the Post-Office ? " answered :—

"I have been considering that in London, at all events, for the purpose of a cheap local telegraph rate, the pneumatic system might be largely extended ; my impression is now, and has been for some time, that London will never be properly served, telegraphically, until the pneumatic system is very considerably extended. I think that at Charing Cross, for example, to which point we have two large tubes of considerable capacity now going, we ought to have a sub-central pneumatic station, with tubes laid to the House of Commons, which would also include an important office in Parliament Street, and likewise that in Westminster Hall, and also to Piccadilly, which would include an important office in Piccadilly Circus, and probably also an office in Regent Street ; and by these means I think that cheap local telegraphy might be secured.   The cost, no doubt, would be considerable at first, but the advantage as regards a system of communication of this kind is, that the cost of laying down, at all events, is final, because there is practically no limit to the 'life' of a pneumatic tube, and we know that underground wires deteriorate almost as much as over-house wires."

"Is it not likely that a large expenditure may have to be incurred in the Metropolis in putting down underground wires instead of over-house wires?"—"I do not know that the expenditure in the area which I contemplate for the pneumatic tube system would be as great as the expense in other parts of London, but no doubt it would be considerable."

And again, in answer to the following question: "Do you mean this pneumatic tube to be applied simply for sending telegraphic forms, or for sending pneumatic letters also?" he said:—

"I can readily conceive of a system whereby a telegram can be written—say in an office in the City—and put in an envelope instead of writing the name of the addressee inside the message, and the envelope would be stamped with the proper payment of the telegram, and sent through the tube and delivered, without any clerical expense whatever."

Further questions:—

"By that system of pneumatic letters, would you not save a great amount of clerical labour and clerical charges?—Yes; a very great deal.

"And might not the expenditure upon those tubes, although the capital might be considerable, be repaid by saving the cost of clerks and other persons?—I should say so.

"Have you been considering, also, the question of sending a less amount of words in ordinary telegrams throughout the country?—I have been considering, as a corollary of the proposal made by me in a report which, I think, has been printed and laid before the Committee, that we should abandon the system of getting the sender's address in the form as an address, and adopt the practice which prevails upon the Continent, and also, as it would appear from Colonel Robinson's evidence, in India, and simply require the signature. If we have the address, let it be put upon the form as a mere record, and not for any purpose of signalling.

"But, supposing the sender desires his address to be sent, do you not think that a little extra payment might be made, so that the address might be sent?—Yes; I think so.

"Will you hand in that form you suggest?—I will.

"According to this form, the signature of the sender is at the end, and the space between is divided into two parts; the address upon the left, if it is not to be telegraphed, is not paid for; whereas, if the sender wishes his address to be telegraphed, it is placed upon the right-hand side?—Yes; it is placed upon the right-hand side, and if the sender wishes it to be sent, it must be paid for.

"Do you think that form would practically give to the public all the facilities which they now possess, and be a great gain to the Post-Office?—Yes; I do. I am quite satisfied that our present system encourages the senders of many telegrams to run to waste with regard to their addresses.

"When you speak of the direct advantage likely to arise from the adoption of that plan, are you referring to a direct increase of revenue or in the way of liberating the wires?—Not so much in direct revenue as in liberating the wires; there would be some direct revenue, of course."

The pneumatic system has now been for years in use in Manchester and Birmingham, and was recently extended to other four of the principal English towns, and has now a length of tube at its command more than ten times greater than what existed ten years ago. London alone, as we have seen, has upwards of 37,000 yards, or more than twenty-one miles, of leaden pipes buried beneath its streets, through which open telegrams are being sucked at all hours of the day and night, which seems astonishing; and yet practical men say that the system should in London be very largely extended.

Other countries have availed themselves of the golden opportunities which the evidence given before our Commission suggested; and we regret that, as regards "pneumatic letters" (*télégramme fermée*), we in England are precisely in the same position as before. We read as follows in a recent article on the subject, and we may well be sorry at the losses and failures on our own part which it points out :—

" Whether the German Post-Office officials have been studying a report intended for our own postal authorities we do not know, but it would appear that the pneumatic letter system, or 'blow-post,' as it is characteristically termed, is in operation in Berlin at this moment, and is in course of being considerably extended. The system, when complete, will comprise twenty-six kilometres of tubing and fifteen stations. The tubes will be of wrought-iron, having a bore of sixty-five millimetres, and they will lie about one metre below the surface of the ground. Wrought-iron tubes are the exception in our pneumatic system, the method generally adopted being a leaden tube enclosed in a cast-iron pipe. We are, of course, unable to pronounce upon the merits of the two systems, although it would appear, on the face of the matter, that the freedom from corrosion, and the smoother surface afforded by such a workable metal as lead, are all in favour of an easier and more rapid working. The exhausting machines and apparatus required for working the Berlin system are situated at four of the fifteen stations. Both compressed and rarefied air, or a combination of the two, are employed in propelling the 'carriers,' or boxes, into which the telegrams, or letters, are placed, and steam-engines of about twelve horse-power are used in condensing and rarefying the air. Each of the four main stations has two engines, which drive a compressing and an exhausting apparatus, and large containers, or reservoirs, are used for the condensed and rarefied air. The tension of the condensed air is about three atmospheres, and that of the rarefied about thirty-five millimetres of mercury; and the former, heated to 45 degrees C. by the act of compression, is cooled in the reservoirs, which are surrounded with water. The letters and cards which have to be forwarded are of a prescribed size, twenty being the complement assigned to each 'carrier.' From ten to fifteen carriers are packed and forwarded at a time—a sort of pneumatic 'train,' in fact; and behind the last 'vehicle' is placed a box with a leather ruffle, in order to secure the best closure of the tube. The velocity of the carriers averages 1000 metres per minute, and a train is despatched every quarter of an hour, each of the two circuits or routes into which the system is divided being traversed in twenty minutes, including stoppages. The entire cost of this novel and apparently complete system is estimated at 1,250,000 marks; and it is always well to remember, in speaking of the cost of a pneumatic system, as compared with that of an ordinary telegraph, that the outlay is as nearly final as possible, there being practically no limit to the 'life' of a pneumatic tube, especially if it be constructed of lead and protected from external injury by an outer coating of iron. A 'blow-post' letter appears to cost threepence in Berlin, or about one-fourth of the cost of a telegram, and the average time of delivery in any quarter of the city is stated to be one hour. Admitting our own Metropolitan telegraphic system to be perfect as far as it goes, it is perfectly clear, from the report of the Select Committee already referred to, that a cheaper rate than one shilling for local telegrams is not to be hoped for so long as the costly machinery of wires, instruments, and clerks is maintained for telegraphing over distances readily compassable by the pneumatic system. What strikes us, on reading an account of the Berlin system, is, that these pneumatic tubes afford an opportunity of combining the postal and telegraph services, in such a way as to confer a *maximum* benefit on the public at a *minimum* of cost. At all events, it will hardly be doubted that what is necessary and possible in Berlin is more necessary, and should be equally possible, in London; and it would seem to be positive economy to replace the wires, which are now happily being removed from housetops in all directions, by leaden tubes to be filled with air, which costs next to nothing, rather than by iron pipes full of a costly and perishable combination of copper and gutta-percha."

This is a subject that well deserves the further serious consideration of the authorities, the more surely that a very influential organ can write in this style :—

"So little has the Post-Office administration of this country entered into that spirit of progress which the example of Paris and Berlin present, that except in London the pneumatic system is practically unknown, and in the Metropolis it is used exclusively as the hand-maid of the electric telegraph, never as its substitute. The tubes laid down there are, if we mistake not, greater in length than those described as existing in Berlin, but they have no pretensions to the character of a circular service, and are simply viewed as a relief from the vast network of wires and service of telegraphists, which the large number of messages, sent up from a few offices to the central bureau, would entail. So long as the blow-post is thus treated as the auxiliary of the electric tele-graph, no progress will be made ; and it seems a matter which our commercial men should take up, in order that a different view of the subject should be attained."

With regard to the general question of reduction of telegraphic rates, the Commission said in their report :—

"In declining at present to make any recommenda-tion for a general reduction to a sixpenny rate for short messages or for local traffic, the Committee are guided by the present condition of the telegraph service of the

State. When the clerks in the office have become accustomed to the management of their own instruments, and when, by a more enlightened system of training, they have an intelligent, instead of an empirical, knowledge of the work they have to perform, the Committee do not doubt that there will be a large increase in the capacity of wires and instruments to transmit more messages than at present. Constant improvements in instruments are being made, and it is difficult to place a limit to the future capabilities of telegraphic operations. Automatic telegraphy, if the work be continuous, gives a greatly increased capacity to a wire, and by a proper combination of this system with hand-worked instruments, the capacity for work of the various offices will be considerably augmented, but at present they might break down under any enlarged strain of work, produced by a sudden development of the system. It is due, however, to the Post-Office authorities, to say that they are constantly improving their telegraphic capacities for work, and that even now messages are transmitted with an efficiency and regularity which, a few years ago, would have been deemed impossible.

"One great point should always be borne in mind, that the postal telegraph system differs from a purely commercial undertaking in this, that as it was taken over by the State primarily for the convenience of the public, all increase of traffic which can be brought about without loss to the revenue adds to the national value of the system. Moreover, as the existing wires and staff are capable of undertaking a considerably increased traffic, and as it is impossible either to maintain or get rid of superfluous wires and operatives without heavy expense and loss, the desirability of developing the telegraph traffic of the country up to the full capacity of the system seems to your Committee to admit of no dispute."

Mr. Fawcett, when waited on by a deputation whose object was to urge a reduction of telegraph rates, practically retreated under shadow of the Treasury. With his views of political economy and progress, he must have felt certain forms of official restriction somewhat painful; for there can be no doubt that there is a great deal of truth in the passage which we shall now venture to quote :—

"Those who oppose the introduction of sixpenny telegrams on Mr. Fawcett's plan are reduced to this argument. They object to the reform because they insist on the Telegraph Department earning more than three and a half per cent. on its capital. Such a contention, however, is untenable, even on Mr. Fawcett's own showing. At the beginning of his speech we find him arguing that it would be unjust to tax the people *en masse* so that some of them might get cheaper telegrams—in other words, unjust that the Telegraph Department should work at a loss for the benefit of those rich enough to use it. Surely by parity of reasoning it is also unjust to compel it to earn a higher profit than that necessary to make it pay expenses, for that must mean the imposition of a tax on the senders of telegrams for the benefit of those who send none."

And again, with quite as effective argument :—

" Mr. Fawcett seemed to think that his hearers might

be disappointed at the effects of the contemplated experiment upon the national revenue. But, whatever
might be the immediate result of the reduction, it is
perfectly certain that the loss involved by the sixpenny
rate would be very soon made good. Moreover, admitting that the item of expense cannot be lost sight of,
it is not, in such a matter as this, of paramount importance. The requirements of the country are the first
thing which the Government have to consider. If
the argument of the purse had triumphed, we should,
as Mr. Fawcett's analogy hinted, never have had the
penny postage system. That reform entailed for thirty-
three years a loss of revenue. The two cases are not,
of course, completely parallel. The necessity of sixpenny telegrams can hardly be compared with the necessity which existed half-a-century ago for the institution
devised by the philanthropic genius of Sir Rowland Hill.
Yet if it can be shown that the demand is as pressing
and as general as the memorial of the Society of Arts
stated, a tolerably conclusive case will have been made
out for the concession."

To the great satisfaction of all interested in social
progress and the development of our trade, the movement for the introduction of sixpenny telegrams was at
last carried, with the allowance of so many words, the
address of the receiver being included. There is no
doubt that under the old system much needless work
was caused through the unnecessary amplification of addresses, full Christian names, titles, &c., &c. If the
change has increased the traffic immensely, it has not,
save in exceptional circumstances, burdened the wires to

the extent that some were inclined to prophesy, and the
organisation has been so efficient that no break-down due
to this cause has occurred, and no delay or confusion
worth noting. The increase of revenue, if not so marked
as might have been expected, is certain, as time goes on,
amply to justify expectations, as the habit of using the
wires for many purposes, instead of writing letters, extends, and the great benefits in the saving of time are more
and more felt by the great body of the community. The
administration will be alive to provide means as traffic
increases. Telegraphing will assuredly have the effect
of superseding correspondence more and more, and will
inevitably form another in the train of causes which have
gone, as some folks say, to cause a marked degeneracy
in the epistolary art. We do not write letters nowadays,
they urge; we only indite messages; and it will form a
very interesting inquiry for some future Macaulay, how
far this assertion is based in fact. The leisurely mood
of mind favourable to the elaborate studied epistle, such
as our forefathers were fond of writing, under the idea
that it was bad economy to pay a shilling to send a few
perfunctory lines to a friend at a distance, is certainly
not directly developed by the use of post-cards and sixpenny telegrams; and a vast social revolution such as
has hardly a parallel is being quietly effected by postal
and telegraphic reforms such as could hardly have been
dreamt of by those who were at the head of affairs only
five-and-twenty years ago.

One incubus the postal and telegraph system still
suffers under, and that is, the position in which it is
placed in relation to general revenue. The Exchequer,

and the necessities of the Exchequer, still dominate ; and if it must be confessed that this does exercise healthy restraint in the direction of putting a check on too hasty changes and speculative enterprises, it is also open to the charge of retarding some of the most pressing and necessary improvements, because of the immediate demands that would be made for capital. Two things are still waiting further development—the extension of the Pneumatic Tube system to form a complete circle round the Metropolis, and the introduction of a system of closed messages or pneumatic letters, such as we have spoken of as being in use in some foreign capitals. Paternal government may have its faults, but given a tolerably honest and efficient administration, it is more apt to carry out a system thoroughly ; whereas we, in this country, are, from many causes, too apt to do things by halves, and hardly reap the full benefit of the ideas which we have been the first to originate and to introduce.

With regard to underground wires, a good deal still remains to be done to put us quite on an equal footing with other countries. Both in France and Germany the main lines, at least, have been put underground, and in France more than 12,000 miles are in daily use, and such little difficulties as are incidental to their position have been overcome by invention. The wires are, of course, perfectly free from damage by wind-storms ; and experience has proved that in the case of electric storms, powerful earth-currents, &c., there is less disturbance than with aërial lines. The main lines in France are, as a rule, laid in trenches four feet deep, with inspection

stations at intervals of about a third of a mile, and it is
found that for lengths of 250 miles the speed of transmission is quite equal to that of aërial lines. By the
use of "relays" at suitable intervals, it is found that the
length of line is practically unlimited, and the Telegraph
Department can afford to laugh at storms which upset
the posts of systems dependent on the aërial method
of carrying wires. Both France and Germany have a
special reason for putting their telegraph wires underground, but the Americans arrived at the same determination from very different reasons, and passed a Bill
which provided that in all cities of half-a-million inhabitants telegraph and other wires should be put
underground before the end of 1885.

After the last great storm which cut off our telegraphic
communications for days with some most important
centres a great agitation was got up; and though some
little was then accomplished, the reform was not gone
into with the thoroughness required to make us absolutely secure. The gaps in our armour are still all too
patent and too prominent to justify us in hugging ourselves on our complete exemption from such another
"accident" as we then suffered from. Perhaps of all
our public departments the Post-Office has, from the
days of Rowland Hill, been the most ably and con-
scientiously administered. Whether Conservative or
Liberal Postmasters-General have been at the head of
affairs—whether Lord John Manners or Mr. Fawcett or
Mr. Raikes—they have all alike devoted themselves with
their whole mind and heart to developing and strengthening the service, with the public interests always before

them; it is the Exchequer, with its persistent demands, like the daughter of the horse-leech, with its incessant cry of "Give, give!" which has mainly stood in the way. The profits of such a public department should surely be at the command of those who have been most influential in making the profits, to improve and to extend it.

Having proceeded thus far, we shall now glance briefly at some of the statistical and monetary aspects of the subject. The extent of telegraph lines in Great Britain is, proportionately to its size, greater than that of any other European State. The length of the electric wires of France is 35,000 miles, of Russia 31,000, of Austria 29,000, and of Germany 28,000, while that of the United Kingdom is 27,000. The average number of telegraphic messages sent in Great Britain is more than double that of any of the nations just named. In France the annual rate is one message to every five persons; in Austria, one to every seven; in Italy, one to every six; in Russia, one to every twenty-two; in Germany, not quite one for every two inhabitants. In Great Britain and Ireland the number of telegrams sent every year exceeds that of the entire population.

Twenty-two years ago the number of miles of telegraph in Great Britain was 3000; at the time of the transfer of the system to the Post-Office there were in existence 15,203 miles of telegraphic line, and 59,250 miles of wire. There are at the present moment more than 26,000 miles of line, and nearly 120,000 miles of wire; while the number of instruments, which stood at the time of the transfer below 2000, has been increased to upwards of 8500. The combined companies forwarded amongst them some six millions of telegrams, and their revenue would be somewhere about half-a-million sterling. In the first year after the transfer of the system to the Post-Office the number of messages had risen to very nearly ten millions; in 1871 more than twelve and a half millions of messages had been forwarded; in 1872 the number had risen to close upon fifteen millions; while for the financial year ending March 31, 1874, the number was over eighteen millions. Thus, the number of messages was tripled in four years, and the revenue considerably more than doubled—the difference of proportion between the increase in the number of messages and the increase in the revenue representing the gain to the British public by the transaction. Since the introduction of the sixpenny rate the number of messages has increased by almost one-half, showing the most remarkable progress and development.

And the following figures will suffice to show how well the telegraphs pay, and how unfair it is that the public should be the losers because of the involvements of past and present, and of multifarious departments. The gross receipts from the telegraphs in 1876 were £1,287,000, while the outlay for working expenses, renewals, &c., was £1,090,000, which shows a profit realised of £197,000. We refer to the year 1876, because it was the year in which that important Select Committee of the House of Commons, presided over by Dr. Lyon Playfair, inquired into the telegraph system of the country. Passing on to the year which closed on March 31, 1880, we find that the gross receipts had increased to no less a sum than £1,471,000, but

that the working and other expenses have not, increased
in anything like the same ratio, owing to great economy
having been introduced into the service and in consequence of improvements in the means of telegraphing.
This largely increased revenue was obtained at a comparatively slight addition of cost. The working expenses had only increased from £1,090,000 in 1876 to
£1,117,000 in the year 1879–1880, so that the profit
for the last financial year was £356,000. The profit
during the four following years has increased from
£197,000 to £354,000. Later figures exhibit an equal
result, which becomes all the more satisfactory when we
turn to the capital account.

Another way of gauging the increase may be found.
The total number of telegraphists employed by the
companies was about 2500, of whom less than 500 were
women; and to this number fall to be added nearly
1500 message-boys, making a total of some 4000
persons. The Post-Office employs nearly 8000 telegraphists, of whom more than 1500 are women, while
the number of message-boys exceeds 4600 — outnum-
bering the whole staff under the companies. It thus
appears that, in all, considerably more than 12,000 persons are employed in the telegraph work of the United
Kingdom, not reckoning the "irregulars" and super-
numeraries.

The great point, as we would earnestly urge, is, that
the question of profit is not the *first* question that ought
to be considered in dealing with the development of the
telegraph system. The public service should be primarily studied. This thoroughly accomplished, the rest

is but a matter of time. In no instance has the liberal and enterprising spirit been in the long-run disappointed in dealing with such affairs ; and the most politic as well as the most profitable method of dealing with the whole difficulty may lie in the boldest and most generous spirit.

X.

A RAILWAY WHISTLE.

IT is sometimes said that the world knows nothing of
its greatest men; it is very certain that the world does
not know much, if anything, of some of its most faithful
servants, or in the least realise what it owes to them.
How few when they hear a railway whistle regard it as
anything but a noisy and unnecessary interruption. Very
few, indeed, are they who know that to the ears of some
it speaks in very definite language, on which they must
act with the utmost decision and despatch. In certain
parts of the Metropolis, where there are railway-lines,
there are recurrent outbreaks of complaint about the
railway whistles, and the tone of most of the angry
letters sent to the newspapers, when the fit is on, has
invariably been such as to encourage the idea that the
railway drivers were a kind of incarnate fiends, who
delighted to make night as well as day hideous by the
use of their shrill whistles, and to torture the ears of the
wakeful. Unfortunate the light sleepers may have been,
placed in such perilous and trying proximity to a railway;
but certainly the railway drivers could not do other than
they did, for they are bound by the very strictest rules,
and must not touch the whistle save when duty calls.

A railway whistle is a definite signal which, amongst other things, brings the driver of the train directly *en rapport* with the signalman in his box. There he stands; you may often catch a glimpse of him when travelling as the train slows into the terminus or junction. He is surrounded by rows of bristling steel handles, all of an exact height. These are the shafts that work the points. They are all carefully numbered. Besides these there are in the box clocks of peculiar construction, right in front of the row of shafts; telegraphic dials and bells, as well as telegraphic despatching desks; books of record, which are most jealously kept and studied. If you had ever spent a few hours with signalmen in their boxes, as I have done frequently, both by day and night, you would find often in their hands a book somewhat resembling a Time-table, but double the size of page, and pretty thick too. This is the "Working Time-table" or "Appendix to the Working Time-table," of the Company which they may serve, so far as it concerns them. This is a document which it would surprise not a few to read—puzzle not a few perfectly to master and remember. It tells all about the stations on the main lines and branches; gives the law of regulation of clocks in signal-boxes; a list of all the stations and signal-boxes connected with the Message Telegraph Circuits; classifies all these stations and signal-boxes which perform train signalling; carefully sets down in tabulated form all train telegraph arrangements, and follows this up with a special list of leading stations in regard to which there are any special points to be attended to; then comes a long catalogue of "Whistles for Engines," then a careful drawing of route-indicators, with the arms in positions for the various signals, and after this a list of all route-indicators. Then follows a list of " Points of Inclines " for intercepting railway vehicles, a list of stations where "ramps" are kept and places where signalmen are responsible for their safety, rules relating to signal-lamps, &c., &c.

All this information the signalman in his box must read, and he must master all of it that bears in the most remote manner on his own station and its relation to others by telegraphs and signals. And as details are constantly being modified to meet the demands of extending traffic, or from other causes, he must keep himself very carefully up to time—so to speak ; he certainly must not be like the Bourbons, "Learn nothing, and forget nothing." And I confess that, when I look at a "Working Time-table," or see a signal-box now, I never fail to have strengthened in me my sense of the responsibility, importance, and ability of the men who labour there.

If we take our start from the railway whistles, we can work round the main circle of a signalman's duty. Strictly speaking, however, we should say that the word "whistle " is a misnomer in the sense we have used it in the heading, but there is no other word that could be popularly used for our purpose. There are whistles and whistles —the long and the short whistle, for example, carefully distinguished, and there is the cock-crow. By the combination of these, or the repetition of them, you have a complete code of signals for all stations for up and down trains, each having its own proper distinctive whistle, unmistakable to the signalman, were it possible that he could for the moment be absent or oblivious. Here, for example, to make matters more plain, are the whistles for Buchanan Street Station, Glasgow :—

From Main Down-Line to No. 1 Arrival Platform.	1 Whistle.
From Main Down-Line to No. 2 Arrival Platform.	2 Whistles.
From Main Down-Line to the Back Road . .	3 Whistles.
From No. 1 Arrival Platform to Main Up-Line, by the Crossover Road south of Signal-box . .	1 Whistle and 1 Cock-crow.
From No. 2 Arrival Platform to Main Up-Line, by the Crossover Road south of Signal-box . .	2 Whistles and 1 Cock-crow.
From the Back Road to the Main Up-Line, by the Crossover Road south of Signal-box . .	1 Long and 1 Short Whistle.
From No. 1 Arrival Platform to Main Up-Line, by Crossover Road north of Signal-box . .	1 Whistle.
From No. 2 Arrival Platform to Main Up-Line .	2 Whistles.
From No. 3 Carriage Siding to Main Up-Line .	3 Whistles.
From No. 4 Departure Platform to Main Up-Line .	4 Whistles.
From No. 5 Departure Platform to Main Up-Line .	5 Whistles.
From No. 6. Carriage Siding to Main Up-Line .	6 Whistles.
From Main Up-Line to No. 1 Arrival Platform, by Crossover Road north of Signal-box . .	1 Cock-crow.
From Main Up-Line to No. 2 Arrival Platform .	2 Cock-crows.
From Main Up-Line to No. 3 Carriage Siding .	3 Whistles.
From Main Up-Line to No. 4 Departure Platform .	4 Whistles.
From Main Up-Line to No. 5 Departure Platform .	5 Whistles.
From Main Up-Line to No. 6 Carriage Siding .	6 Whistles.
From No. 5 Departure Platform to Siding at back of Signal-box	1 Cock-crow.
From No. 6 Carriage Siding to Siding at back of Signal-box	2 Cock-crows.

There are, of course, emergencies when engine-drivers may be forced to use the whistle, such as a person on the line, or other risk of " danger," and then a margin must be allowed to the discretion of the driver ; but the rules are imperative that the driver is not to whistle more than is absolutely necessary, and for a very good reason,—the more he whistles the more he may confuse.

This is a common form of direction in Working Time-
tables :—

"The signalmen at So-and-so, guided by the Time-
table, by indicators on engines, and verbally by the station
officials, being in possession of information as to the trains
for which points are to be put in position and signals
cleared, drivers are not to sound the engine-whistle more
than absolutely necessary—such as a short whistle before
putting on steam when the starting-signal is given, a
whistle to warn any one who may be on the line, or when
instructed by any of the station officials to give any particular whistle as a signal to the signalman or otherwise;
and it must be distinctly understood that no such thing
as long and repeated whistling for signals to be taken off,
or from any other motive, except in some extreme emer-
gency, can be allowed at So-and-so."

In the daylight, therefore, the railway whistle has its
own special significance wherever heard, and is never
a sound at random; but in the darkness of night or in
fog, when other signals cannot be seen, it soon becomes
evident of what use and importance it is. It is, then, one
of the most available links between drivers and signalmen. In fact, railway traffic, as now conducted, would
not be at all possible without it, and the codes on
which it rests. A signalman, then, is a man on whom
a vast deal of responsibility lies; he must have a clear
head and a good memory, a cool nerve and a steady
hand. This is his ordinary duty: he must look to open
signals the moment any train is telegraphed to him, and
enter the same with exact time in the proper column of
a book. Then he must set his points, where this is

necessary, and when the train has passed he must telegraph on to next station, enter the time and fact in
another column of his book, and then relieve his points
again to be ready for the next train. Every one knows
the semaphore formula, " Up arm for danger; down arm
for clear line." And it should be borne in mind that this
is not only the procedure for passenger trains, but for all
trains whatever; nay, even for light engines, or for pilot
engines and ballast engines, and engines passing for purposes of relief, or for a hundred other reasons; all are
telegraphed, signalled, and entered without "respect of
persons," because to the signalman the returning coal or
ballast engine is just of as much importance as an express
train—it may wreck an express train if by any oversight
it were getting wrong or run on the wrong metals. The
signalman's book is therefore a complete record of everything that goes on by the metals past his box, and his
primary duty is to keep his section clear, or, if blocked,
to let all concerned clearly know it.

In some cases, as in that of big towns and extensive
junctions, the work goes on as ceaselessly by night as by
day. Then the goods trains roll along, then the empty
trucks come back, then the extra engines come in. All
have to be dealt with in the way we have described and
entered in our signalman's book, which is an extended
index of all the traffic of the company at the point with
which it deals. There is no end of extra or special
things to which the signalman must attend and have always
in readiness—one of them is the fog-signal, which is most
important. In the depth of winter or in thick fogs the
signalman then has to trust almost wholly to his ears.

Immediately that he has cleared one train and got his points straight, out he goes a little distance up or down the line, as the case may be, for the next up or down train, and there he attaches by a sort of wire fixture to the metals a kind of slightly raised band containing an explosive material. This is the fog-signal, which stands to him in the place of an engine-indicator in the daylight. When the first wheels of the engine pass over it, it explodes and gives the signal.

Every signalman must be a fair telegraphist; for though in many cases telegraph-boys are kept, he must supervise and watch them. "It is imperative that every signalman be able to work the needle instrument expeditiously," and "signalmen are held responsible for the telegraph-boy's attention to duty." In cases where there is no telegraph-boy, which, of course, happens at what are deemed the less important stations, the signalman is also the telegraphist, and he is thus directed: "Messages to signal-boxes where there are no boys must be telegraphed very slowly and distinctly, to enable the signalman to read them."

But the signalman's judgment has of necessity a good deal left to it, and that in circumstances that may be most trying. Now and then we come on directions "not to use the wire save when necessary." And to give some idea of the work that in special cases and cases of danger may arise the following may be cited:—

"In the event of a line being blocked near a telegraph box, information must be sent along the circuit at once, stating the time the line is likely to be blocked, and the stations on the circuit must be advised when the line is again clear."

The signalman's vigilance is constantly called for, whether the line be worked by "train tablet," as is usual now on single lines, or by what is now known as the Absolute Block System. He must be always on the alert. But so important now is the Absolute Block, that it may be well to describe it a little more fully for clearness' sake.

Its object is to prevent more than one train or engine moving in the same direction between two signal-boxes at the same time. This is done by bell and gong—the bell for up-trains, and the gong for down-trains; and there is, of course, in this a complete code of signals by arrangement of beats applied to indicate exact advice. Thus, for a passenger train, three beats on bell or gong; for goods train, four ditto; for mineral train, five ditto; for light engine or engine and van, six ditto. The semaphore arm which has been raised in advance is to stand at "Danger," and is to be lowered only by the signalman in the signal-box in advance in acknowledgment of the advice of the "Preparatory Signal" of an approaching train or light engine. All outdoor fixed signals are so worked as to show to drivers of approaching trains the same signals as those shown at the same time on the Block Telegraph instrument. No signal is cancelled until after it has been acknowledged. In the copy of "Working Rules" in our hand, which was in use by a man of long experience on one of the Scotch lines, the following has been carefully underlined by him, and will exhibit the systematic observation and despatch required of the signalman :—

"When a train having an engine assisting behind passes a signal-box, the signalman, *after* having transmitted the Block Signal, and after having received the acknowledgment thereof, must give one beat on the bell or gong to the signalman in *advance*, to let him know that the train has an engine behind it, *which must be acknowledged by one beat, and registered in Train-Book accordingly, under the heading of Remarks.* If the train passes the next signal-box without the assisting engine, the signalman there must conclude that it has broken down on the section, and must not lower the semaphore arm in the signal-box in the *rear* until the engine has been removed from the section.

"When a train or light engine passes a signal-box without having a tail lamp on the last vehicle as a 'last vehicle' indicator, the signalman must not lower the semaphore arm in the signal-box in the *rear* until he has given nine beats on the bell or gong (the signal to stop train and examine it) to the signalman in *advance*, and ascertained from him by means of the needle instrument that no part of the train has broken away, although it has no 'last vehicle' indicator upon it."

In addition to the duties we have named, the signalmen on most lines are charged with the duty of taking at the signal-boxes the numbers of the engines under their direction:—

"Signalmen must, as far as possible, ascertain the numbers of all engines which stop at their boxes, and enter the same in their train-books. This is necessary to enable the working of the engines to be correctly traced."

When trains are late signalmen on duty must be late too :—

"When trains are late, signalmen must remain on duty, if necessary, until they are past, and at all signal-boxes and goods and mineral yards, stations and junctions where shunting engines are employed, and goods or mineral trains late in arriving, signalmen must not go off duty till the work is finished."

The following paragraph about arranging transfer from day to night duty, and *vice versâ*, will indicate that the signalman does not enjoy the luxury of short hours, whatever else he may enjoy :—

"In double-shifted signal-boxes, where there are no relief signalmen, the change from night to day duty must take place on the Sunday preceding the pay. For example, the man who has been on duty for the fortnight will be relieved at 6 P.M. on the Saturday by the man who has been on night-duty, and who will remain on duty until the traffic permits the box to be closed at midnight on Sunday morning, as the case may be. The man who has been on day-duty for the previous fortnight will open the box on Sunday night or Monday morning as the traffic demands, and will be relieved at 7 P.M. on Monday by the man who has been on night-duty. The shift from night to day duty for the fortnight will then take place at 7 A.M. and 6 P.M."

There may be some differences in detail in the working of different lines, but in the broad the same principles hold for all. The signalman in all cases has not only to receive the signal, clear, and telegraph, but to keep exact and faithful record. The least slip on his

o

part might at any moment be fatal. In some cases
there are in a single box as many as forty or fifty shafts,
which have to be constantly in use. The putting of the
hand on one instead of on another, separated only by a
few inches, might be the cause of a collision, with death
and injury and miserable torture to hundreds of men,
women, and children.

Talking to a man who has been pretty nearly all
his life employed on a railway the other day, he said,
"Well, so far as I know railway work, I can't understand why the signalman should be so poorly paid. All
the signalman gets is about one-half the pay of a driver.
Now, I do not say as the driver don't deserve all he
gets, but I do say as the signalman ought to get more.
A good driver has some 7s. or 7s. 6d. a day, often
working on Sundays, thus making something like from
£2, 5s. to £2, 10s. per week regular. Your signalman,
even though a first-rate hand, has only from 23s. to 25s.
per week, and less experienced men acting as assistants
only from 18s. to 21s. Now, it can't be said as I'm
an interested party, becos I never worked in a signal-
box, nor any of my folks, and my own father is a driver,
and 'ave been so nearly all his life, leastways all my life,
and long 'fore I was born. I speak what I feel about
a set of men as deserve much better nor they get, but
that ain't sayin' much now'days, though, after all, 'tis
a'most sayin' everything. They have long hours, hard
work, and little pay, and they work with the head just
as much as the manager of the line does. The slightest
slip on their part might lead to no end of disaster—loss
of life and loss of limb, and pain and sorrow all round.

And yet how often do we hear of efforts made by the poor signalmen to get 1s. or 1s. 6d. a week advance of wages! Why, we should hear something else than complaints about whistles if the public only knew what rests continually on the signalman's care and correctness; that is, the safety and lives of themselves, their wives and children, their friends and relatives, for everybody travels nowadays, at least goes down once a year to get a whiff o' country air or a waft o' sea-breeze; and certainly they could not get to their destinations with despatch, and in safety and peace, if it were not for the care and attention of the signalman in his box, with his clocks and telegraphs, his shafts and record-book, and all the rest of it."

I quite agree with my friend in this plea for the railway signalmen of the United Kingdom. There is not a class of men on whom more depends, nor a class who get less recognition for their labours. The life of the Queen herself is constantly committed to their care; for on a railroad, as elsewhere, all things work together; and though, no doubt, special care is taken for Her Majesty's train, yet even Her Majesty's train must be prepared for—the way kept clear for it; and, however much your manager, and secretary, and guards, and station-masters, and drivers may do, a lapse on the signalman's part might ruin all.

Notwithstanding all the care that *can* be taken, unexpected things will occur, which, even in the case of the Queen's train, throw the whole *onus* on the driver and signalman. On one of the Queen's journeys from Balmoral to Windsor in the summer of the year before last, for instance, a strange and perhaps unexampled thing happened. We take the account of it from the *Westmoreland Gazette :*—

"The signalman at Hincaster Junction, about five miles south of Kendal, had his lamps lit, and all appeared right until a few minutes before the approach of the royal train. As the train got near the junction the down distant signal, which was to guide the driver of the royal train, was in darkness, and for the purpose of ensuring safety the train was brought to a standstill. On making an inspection of the signal-lamp it was found to contain a grand swarm of bees, the great number having had the effect of putting out the lamp, which the signalman was unable to light again. The bees had evidently been attracted by the light. Dewhurst (the signalman) regrets that time would not allow of the swarm being secured in a box and sent forward with the royal train."

About Christmas-time last we read in the newspapers that some people declined to give the railway porters Christmas-boxes, on the ground that they could not get at the signalmen to make their presents to them, though they held that these workers quite as much deserved them, or even more. We would not counsel any niggardliness towards the porters—a most deserving, energetic, and obliging body of men—but we do wish some concerted method could be adopted by which the signalmen might share more practically in the good-will agoing at that festive season, for here again they are at a disadvantage with those who are brought more directly in contact with passengers.

Let us, then, when we hear a railway whistle hereafter,

think of the signalman in his box, for whom it has a special meaning and message; and let us do what in us lies to get further encouragement and recognition— shorter hours and better pay—for a worthy, intelligent, and highly responsible class of men who are at present hardly better paid than a warehouse porter, and certainly very inferiorly paid to a good junior London clerk. Not a few of the railway accidents that have happened have been due to the weariness, and it may have been private troubles, of the signalman; and to keep a wife and family of perhaps six children on 23s. to 25s. a week, as in some cases that I know of, "is no easy matter, gentlemen," as Sarah Gamp was wont to put it; and if you have a man preoccupied and troubled in a signal-box, you certainly increase by fifty per cent., or more, the risk of accidents. The public are more powerful than the railway companies, strong as they are; and it is the public, after all, who are most directly concerned in the perfect comfort and peace of mind of the railway signalmen.

XI.

SOME HISTORICAL BEDSTEADS.

It is a very remarkable fact that more than five thousand years elapsed before mankind reached the idea of a "proper bed." Previous to that men and women, even those of highly civilised nations, were fain to content themselves with something in the nature of a couch merely raised above the ground, with a head-rest of wood or other material. This was the case in Greece and Rome; and though we have testimony through Mark Antony that the "Beds o' the East were soft," we have no reason to conclude that they were anything more than very improved versions of those of Greece and Rome, and certainly not in any way approaching the bed of modern days. Sir Gardner Wilkinson thinks that the ancient Egyptians usually slept on their day-couches, which were long and straight, sometimes with a back, sometimes with carving of the heads and feet of animals at the ends, made of bronze, of alabaster, of gold and ivory, of inlaid wood, and richly cushioned. When these were not in use mats replaced them, or low pallets made of palm-boughs, with a wooden pillow hollowed out for the head. In our own country something more like a sofa than anything else was the only sleeping-place of our forefathers for centuries. When they went to bed, it could hardly be said that they "lay down." The sofa-head prevented that. Then, even after bedsteads were invented, and no end of skill in decoration had been lavished upon them, the sleepers lay in bed without night-dress, that article of luxury (however necessary and common now) not having then

BED OF THE MIDDLE AGES.

been thought of. The sleepers took off their clothes, and the poorer ones used them as bed-clothes, and even with the richest much that the poorest now considers necessary was not then to be had. There were no sheets, properly speaking, nor was there any bolster, these being refinements that came very late—not, indeed, being known at all till the end of the thirteenth century, and not in general use till the end of the fourteenth. How odd it is to think of all the generations that passed without having known the comfort of well - arranged sheets and bolsters! Truly we have much to be thankful for; and yet perhaps not so much. There are no such things on this earth as unmixed advantages. If the earlier sleepers did not enjoy some of the luxuries that are commonplace and general with us, their want of constructive art in this department stood them in good stead. If they did not have sheets and bolsters, each at least had a "bed" to himself. The later developments soon ran into defiance of all laws of sanitation. No sooner did people get the idea of a four-poster than they tried to excel each other, not in beauty so much as in bigness, till it is clear that whole families could have slept in one bed, if they did not actually do so. One of our historical beds is a valuable witness on this point. This is the Bed of Ware. It was said to be capable of containing twelve persons, and tradition assigns it to Warwick, the kingmaker. It is still preserved, we learn, in an inn at Ware, in Hertfordshire. It is more than twelve feet square, and has a remarkably curious and richly-carved back, which by means of two massive pillars at the foot supports a heavy canopy, enriched with elaborate carved work. Before the time of Shakespeare it was proverbial; for we find Sir Toby Belch, in "Twelfth Night," saying to Sir Andrew Aguecheek about the writing of a certain letter, "It is no matter how witty, so it be eloquent and full of invention; taunt him with the license of ink; if thou thoust him some thrice it will not be amiss;

and as many lies as will lie in thy sheet of paper, although the sheet were big enough for the Bed of Ware in England, set them down."

From this it is quite clear that, contrary to the idea that some would-be historical fictionists have of the use of the *thou* in the English common speech of that time, the "thou," whether used systematically in other ways or not, was used as in the German "Du bist ein Knarr!" as a term of insult or offence. For this we have Shakespeare's clear authority here. And we have Shakespeare's clear authority in another matter bearing more directly on our proper subject; for by his will he made a bed historical, and no end of difficulty and dispute have arisen regarding it and his motives in reference to it. To his wife, Anne Hathaway, he devised his "second-best bed" with all due formality. At first one has some vague fear that by this, in spite of apologies, Shakespeare did her no great honour. But a slight glance at antiquities may help to dissipate that idea. Beds had become the chief domestic glories of the time, and immense sums were spent to adorn them. They were even thus specifically named in the wills of sovereigns and of the chief nobility. Anne, Countess of Pembroke, in 1387, bequeathed to her daughter a Bed, "with the furniture of her father's arms." In 1368 Lord Ferrers left to his son his "green Bed with the arms thereon," and to his daughter his "white Bed and all the furniture, with the arms of Ferrers and Ufford thereon." Edward the Black Prince bequeathed to his Confessor, Sir Robert de Walsham, a large Bed of red camora, with his arms embroidered at each corner, while to another friend he left another Bed of camora, flowered with blue eagles; and in 1385 his widow gave "to my dear son the King, my new Bed of red velvet, embroidered with ostrich feathers of silver, and heads of leopards of gold, with bows and leaves issuing out of their mouths." So that even the Second Best Bed of our great dramatist may have been a very fine affair, and that he did not wish in any way to reflect on Anne Hathaway by thus leaving it to her. Let us hope so.

There was up till a few years ago in the town of Leicester a very old-fashioned, picturesque house, with old oak beams showing here and there through the brickwork. It was one of the inns of the town, and before the era of railways enjoyed the presence of many a guest-traveller. The best bedroom contained an old oak bedstead, very curiously carved. It was said that on this bedstead King Richard the Third lay (whether he slept or not) the night before the battle of Bosworth Field. The bedstead is in existence still, and is called King Richard's bedstead. It was his own property, and he was in the habit of having it carried about with him from place to place. But after the fatal battle of Bosworth Field the bedstead remained in the possession of the landlord of the "Blue Boar," who claimed it as his perquisite. Something over a hundred years afterwards the bedstead came into the possession of a woman, who was fortunate enough, or unfortunate enough, to make a great discovery. As she was making the bed one morning she heard a chinking sound, and saw, to her great delight and surprise, a piece of gold drop on the floor. Of course, she then began carefully to examine the bedstead, and found that the lower part of it was hollow, and had been the King's repository of funds for immediate wants. Three hundred pounds—a fortune in these days when money went so much further than it does now—was brought to light, having remained hidden there all these long years.

As King Richard was not there to claim the gold, nor any legitimate representative for him, the woman quickly possessed herself of it. But she had much better have remained in ignorance. With that strange irony which often follows lucky finds and discoveries, as soon as the matter became known one of her servants, in order to rob her of the gold, murdered her. Thus it was said in the neighbourhood of King Richard's gold, that it did nobody any good.

Visitors to Versailles will remember the elaborate, beautiful canopied bed of Louis XIV., on which, as he lay, no doubt he revolved in his mind the schemes which did so much to affect the history of France, and even of the world. At Versailles, too—that is, at Trianon—is to be seen the bed prepared for our own Queen Victoria when she paid her memorable visit to the then Emperor of France, when the Prince Consort, as confessed in his Memoir, had his own doubts and some little uneasiness about the "Man of Destiny," and could not quite bring himself fully to share the Queen's faith in him.

Beds associated with Peter the Great of Russia are many ; and some doubts may arise about the genuineness of some of them. There is one at Amsterdam, and another at St. Petersburg, which may, however, be accepted as genuine.

Then there is the bed of Mary Queen of Scots at Holyrood Palace, Edinburgh, in which we can more readily believe than in that spot of blood which is pointed out to us in the floor near by as being the literal witness of the rough death which befell her friend Rizzio.

And what could be more affecting than to look on that plain little camp-bed of the Emperor William of Germany at Potsdam? As we gaze on it, we feel how much of the man's character was expressed in that bit of furniture, to which he was so greatly attached.

Turning from royal beds, we think of that solid carved four-poster on which the great Rubens lay, and which is to be seen in the Musée at Antwerp, as well as many of the articles associated with his daily life. How the sight of such things sends the imagination careering over the by-ways of biography! How the fancy dances and rejoices in the sense of an affectionate intimacy with the great and good!

Of course, if we chose to take our readers through the state bedrooms of Buckingham Palace and Hampton Court Palace, not to speak of Windsor Palace and St. James's and Marlborough House, we should find plenty of beds made historical by the fact that royalty has lain in them. But that process would be endless, or almost so. For it would look very insular indeed if we did not somewhat extend our view, even if we did not carry it quite so far as China and Peru, and glance in the same way at the historical Beds of France and Germany

and Belgium and Italy. That must wait a more auspi-
cious occasion; what we meant to do at present was
merely to draw attention to some of the Beds that had
become famous in literary record; and our readers, we
trust, will admit that we have done so. Only a few of
royal Beds, as of other Beds, have been raised to this
happy pre-eminence.

XII.

KNIVES AND FORKS.

"KNOWLEDGE comes, but wisdom lingers," says the Laureate. Truth to tell, on a broad view of human nature and history, even knowledge seems to come slowly. In saying this, we refer rather to the small than to the great things of life, to matters of domestic convenience and comfort rather than to great discoveries. Even a good bed, as we would judge it, was a very late affair, and followed long after the discovery of gunpowder and the timepiece. And then it is certain that up to a comparatively recent date the luxury of knives and forks was unknown, and the manner in which a person ate out of the dish with the fingers was a mark of position or of culture. How do we know this? From the records of literature most pleasantly; from dry-as-dust historians less pleasantly. Chaucer affords us a naïve proof that in his time this was so; for he gives us this passage in his portrait of "The Noune Prioress:"—

> "At mete well i-taught was sche withalle;
> Sche leet no morsel from her lippes falle,
> Ne wette hire fyngres in hire sauce deepe.
> Wel cowde sche carie a morsel, and wel keepe,
> That no drope fil uppon hire brest
> In curtesie was sett al hire hest.

Hire overlippe wypud sche so clene,
That in hire cuppe was no ferthing sene
Of grees, when sche dronken had hire draught."

Forks were not introduced into England till the
fifteenth century; and for a long time the use of them
was looked upon as a piece of affectation, if not super-
fine foppery. Even Queen Bess, of glorious memory,
hesitated for a long while to use a fork; and when she
did begin she was very chary of its use, and was not
guiltless of falling back now and then on the fingers as
the most effective aid to the spoon and knife. In truth,
the Fork had a severe fight for existence during the next
half-century, and was once more dropping out of use,
when it was reintroduced by an adventurous and obser-
vant gentleman named Thomas Coryale, who had been
in Italy, and came away enamoured with the neatness
with which the Italians used the fork. He had a fork
made for himself, without which he never travelled,
and had to bear a good deal of chaff, if not offensive
ribaldry, from the bucks of the time. They dubbed
him Furcifer, or the fork-bearer, and made much mirth
at his expense. But Thomas persevered. He was not
content with practice, but brought the pen to his aid
to commend the novelty to others. In an account of
his travels in Italy, Spain, and Switzerland, quaint and
amusing enough, if not very vigorous or original, he
says :—

"The Italian cannot by any means endure to have
his dish touched with fingers, seeing all men's fingers
are not alike clean. . . . They do always at their meales
use a little fork when they cut their meate. For, while

with the knife, which they hold in the one hand, they cut the meate out of the dish, they fasten their forke, which they hold in the other hand, upon the same dishe."

But the Italians are not to be credited with the first discovery of the fork. It really belongs to the Chinese, and travelled northward from China, through Italy and France, to England. The fear of being accused of effeminacy deterred not a few at first from trying the new device for neatness and cleanliness at table. The satirists were down upon it. Broadsheets of the rudest kind caricatured it. The dramatists did not scorn to ridicule it, if they did not make a dead-set against it. John Fletcher, in his "Queen of Corinth," speaks of the "fork-carving traveller;" and Jonson says in his "Volpine"—

> "Then must you learn
> The use and handling of your silver fork,"

which shows that even thus early the silver fork was in use in the higher circles, and that the two or three pronged iron fork was the refuge of the lower classes only. In village inns and rural districts the patience of the traveller is sometimes still severely tried by the two or three pronged iron fork, which has at several periods vainly endeavoured to hold up its head and to contest place with the silver four-pronged one. The truth is, that a large trade was interested in the production and sale of steel forks; and notwithstanding that the fork-grinders were the most short-lived class in England, they fought for their freedom slowly to kill themselves off at their trade with a unanimity and determination alike noticeable and remarkable. Steel forks are doomed, however; their day is past, and very soon the few employed in making them will find themselves, like Othello, " their occupation gone."

Trifles have often determined great questions—often occasioned momentous events. The length of Cleopatra's nose produced a great war. So it is in the opposite direction sometimes. Great crises affect trifles, and fashions come into existence often because, like straws, they are caught in some backwater or side-eddy of some great movement and are finally sucked down. Steel forks were more in use in America than elsewhere prior to the great American Civil War, and especially did the steel fork hold its place in the South. The negroes had no objection to cold steel, at all events before the war, and cleaned and scoured assiduously at the steel forks. But the "helps" who took the place of the black servant in the North, and of the slave in the South, had great objections to cleaning them—so great that their will and the little ruses resorted to by them to show the disadvantages of the steel fork soon told. Nowadays steel forks are as seldom met with in the United States as elsewhere.

The fork is the direct descendant of the Chinese chopsticks. The knife was already an article of common use in England, and, just as in other things, wise compromise at last won the day. The awkward movements necessitated by the chopsticks—very difficult indeed to learn the mastery of—were got rid of by the improved chopstick alongside of the fork. One did not then need cunningly to shove or bundle the meat into the mouth, so to speak, but could cut it up into the smallest

P

portions, and convey them to the mouth in the most leisurely way separately. That this was not possible with the chopsticks is evident when we think of the position of those using them. A number of little saucers are placed in front of the diner, with vegetables and little bits of meat of different kinds already neatly cut up in them. The Chinaman, holding his basin in one hand, picks up a piece of meat and vegetables with his chopsticks, and dropping it in amongst the rice, holds the basin close to his chin, and pushes rice, meat, and vegetables all together into his mouth with a sidelong movement of the chopsticks.

Eastern hospitality, and, indeed, some of our own early social life, would be shorn of much of their poetry and romance if we did not clearly realise that knives and forks were not in fashion then. Our Saviour Himself spoke of one that ate out of the same dish with Him betraying Him; and thus we are made to feel that eating together in the East implies a much closer and more intimate relation than it can possibly do with us nowadays, when each individual has his own proper dish and his knife and fork. A traveller in the East, mixing among the people of the upper class, describes his sensations when those who were at meat with him (we cannot say table, for there really was none), when they observed what they deemed any cessation of eating or failure of enjoyment, as they fancied, on his part, would with their fingers pick some tit-bit out of their dish and put it in his mouth. Very kindly meant, but rather trying, as you can conceive, to one used from childhood to a knife and fork. But the whole spirit of

Eastern hospitality is in it, and the eating together of the New Testament cannot be fully realised unless we get thoroughly rid of the accompaniment of knives and forks and their associations.

It goes without saying, therefore, that if we got the original idea of the table-fork from China, we have greatly improved upon the original, as it is our wont to do. Our four-pronged silver forks are really all that could be desired for their purpose, and there is little likelihood that much improvement in that direction will be possible even to advanced science. But we also see from the history of forks how long humanity has had to wait for the most ordinary discovery in small affairs of personal comfort; how loth it was to adopt the improvement; and how, suddenly adopting the new method, it contentedly settles down to enjoy it, too often forgetting even the names of the first innovators who had to fight for freedom in doing it a service. So we need not be too proud of our forefathers (or of ourselves?) when we wield our knife and neat silver four-pronged fork.

XIII.

ARSENIC IN INDUSTRY.

ARSENIC has a bad repute. It is better known as a poison than as a useful article in many industrial arts. And even in these arts, at all events in some of them, a bad odour goes with it. It is apt to reveal itself in many unpleasant phases, and to make the medium to which it is conveyed a mere minister of poisonous influences. Wall-papers especially have been its agents for evil, giving off dust that poisoned people. It has infected others through the skin when used as an element in the dyes of gloves and underclothing; and, on the whole, save in the hands of the chemists and doctors, it is a thing to keep clear of by any means one can. Nevertheless it has its own uses; and some of these we shall proceed to illustrate, as well as some of its delinquencies when foisted upon us by none too scrupulous traders in the amiable and attractive disguises which evil of whatever sort is only too apt to assume.

To understand better what we have to say, we may, in the outset, as well try in a simple way to answer the question, What is arsenic? and How is it produced?

Arsenic is a powder derived from the slow combustion of certain metallic substances. These are called arsenical pyrites or leuco-pyrites, and all alike carry in them colouring elements which are almost essential to the production of certain shades alike in paints, dyes, and coloured papers. It may be that now, through the wonderful developments of the coal-tar dyes, we may feel a little more independent of arsenic, yet in some colours and in some mediums, if we will have certain shades and tints, we must run the risk of the presence of arsenic in greater or lesser proportion, though it must be added in justice that all the coal-tar dyes are not innocent of poisonous effects.

Arsenic is a whitish crystalline powder which feels decidedly gritty, like fine sand, when placed between the teeth, and it has a well-marked taste. It is exceedingly heavy; if you were to try to lift up a bottle of it, you would be surprised, and fancy it was solid lead instead of a white powder till you looked again and assured yourself. Nevertheless, though so heavy, it does not wholly sink in water, but conducts itself under these new circumstances very much as ordinary wheat-flour would do. A large proportion of it would float on the top, and what of it did sink would roll itself into little round pellets, wetted only on the outside, and with a little compact mass of flour still within.

The substances from which it is obtained, termed arsenical nicheloses, surrender it by a process of roasting in great iron cylinders; rising as vapour into a somewhat cool flue, it is there deposited. The raw material is found extensively in Cornwall and Devonshire, and is also distributed over sections of the Continent, especially in parts of Germany, where it is extensively produced. One of the largest places of production in our country is the Great Devon Consols Mine, of which Dr. Oxall is or was the able superintendent. The first thing that is introduced to your notice in going over the works are gigantic revolving or cylindrical furnaces or calciners. Within these may be seen great masses of incandescent metal, glowing with hues that might well be deemed unearthly. In the interior of the cylinder great iron spikes at regular intervals toss the glowing mass about, the friction serving to maintain the combustion. Duly regulated by a proper proportionate mixture of the arsenical pyrites with sulphur, the combustion can be kept for days without using a single pound of coal.

These gigantic cylinders, we were told, were formed of disused boilers. Their use is to extract and refine the arsenic, which, after fusion in the calciner, passes in vapour, as already said, into flues, only kept at a cooler temperature, from which it is collected and reduced to that fine powder, so dangerous, yet, from its resemblance to flour, might so easily be mistaken, or mixed with murderous intent. Of this deadly stuff no less than 200 tons per month were turned out here at the time of which we speak (some years ago), reaching the grand total then of 67,000 tons since the mine was opened, sufficient or more than sufficient, probably, to poison the whole human race. What marvellous powers are indeed lodged in the hands of man! Any incipient Williams, or Brinvilliers, or Mrs. Manning would be a dangerous person to have free access to these stores!

Piles of barrels lay in the yard, ready for shipment to various parts of the world; a small army of men employed in filling, closing the casks, and rolling them about—men who did not, on the whole, look as though the work had such a very deleterious effect upon them, though it must be admitted here and there one looked pale, emaciated, and without energy. Inquiry, however, brought the information that, on the whole, things were in this respect far better than might have been expected. Like everything else, arsenic has some redeeming qualities, at least looked at as a material to work among. The employés were reported remarkably free from everything in the shape of asthma, and could walk long distances without fatigue. One man, who had formerly worked in a lead-mine, declared that he regarded the lead as more unhealthy than the arsenic, but he may have been a person with some peculiarities of constitution.

The ore in this mine consists of three parts copper, fifteen of arsenic, fifteen of sulphur, and sixty-seven of iron and silica. Of these the copper and arsenic are the most valuable. Of course, before the ore is exposed to heat it has to be broken down. Great masses of ore are delivered to the *balmaidens* or *cobbers*, who sit with a large iron hammer in one hand, whilst the other is strongly cased in leather or carpet, to prevent any accident, and with the hammer they chip small pieces from the vast blocks, which give out a sharp metallic ring when struck. These small chips are immersed in water, and thrown in heaps upon long wooden tables. On each side of these recline a row of young girls, who, with three small wooden trays and a bent piece of hoop-iron before them, deftly sort out the chips, and dexterously place them in the proper trays according to the several kinds of ore,—throwing down beneath the table the less valuable material, which, however, undergoes its own proper treatment, that the merest atom of wealth may be extracted from it.   These pieces, put into the trays, then go to the calciners, or are made to undergo some other process that has the same practical results.

Even the waste from the washings is utilised.   It is conveyed by wooden gutters or spouts into shallow pits where pieces of old iron are deposited to attract and absorb the latent copper, &c., that may be there.   This is scraped from them frequently, and we were informed that the quantity obtained was estimated at from four to seven grains per gallon, amounting to many tons in the course of the year.   The whole process carried on here contrasts very forcibly with the old smelting, by which no end of valuable chemical constituents were lost, which now, at the beck of science, come forth to be of the utmost service in manufacture, the arts, and in medicine.

There can be no doubt that arsenic as a pigment in many forms is deleterious to health.   Mr. Henry Carr, a member of the Institute of Civil Engineers, but retired from the active practice of his profession, some years ago became convinced, from circumstances within his own experience, that the evil was much more common than was generally supposed, and set on foot systematic inquiries on the subject.   The result was such as to confirm him in his agitation against the use of arsenic in wall-papers, gauze, tulle, curtains, and even gloves and under-garments ; and he collected quite a volume of attested information on the subject, which he has printed in the form of circulars and pamphlets, and as a lecture which he delivered before the Society of Arts. He says that "arsenic is, in fact, present in such a variety of dyes and colours as to render any judgment from colour on the part of the general public entirely out of the question;" and he adds: "It should be observed that it is not arsenic merely that renders aniline colours poisonous, some being found highly injurious, where, after careful analysis, there was clearly no arsenic present in the fabric."

"In the case of wall-papers," he goes on, "the green, as a rule, contain more arsenic than others; but colour, whether in papers or other fabrics, is no guarantee of freedom from arsenic. . . . In all probability arsenic, as a pigment, was first used in greens, and this may have given rise to the erroneous impression that it is green alone that is injurious, whereas colour is no guide whatever to the purchaser. The danger is simply in proportion to the quantity of arsenic, and in proportion to the facility with which it may be removed from the fabric, either as dust or as gas. . . . The question whether one is poisoned by dust or gas is a matter of interest to the medical profession, but it is of little consequence to the public, the practical fact for their consideration being this, that great numbers do suffer more or less, many most severely, from poisoning by arsenical fabrics; and that, when the mischief has gone too far, they do recover on removal of the arsenical paper or other fabric, thus demonstrating the origin of the malady."

The following, in the shortest possible compass, are

set down as the ordinary symptoms of arsenical poisoning :—

"The symptoms of chronic poisoning by arsenic begin with what appears to be an ordinary cold and cough ; dryness and irritation of the throat and frequent headache; extreme restlessness; great debility, accompanied by cold clammy sweats; cramps of the legs; convulsive twitchings; and a group of nervous symptoms, varying in each case. Inflammation or irritation and smarting of the eyes and nostrils is often the most marked symptom, lasting for days, weeks, or months, sometimes accompanied by irritation of the whole mucous tract, short dry cough, sore throat, running on to diphtheritic throat; ulceration and soreness of the mouth and tongue; irritative fever, which if persistent exhausts the patients, and death takes place by collapse, coma, or convulsions. Among the symptoms there has been occasionally irritation of the skin, accompanied with eruptions."

Mr. Carr collected the most valuable testimony from medical men on the subject; perhaps as curious and interesting a case as any was that of Dr. J. Lauder Brunton, Lecturer on Materia Medica to St. Bartholomew's Hospital, and editor of the well-known medical journal, "The Practitioner." Dr. Brunton wrote :—

"The paper which caused such an injury to my own health was a dull green, such as one would hardly suspect to contain arsenic—arsenical greens being generally thought to be bright greens only. I have heard that many other colours contain arsenic, but have no personal experience on this subject. It is not a combination of arsenic and copper only which is injurious, but arsenic when present in wall-papers as a pigment of any kind will do mischief, the injurious action being due to a combination of arsenic with the paste by which they are fixed to the wall. An organic compound of arsenic is thus formed which is exceedingly poisonous, much more so apparently than arsenic itself. For a long time I did not believe in the injurious effects of arsenical wall-papers, because I knew that patients could take, as a medicine, without any bad result, more arsenic than they were likely to get from the paper of their room; and it was only after I had learned to my cost, how very powerful for evil arsenical wall-papers are, that I became acquainted with the explanation. The most marked symptoms in my own case were severe griping followed by dysentery, although running from the nose and dry cough were not absent."

"Death in the pot" was an old phrase; death in the walls and in dress, it would seem, should become a new one. Wall-papers which contain arsenic have been frequently offered to customers and sold as non-arsenical; and it certainly seems that something should be done of a more strict and thorough kind than has yet been done to deal with the sale of these domestic poisons. Mr. John Bright was strong in his dictum that "adulteration was only another form of competition;" but surely he would have desired to make such things as these impossible.

Besides the uses to which arsenic is applied in industry already noted, we may mention that, in combination with potash, it forms an efficient sheep-wash. A combination of arsenious acid and the oxide of copper is a pigment largely used as a cheap new paint. A great deal of arsenic is used for poisoning wild animals and birds. The rooks in some localities at certain times have suffered much from grain steeped in a solution of arsenic being thrown down to them; and cows and horses have also been injured through partaking of it.

Arsenic is also used, more extensively in some countries than would be believed, to improve the complexion, and its devotees in this respect (who, like opium-eaters, by persistence in their dose, come not only to bear it, but to like it) attribute to it other good effects on health, and say that it increases the capabilities of endurance in many ways, enabling them, by adding to the powers of respiration, to carry loads and to climb hills with greater ease and springiness. Though the practice of arsenic-eating is not unknown in England, we learn that others abroad outstrip us in this taste, and that in some parts of Austria, more especially in Syria, Carinthia, Salzburg, the Tyrol, Lower Austria, and the Erz-Gebirge, arsenic-eating is not only extensively used by the peasant-girls, with the view of increasing their personal attractions, but is largely eaten by the men also, with the ends we have named above chiefly in view, though male vanity as to clear complexion may also have a share in leading to the beginning of the habit. It is said the arsenic-eaters do not shorten their lives by the indulgence. Truly, what is one man's poison is another man's meat; for those whom we have met with who were compelled to take arsenic for various forms of eczema did not speak of it as very attractive, but as producing sensations the reverse of pleasant or likely to lead to indulgence in the drug. At first a dose is taken once a week or so, afterwards more frequently, till, as the constitution accommodates itself to the action of the drug, it may be taken daily. Authorities tell us, indeed, that there are authenticated cases of men who take six grains—enough to poison three men—at one dose without inconvenience, and with the best effects on the digestive organs and the breathing. The penalty has to be paid, however, as in all such cases of indulgence. The arsenic-eater, like the opium-eater, cannot relinquish the dose when he has once begun and has made it a habit. He is the slave of his own indulgences, and the tendency is always to increase. "Terrible heart-gnawings invariably follow any attempt gradually to stop the practice; and sudden cessation causes death. That arsenic can be taken habitually for any length of time with impunity was formerly regarded as a physiological impossibility; and yet the fact is established on unquestionable evidence."

"The production of arsenic in this country," says Mr. Carr in his lecture before the Society of Arts some years ago, "is on a scale that will surprise most people; when it is borne in mind that two or three grains will destroy the life of a healthy man, an output of 4809 tons, value £30,420, in one year, does indeed seem a large quantity to be dealt with. This quantity of arsenic is produced from twenty mines in Cornwall and Devonshire; it is an ingredient of copper and tin ores, and has to be separated from the metals in the process of smelting. The arsenic sublimed in the furnaces is de-

posited in a crystalline form in long galleries, through
which the fumes are made to pass. The crude arsenic
thus deposited is collected at long intervals and passed
on to the refiners. There are but six firms of refiners;
from these information has been sought as to the quantity of arsenic used for colour manufacture and for
dyeing, but no replies have been received. A reply to
the inquiry as to how much of a virulent poison is sent
out annually for use in our domestic fabrics was, perhaps, hardly to be looked for. The withholding such
information is certainly no ground for complaint; at the
same time, it may be gathered that the less the public
know about this matter the better for the trade.

" As the arsenic must be separated from the metal, the
expense of collection probably is small, and the bulk of
the £30,420 per annum may be looked upon as profit.

" Large quantities of arsenic are used for sheep-wash,
for poisoning seed grain, in the manufacture of glass,
for killing vermin, for preserving anatomical specimens,
&c., as well as in pigments and dyes; but what the
proportions used for the different purposes are, or how
the 4809 tons are distributed, there is no information
to show."

This subject, "Our Domestic Poisons," arsenic in
particular, has been considered of such importance that
the Medical Society of London thought well to appoint
a special committee to investigate the subject, with a
view to bringing the matter under the consideration of
the Local Government Board. A paper was also read
before that Society, on the medical view of the question,
by Mr. Jabez Hogg, M.R.C.S.

With a view to the investigation of the action of arsenical fabrics, experiments have been made to test the presence of arsenic in air exposed to arsenical papers. Mr. Phillips, in the second report of the Commissioners of Inland Revenue, 1858, gives the result of his attempts. He failed to detect arsenic in gaseous combination, and goes on to say :—"It is probable that persons have been affected by inhabiting rooms papered with arsenical hangings, not because the arsenious acid has been volatilised, but from minute particles of arsenite of copper dispersed in the air ;" thus upholding the dust as against the gaseous theory. Dr. Alfred Taylor also considers the arsenical dust as the principal cause of mischief, though in some cases, arseniuretted hydrogen might be evolved.

As no effectual chemical antidote to arsenic has yet been found, it is the more needful for the public to be cautious.

XIV.

SOME FAMOUS DIAMONDS.

MANY readers doubtless felt that Mr. Wilkie Collins's
" Moonstone " was exceedingly sensational and overdone,
with its many episodes, narratives of different persons,
its sleep-walking scenes, its mysteries, and all the rest of
it. But, indeed, the stories of some famous diamonds
are almost equally sensational, full of incidents, plots,
surprises. As in Mr. Wilkie Collins's story, they have
flashed in the eyes of idols; been stolen, hidden, buried
in the earth or thrown into the sea; have travelled from
country to country, been lost for ages, and most unex-
pectedly and wonderfully recovered, to figure over again
on idols or to adorn the crowns of kings,—inwoven with
the histories of famous dynasties. They have under-
gone transformations manifold, been even cut in two,
and, long after, the parts recovered and brought together
from distant points, anew in company to flash and dazzle
and excite the admiration, wonder, and cupidity of men
and women, as in the former times. They have even
been swallowed under murderous attack, and found afterwards in the body of the victim.

It is no wonder, then, that the most extraordinary
romances have been woven round these precious stones,

nor that the ancients, knowing little or nothing of the chemistry of the subject, should cherish the most extraordinary beliefs as to their properties. It was believed that they were incombustible, and that no force could break them. The hardness of the diamond is proverbial, embodied in the common phrase, " Diamond cut diamond," which simply asserts one remarkable property the stones possess ; but incombustibility and unbreakability are not among them, though, as we shall see, these beliefs have sometimes resulted in great loss and disappointment. " All diamonds," writes Pliny, " are tested upon an anvil by blows from a hammer, which they resist to the extent of causing sparks to fly from all sides, and the anvil is oftentimes destroyed." Pliny died in the year 69 A.D., but for centuries the belief remained in full strength. We read that, even in 1476, during the battle of Morat, the French burst into the tent of Charles the Bold and discovered a treasure of diamonds, which they proceeded to test by beating them with heavy hammers, with the result of utterly destroying them all.

The theory of the incombustibility of the diamond has been completely exploded by the experiments of chemists. Lavoissier, Morren, and Dumas have established the fact that diamonds, upon exposure to great heat, do not melt, but burn away in layers. The experience of glaziers, too, suffices to prove that the diamond wears away under continued friction. A diamond in continual use for glass-cutting is exhausted in about six weeks. Experts, however, have by calculation come to the conclusion that a diamond will travel over some

Q

thirty miles of glass before it becomes useless for this purpose. Not every diamond, however, will cut glass, but only that of naturally acute angles. Science tells us that the diamond cannot be acted on by any acid, however strong.

One other use to which the diamond is put we must notice in a word or two. This is its employment in an

DIAMOND STONE-SHARPENING MACHINE

apparatus for the sharpening or putting an edge upon millstones. The diamond is fixed in a well or socket, and the edge of the stone in some degree exposed to it as it revolves quickly—some 6000 times per minute. Our illustration will give some idea of this useful and ingenious contrivance.

Diamonds are found of all colours—white, yellow, orange, red, pink, brown, green, blue, black, and opalescent. The most valuable are those of pure white. Sir David Brewster made many experiments on diamonds, particularly as relative to their refracting power. He found that they did not polarise light, but sometimes it underwent a slight change in passing through ; and to this the diamond owes its great brilliancy and play.

India, which once produced the great supply of diamonds, has now become almost, if not altogether, exhausted. Many thousands of persons were at one time employed in the Golconda mines, and in cutting, splitting, and polishing diamonds—two special classes, distinct and separate, having indeed monopolised the latter industries ; a people with a mixture, it is said, of Arab and negro blood. The Indian diamond is different in specific gravity from the diamond of Brazil (which country came in with the supply on the failure of the Indian source), and even when only of equal whiteness, seems to possess more lustre and brilliancy, and they are worth more, than the Brazilian.

Two elements decide the value of diamonds—their purity and brilliancy, and their size. Given the former qualities in the first water, the size decides, in a general way, the price, and this increases in proportion to the square of their weight. A stone of two carats is worth four times as much as a stone of one carat, and one of three carats nine times as much, and so on by precise arithmetical calculation. A diamond of one carat is about the size of an ordinary pea, and it may be worth about £20.

Of late there has been great increase in the supply of diamonds through the opening of the diamond-fields at the Cape and elsewhere (Mr. Anthony Trollope, in one of his travel-volumes, gives a vivid description of the manner of mining at Kimberley, and of the mode in which the diamonds are transported and guarded on the way down from the diamond-fields there); and they have caused a kind of glutting of the market in diamonds within a certain range of size, so that it is said the price will hardly cover the cost of production; and it has even been recommended that some limit should be set upon the output. " Were the four great mines of the diamond-fields worked as one concern," says a correspondent at Johannisburg, writing to a morning paper, " the directors could do something effective in control. It is even possible that the costly gem may be found in many fresh places, and become so common that it will not pay to mine unless some fresh use should be found for it similar to that for boring purposes—some practical use, in fact, that will consume a great many stones and keep up the price." So that it is evident diamonds, like other things, in the last result, obey the ordinary law of supply and demand.

Notwithstanding the antiquity of the diamond and the immense value set upon it, the art of diamond cutting and polishing, as we know it now, is of comparatively late date. From India we have nothing to learn. The diamond-workers there were inclined to sacrifice almost everything to secure weight, and never thoroughly mastered the principle of increasing the brilliancy by multiplying the facets. Many of the finest old Indian diamonds have been recut by modern hands. In 1456 the good fortune of developing the modern system of cutting diamonds into regular facets was discovered by Louis van Berghem. The famous "Sancy" was one of the jewels he recut, committed to him by the French King for this purpose from his treasury. Berghem's pupils established themselves at Antwerp and Amsterdam (he belonged to the latter place), which thus became centres of the diamond industry; Amsterdam even at this day maintaining its pre-eminence in this respect.

The system may well demand a word. The diamonds are fixed into the prepared end of sticks like hammer-handles with a powerful cement. "The workman, who has leathern gloves on his hands, as well as a leathern stall on the right thumb, takes a stick in each hand, and leaning them against two upright pieces of iron fastened on the edge of the cutting-bench, rubs the two diamonds together until he has produced a flat, even surface (which is a facet), instead of the concave or convex form of the natural stone. By this means two facets are cut on two different stones at the same time. The dust or diamond powder which falls is received in a small box containing oil, and the powder is burnt before being used, to free it from the particles of cement that become mixed with it."

The process of cutting only gives eighteen facets; the after-work which secures the rest is called polishing, and this is done by means of diamond powder on a steel dish called "skaif," which is made to revolve very quickly, by means of steam or horse-power.

Diamonds, when the natural form is bad, are split; the workman, being very skilled, knows well the lines of natural cleavage, and works on them. "In order to split a diamond, it is fastened into a stick, the top of which contains cement, and the part to be split off is left unsevered; to avoid missing the proper plane of cleavage, a line is scratched on the surface with another diamond, to mark the exact place. To make this line three diamonds are used successively; the first a complete crystal, which marks out the direction; then a sharp splinter, to deepen the impression; and lastly, a very fine splinter, to make a very deep mark. The cement-stick is placed upright in a piece of lead fastened to the workman's bench, a very fine knife is then inserted in the mark made, and the stone is split by a smart blow from a hammer." *

The fact of the purely geometrical forms of the diamond due to crystallisation determines the principles of cutting. Every part of a diamond, into however great a number of facets it has been cut, has a definite name, and every form into which a diamond can be cut has also a definite name. There are single-cut diamonds and double-cut diamonds, table diamonds and star diamonds, rose diamonds and shell-cut diamonds, briolets, and others, as our illustration will show.

Small diamonds are common enough, but Nature here seems to exult in her prudent illustration of the maxim that "fine things are rare," and "good gear is tied up in little bundles," as the Scotch have it. Not one in ten thousand exceeds ten carats or is more than half an inch in diameter. Those that exceed this could almost be counted upon the fingers; and they are each historical—spoken of, with an assumption of knowledge

* H. Emanuel on Precious Stones.

VARIOUS FORMS OF CUT DIAMONDS.

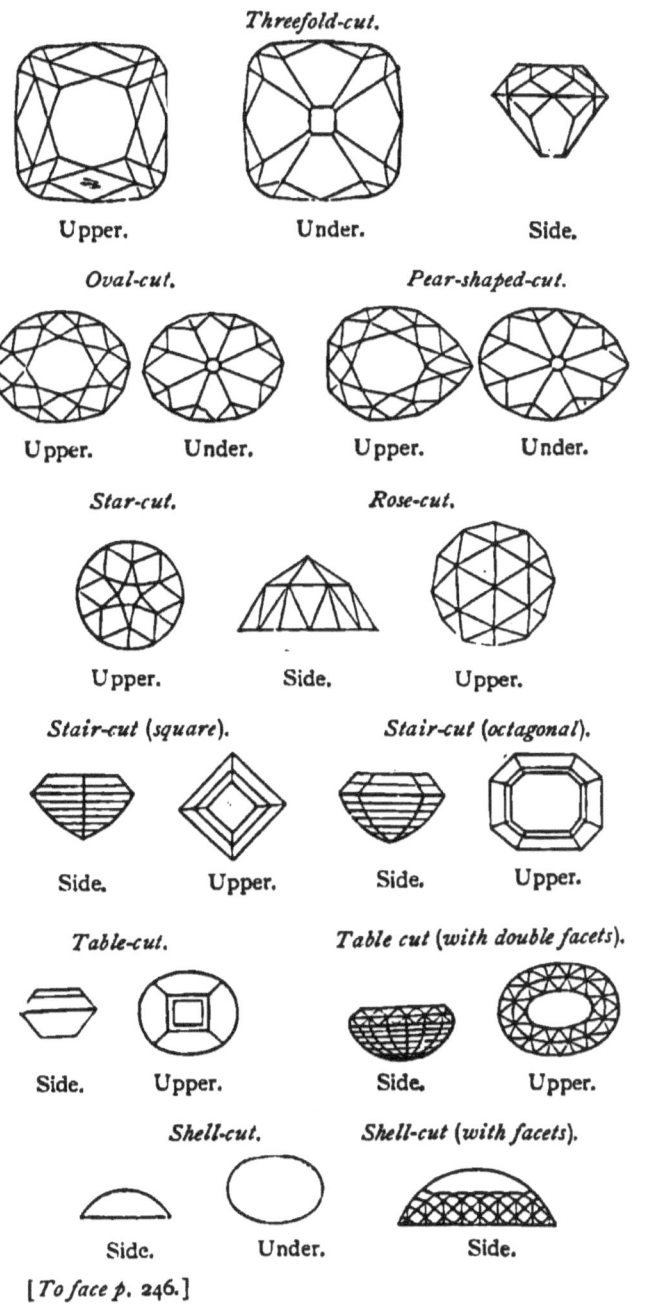

Threefold-cut.

Upper.   Under.   Side.

Oval-cut.   *Pear-shaped-cut.*

Upper.   Under.   Upper.   Under.

Star-cut.   *Rose-cut.*

Upper.   Side.   Upper.

Stair-cut (square).   *Stair-cut (octagonal).*

Side.   Upper.   Side.   Upper.

Table-cut.   *Table cut (with double facets).*

Side.   Upper.   Side.   Upper.

Shell-cut.   *Shell-cut (with facets).*

Side.   Under.   Side.

[*To face p.* 246.]

on the hearer's or reader's part, precisely as world-famous men in their own epoch are—"familiar in their mouths as household words." Who has not heard of the "Koh-i-noor" or "Mountain of Light," of "The Great Mogul," of the celebrated "Regent" or "Pitt Diamond," of the romantic "Sancy," of the "Pigott," of the "Orlow" and the "Nassac"?

"The Great Mogul" is now in Persia. It is of the shape and size of half a hen's egg, and weighs 280 carats. It is estimated to be worth some £480,000—the largest and most valuable gem in the world.

The celebrated "Regent" or "Pitt" diamond perhaps comes next in rank, though much smaller in size. It is perhaps the most brilliant diamond in existence. It is said to have originally weighed 426 carats, but after two years' continuous labour was reduced to 136¾ carats, at a cost of £6000 for cutting. It was purchased for the sum of 3,375,000 francs by the Duke of Orleans, Regent of France during the minority of Louis XV. This gem was stolen with the other crown jewels in 1792, but with others it was recovered. We shall speak of it more fully further on.

The most romantic history of the "Sancy" diamond would almost give it a place apart. It was among the treasure seized by the Swiss in the disastrous fight of Granson, when Charles the Rash was so ingloriously defeated.

The gleam of diamonds occasionally moves along the forefront of history like the glittering lines that on sandy sea-coasts foretell the advance of the tide. This has certainly been the case with the "Sancy." Here is a passage from Professor Thorold Rogers's recent valuable addition to the "Story of the Nations" Series, on Holland, which will, we think, illustrate this :—

"At last Charles the Rash quarrelled with the Swiss. He had appointed one Hagenbach as his deputy in a district of Alsace which was frequented by Swiss merchants. The deputy plundered them, and Charles paid no attention to the complaints of the Swiss envoys. In 1474 the inhabitants of Brisach captured Hagenbach, tried him, and executed him. On November 13th they first came into collision with the Burgundians, near Hericourt, and routed them decisively.

"Charles did not attack them in person till the beginning of the year 1476. On March 3rd he met them at Granson, near the Lake of Neufchâtel. When the battle had raged nearly six hours, when no impression had been made on the mountaineers, and some of the best of the Burgundian captains had fallen, the mist which hung over the battle rose, and the astonished army of Charles saw the second division of the Swiss peasants descending upon them, fresh and eager for the fight. A panic seized the Burgundian army. Charles himself was hurried away in the rout, and all his treasure fell into the hands of the Swiss. His diamonds [of which the "Sancy" was one], we are told, were sold by the captors for trifling sums. They imagined that his vessels of gold and silver were copper and tin. Of these diamonds the three largest came ultimately into the possession of the Pope, the Emperor of Germany, and the King of France, and are still in the tiara and crowns of these potentates.

"The soldiers of Charles, whom he summoned to his standard by the threat of punishing them as deserters, reassembled at Lausanne and marched to Morat, near Berne. Thither the Swiss confederates also marched. On June 22nd the battle was joined, and the Swiss again defeated Charles with immense slaughter. Charles again had to fly, and did not draw bridle till he reached the Lake of Geneva.

" He was beside himself with rage, and henceforth his actions were those of a madman. He had been twice beaten by peasants whom he despised, and had lost his treasures and his artillery. The rich cities of the Netherlands could make good his losses, and he resolved on a third attempt. On October 22nd he undertook the siege of Nancy. On Christmas Day the Swiss marched to relieve it. On January 5th he met his enemies and perished. Two days afterwards his body was discovered, or was thought to be discovered, among a heap of slain, and frozen into a muddy stream. The end of no person in that age was more tragic. He seemed at one time to be the foremost man in Europe." *

In 1479 the "Sancy" was bought by the King of Portugal. In 1489 he sold it to Nicolas de Harly, Baron de Sancy. This Sancy was Colonel-General of the Swiss and Superintendent of Finances, and raised an army of Swiss for the service of Henri III. in 1589. Colonel Yule says it is not known where he got it. In 1604 he sold it to our James I. ; and during the Civil War Queen Henrietta Maria carried it to France and pledged it, with another famous diamond, called the "Mirror of Portugal," to

* Thorold Rogers's " Holland," pp. 38, 39.

the Duke of Epernon for 460,000 *livres*.* In 1657 Mazarin paid off the Duke, and with the Queen's consent took possession of the diamonds. He bequeathed them, with other five stones, to Louis XIV. There is a story told to this effect, that Sancy sent the diamond known by his name to the King as a present by the hand of a servant; that the servant was attacked by robbers, swallowed the stone, and after his death the stone was found in his body. Something of the same story is told of some Indian diamonds, and doubtless with foundation in fact in at least one of the cases; but if this were so, it would seem that Sancy after that himself kept possession of the diamond, else he could hardly have, in 1604, sold it, as it is clear that he did, to our James I.

In 1792, as has been said, along with other stones, it disappeared, but apparently was, with some of the others, recovered.

"The history of the Sancy since the robbery of 1792," says a good authority,† "seems to be somewhat obscure. After its recovery by the national depository, it was (as M. Bapst states) apparently disposed of, with other portions of the rescued spoil, to meet expenses of the great campaign of 1796, and since then has not been among the national jewels. It made its appearance in Spain in 1809, and passed into the possession of the Demidoff family, with whose representatives it is believed still to remain."

The "Mattam" diamond, pure and brilliant, weighs 367 carats, is pear-shaped, indented at the thick end. It was

---

* The *livre* was then worth about 1s. 4d. sterling.
† Colonel Henry Yule, C.B.

found in 1760 at Landak, in Borneo, and has been the cause of a sanguinary war. It still remains in the possession of the Rajah of Mattam. The Dutch governor of Batavia offered two gunboats, with stores and ammunition complete, and £50,000 for it, but the offer was refused, the Rajah replying that the fortunes of his family depended on it.

The "Orlow" is supposed to have formed one of the eyes of an idol in a Brahmin temple. It was said to have been torn by a soldier from the eyes of a Brahmin idol in a temple at Seringapatam. It is also said to have been set in the famous peacock throne of Nadir Shah. It is certain that a Frenchman sold it in Malabar for £2800. It was purchased by an Armenian, Schaffras, who sold it to the Empress Catherine II. in 1774 for 450,000 roubles, a pension of 20,000 roubles, and a patent of nobility. It is now in the Russian Imperial sceptre.

The "Nassac" is a triangular stone, and was in the possession of the Maharajah of Malabar, and it was valued at £36,000.

The story of the "Koh-i-noor," which is now among the crown-jewels of England, is well known, and the same may be said of the famous "Star of the South."

A wonderful white diamond, weighing 457 carats in the rough state, was found in South Africa in 1884. It was subsequently purchased by a syndicate of London and Paris merchants. The gem was entrusted to the care of one of the most skilful cutters, and turned out very brilliant and beautiful. The stone in its first finished state weighed 230 carats, but it was resolved, in order to bring out its fullest lustre, to reduce it still further, and in its last stage it weighed about 200 carats. It is next to the largest diamond in the world; only the "Great Mogul" beats it for size; but it is said that this giant gem needs further cutting, which would certainly

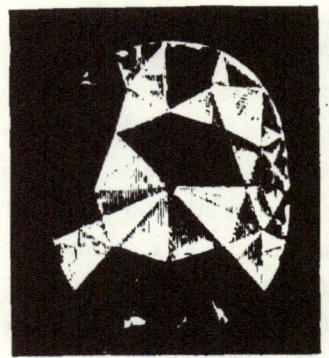

THE KOH-I-NOOR.

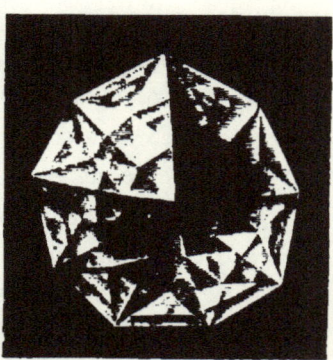

THE FLORENTINE.

THE POLE-STAR.

reduce it by as much as its excess over the South African diamond, if not much more. The "Koh-i-noor" now only weighs 106 carats; the "Regent," as we have seen, 136¾ carats; the "Star of the South," 125; and the "Pigott," 82¼.

Instead of a more detailed and bald recital of circumstances connected with each of these diamonds (for the
story of each of them could be expanded into a much
longer chapter than we can write here), we prefer, for
a good reason, to devote our remaining pages to a fuller
account of the "Regent" or Pitt Diamond. That inde-
fatigable Oriental scholar and antiquary, Colonel Henry
Yule, C.B., whose knowledge of out-of-the-way facts is
as remarkable as his patience and polished style, has
recently devoted himself to tracing out and printing
the history of this stone, with a very large amount of
correspondence of the most curious kind respecting it,
and has been so good as to present to us one of the
fifty copies of his first pamphlet respecting it, prepared
for issue by the Hakluyt Society.*

The diamond takes its first name of Pitt from the
gentleman who bought it and sent it to Europe. Thomas
Pitt was governor of Fort George, and seems to have
had a commission from one Sir Stephen Evance to find
such gems for him, as is shown by a letter from Pitt, in
Madras, to this gentleman dated October 18, 1701 :—

"I have alsoe heard that there are two or three large
stones up in the Countrey, which I beleive had been
here, but that the troubles of the Countrey have prevented it, besides they ask soe excessive Dear for such
Stones that 'tis Dangerous medling with 'em, but if that
Stone comes hither shall as near as I can follow your

* The History of the Pitt Diamond. Being an Excerpt from "Docu-
mentary Contributions to a Biography of Thomas Pitt." Prepared for
issue by the Hakluyt Society. Edited by Colonel H. Yule, R.E., C.B.,
LL.D., President of the Society. Fifty Copies printed for Private Distribution. London, 1888.

advice and orders therein, and should I meet with it here is little money to be taken up, besides you have given your orders to soe many in this matter that we shall interfere one with another."

Colonel Yule remarks that "diamonds at this time seem to have constituted one of the most usual means of remittance to Europe, and by far the largest part of Pitt's shipments on account of other parties consisted of diamonds."

In the next letter we have *the* historic stone appearing :—

" *To* Sir STEPHEN EVANCE, Knt.

"FORT ST. GEORGE, *Novr. 6th*, 1701.

"SR : This accompanyes the Modell of a Stone I have lately seene ; itt weighs *Mang.* 303 and *cartts.* 426. It is of an excellent christaline water without any fowles, onely att one end in the flat part there is one or two little flaws which will come out in cutting, they lying on the surface of the Stone, the price they ask for it is prodigious, being two hundred thousand *pags:* tho' I believe less then one (hundred thousand) would buy it. If it was designed for a Single Stone, I believe it would not loose above ¼ part in cutting, and bee a larger Stone then any the MOGULL has, I take it. *Pro rata* as Stones goe I thinke 'tis inestimable. Since I saw itt I have been perusing of TAVERNIER, where there is noe Stone soe large as this will bee when cutt. I write this singly to you, and noe one else, and desire it may bee Kept private, and that you'l by the first of land and sea conveighance give mee your opinion thereon,

1. THE PITT OR REGENT.
2. THE SANCY.
3. THE SOUTH STAR.

4. THE ORLOW.
5. THE GREAT MOGUL.
6. THE SHAH.

To face p. 254.]

for itt being of soe great a vallue I believe here are few
or none can buy it. I have put it (*i.e.* the model) up,
Inclos'd in a little box and mark'd it S: F: which the
Capt. will deliver you, my hearty service to you, I am
Sr: Your most oblidged humble Servant,

" T. PITT."

From Sir STEPHEN EVANCE *to* T. PITT.

" LONDON, *August 1st*, 1702.

.   .   .   .

" I have received yours with a modell of a great
diamond weighing 426 *Car*, therein you give   an
account of itts Water and goodness, certainly there
was never such a Stone heard of before, and as for
Price, they asked for 200,000 *Pas.*, though you beleive
less than 100,000 would buy. Wee are now gott in a
Warr, the French King has his hands and heart full,
soe he cant buy such a Stone. There is noe Prince
in EUROPE can buy itt, soe would advise You not to
meddle in itt, for the Interest Yearly would come to a
great sum of Money to be dead. As for the Diamonds
received per *Dutchess*, cant Sell them for 8s. a Pagoda.
Mr. ALVARES tells me he received some diamonds from
Mr. MEVERELL that he sold for 6s. a pagoda, soe there is
noe encouragement to send for diamonds."

Notwithstanding this discouraging report from Sir S.
Evance, Pitt, on his own account, purchased the stone,
and afterwards gave the following narrative of the transaction :—

" I have been often thinking of the most unparalleled

villainy of WILLIAM FRASER,* THOMAS FREDERICK, and
SURAPA,† a black merchant, who brought a paper before
Governor ADDISON in Council, insinuating that I had
unfairly got possession of a large Diamond, which tended
so much to the prejudice of my reputation and ruin of
my estate, that I thought it necessary to keep by me the
true relation how I purchased it in all respects, that so,
in case of sudden mortality, my children and friends
may be apprised of the whole matter, and so enabled
thereby to put to silence, and confound those, and all
other villains in their base attempts against either. Not
having got my books by me at present, I cannot be
positive as to the time, but for the manner of purchasing
it I do here declare and assert, under my hand, in the
presence of GOD ALMIGHTY, as I hope for salvation
through the merits and intercession of our Saviour JESUS
CHRIST, that this is the truth, and if it be not, let GOD
deny it to me and to my children for ever, which I would
be so far from saying, much less leave it under my hand,
that I would not be guilty of the least untruth in the
relation of it for the riches and honour of the whole
world.

"About two or three years after my arrival at MADRAS,
which was in July 1698, I heard there were large
Diamonds in the country to be sold, which I encouraged
to be brought down, promising to be their chapman, if
they would be reasonable therein; upon which JAUR-

---

* WILLIAM FRASER, one of Pitt's colleagues in the Council of Fort
St. George.

† In all the repetitions printed *Smapa*, which I have ventured to
correct as above. SURAPA was a well-known merchant, and an ally of
Fraser's. [Col. Yule.]

CHUND, one of the most eminent diamond merchants in those parts, came down about December 1701, and brought with him a large rough stone, about 305 man-gelins,* and some small ones, which myself and others bought; but he asking a very extravagant price for the great one, I did not think of meddling with it when he left me for some days, and then came and took it away again; and did so several times, not insisting upon less than 200,000 pagodas; and, as I best remember, I did not bid him above 30,000, and had little thoughts of buying it for that. I considered there were many and great risques to be run, not only in cutting it, but also whether it would prove pale or clear, or the water good; besides I thought it too great an amount to be adventured home in one bottom. But JAURCHUND resolved to return speedily to his own country; so that (as) I best remember it was in February following he came again to me (with VINCATEE CHITTEE, who was always with him) when I discoursed with him about it, and he pressed me to know, whether I resolved to buy it, when he came down to 100,000 pagodas and something under before we parted, when wee agreed upon a day to meet and make a final end thereof one way or other, which I believe was the latter end of the foresaid month, or the beginning of March; when we accordingly met in the Consultation Room, where after a great deal of talk I brought him down to 55,000 pagodas, and advanced to 45,000, re-solving to give no more, and he likewise resolving not to abate, I delivered him up the stone, and wee took a friendly leave of one another. Mr. BENYON was then

* Always in the copies *mangelius.*

R

writing in my closet, with whom I discoursed on what had passed, and told him now I was clear of it; when about an hour after, my servant brought me word that JAURCHUND and VINCATEE CHITTEE were at the door, who being called in, they used a great many expressions in praise of the stone, and told me he had rather I should buy it than anybody, and to give an instance thereof, offered it for 50,000; so believing it must be a penny-worth, if it proved good, I offer'd to part the 5000 pagodas that was then between us, which he would not hearken to, and was going out of the room again, when he turned back and told me that I should have it for 49,000, but I still adhered to what I had before offered him, when presently he came to 48,000, and made a solemn vow he would not part with it a pagoda under, when I went again into the closet to Mr. BENYON, and told him what had passed, saying that if it was worth 47,500, it was worth 48,000; so I closed with him for that sum, when he deliver'd me the stone, for which I paid very honourably, as by my books appear."

Though Sir S. Evance did not enter into any responsibility about the purchase, Pitt evidently looked to him for aid in its disposal; for we find Pitt writing this letter :—

" *To* Sir ST. EVANCE.

"*ffeby. the* 3d, 170⅝.

.   .   .   .

" I hope my Concerne on the *Loyall Cooke*, will come Safe to your hand and doubt not but you'le doe all you can to Contribute to the well disposall thereof, 'tis a very good Water, ffree from all foules and noe flaws but what will be worked out, and the Shape is not bad, and upon the best enquiry I can make 'tis Certainly the finest Jewell in the World, and worth an immense Sum, and I hope you'le never part with it but for its reall value, which it may be you'le not be able to get dureing the Warr, to which God send a happy and Speedy conclusion, when I doubt not but you'le have Chapmen enough for it, for Princes generally covet Such Jewells as cannot be parallel'd, and I am sure that cannot, for its excellency and magnitude, and 'tis my opinion 'tis best to keep it in one Stone, which I leave wholly to you and the rest consign'd to."

Again we find him writing six months afterwards :—

" *To* Sir STEPHEN EVANCE *and* Mr. ROBERT PITT.

" FORT ST. GEORGE, *Sept.* 12*th*, 1704.

.　　.　　.　　.　　.　　.　　.

" 'Twas Well come news to hear of the Safe arrivall of that concerne of mine, and observe the progress you have made in Cutting it, of which you should have wrote me fully in your joynt Letter, of which there is a Smattering thereof in both your particular, 'tis very fortunate that it proves soe good, and 'tis my desire that it be made one Brillion which I would not have sold (unless it be for a trifle) less then fifteen hundred pound a *carrat*, tho by all Computation that I can make from Presidents that nature, 'tis worth much more. 'Tis my whole dependance, and therefore it must be Sold to the best advantage, for which reason I have trusted it in the hands of a ffriend and a Sone, whose care I doubt not, but will likewise preserve it from Any accident of ffire or any other event, and I approve of your locking it up, and defer the Sale till after the Warr."

"*To* JOHN DOLBEN, Esq., London.

"*Feby. the 5th,* 170$\frac{8}{9}$.

. . . .

"I observe what you wrote to my Sone, who I perceive minds very little of my busyness, in which I wish he do's not neglect his own. He has wrote me about the grand affair, as alsoe Mr. ALVEREZ, Mr. COPE, and Sr: STE: in which I am fully Satisfy'd.

. . . .

"With concern I read what you write of the Lieut: Generall. My Sone had noe Commission to impart my affairs to him ; and for God sake prevent any misfortune that may attend me from any thing that shall befall Sr: STE: of which I gave you a hint in my last; and I am not a little Jealous too of my Sone, who has allready made too bold with me on severall occasions, therefore pray take care now that he do's not strip me. I am of your opinion of these two gentlemens charecters, and wish that My Sone may deserve a better. I wish it was bought for that small sum the Generall mentions, and for that use. I heard from Lisbon, that upon the Union with SCOTLAND passing our Parliament, 'twas intended to present the Queen with the Royall title of Empress. I am sure no thing is soe proper to accompany it, being the best and the biggest in the world. In this matter I rely wholely on your kindness and management, and I hope on your arrivall you tooke effectuall care to Secure it from either of the Sharpers."

Evidently, there was not a little excitement in London about the diamond, for we find Lady Wentworth thus writing to her children under date December 15, 1700 :— " My dearest and best children, for all the great Scairsety of mony, yett hear will be a gloryous show one the Queens birth day, wonderful rich cloaths ar preparing for it ; thear was one that see Mr. PITS great dyomont that I writ you word of, and they say its as big as a great eg ; I would have the Sety of LONDON bye it and mak a presant of it to put in the Queens Crown " (*Wentworth Papers*, pp. 164–5).

Pitt had invested so much of his private means in the purchase of the diamond that, as he regarded it, the whole future of himself and his family depended upon its profitable sale ; and his anxiety may be imagined when he found that he must wait for an indefinite period (till the war was ended) before he could realise, and that his son, who ought to have been his trustworthy representative, was not to be depended on. Even the pathway of rich men able to speculate in unique gems is not strewn wholly with roses ; some thorns mingle with them.

" The Diamond," writes Colonel Yule, " remained in Pitt's possession till 1717, when it was sold to the Regent Duke of Orleans as a jewel of the French crown." The following particulars regarding this transaction are noted in a memo, in the handwriting of Philip, second Earl Stanhope, Pitt's grandson, and " for this memo," says Colonel Yule, " I am indebted to the favour of the present Countess Stanhope, communicated through my kind friend, Mr. Robert Scharf, C.B."

"Diamond sold in 1717 for 2,000,000 *livres*.* Before it was sent over to FRANCE £40,000 (sterling) was deposited in ENGLAND, to be taken in part payment of the diamond. When carried to FRANCE, should be agreed to be bought, but otherwise £5000 of the deposit money was to be allowed to my Grandfather for his expense and risk.

"It was cut by HARRIS, and not by VAN HUFLIN. The expense of cutting was £6000. The chips were valued at £10,000, though not all sold. It was carried over to Calais by my Grandfather himself, accompanied by his two sons, Lord LONDONDERRY and Mr. JOHN PITT, and by his son-in-law Mr. CHOLMONDELEY, who were there met by a Jeweller of the FRENCH Kings appointed to inspect and receive the Diamond, and to deliver in return some (I think three) boxes of Jewels belonging to the Crown of FRANCE, as a security for the payment of the overplus of the purchase money above £40,000 before deposited, which payment was agreed to be made at three several times fixed upon by the Parties concerned.

"The Diamond after it was cut weighed 128 *Carats.*

"My Grandfather's letter, dated at BERGEN, July 29th, 1710, about his purchasing the diamond in the EAST INDIES, was copied from the Original after his death at SWALLOWFIELD by Mr. CHOLMONDELEY's Chaplain, and the Original was sent to Mr. ROBERT PITT my Grandfather's eldest Son."

"The 'overplus of the purchase money' was never paid," adds Lady Stanhope, "and when it was claimed

---

* The value of the *livre* at that date may be taken at 1s. 4d. sterling.

from the French Government by the children of Governor
PITT, the debt was fully admitted, but it was pronounced
impossible to enter into the past transactions of the
Regent."

This being so, the price really received by Pitt must
have depended on the value of the three boxes of jewels
pledged as security, respecting which there seems to be
no evidence forthcoming.

Colonel Yule then follows on with these details :—

"The first prominent place occupied by the *Regent*, as
the diamond was now called, was in the circlet of the
crown made by Ronde * for the coronation of Louis
XV. in 1722. Beside the *Regent* were others of the
diamonds known as the *Mazarins*, including the *Mirror
of Portugal;* whilst the middle point of the fleur-de-
lis, which formed the apex of the crown, was the famous
Sancy.

"In 1791, by votes of the 26th and 27th May and the
22nd June, the National Assembly decreed that a complete inventory of all the jewels of the Crown then existing should be drawn up for publication, in presence of
commissioners and experts named for the duty. This
report consists of not less than 300 pages, of which 100
are devoted to the diamonds. At the head of these
figures the *Pitt*, with this description :—

"'Un superbe diamant brillant, blanc, appelé le *régent*,
forme carrée, les coins arrondis, ayant une petite glace
dans les filets et une autre à un coin dans le dessous,

---

* Laurent Ronde, from 1689 jeweller to the King, was succeeded by
his son Claude Dominique, who made a famous crown for the coronation of Louis XV.

pesant 136 *carats* $\frac{13}{18}$ (environ 29 gr. .617), estimé 12 millions de livres.'

"The inventory was drawn up in August 1792, whilst the treasure was deposited at the *Garde-Meuble*, where the jewels were shown on Mondays to the public.

"The Legislative Assembly ordered the sale of the diamonds, but meantime the bulk of them, to an estimated value of a million sterling, including the *Regent* and the *Sancy*, disappeared.

"The history, which follows, of this audacious burglary, is condensed from the communications of M. Bapst:

"Paris was in the utter demoralisation and anarchy which followed the September massacres; and lay open to any violent enterprise. The Municipality had set an example of pillage; and though many real criminals had been murdered in the prisons, many roamed the city without restraint, and the police was reduced to nullity. Meanwhile practised thieves had made good use of the Monday exhibitions to reconnoitre the interior of the *Garde-Meuble.*

"Under these circumstances, during six days in succession, beginning from the 11th September, a band composed (at least on the last of those days) of some 30 or 40 individuals, made their way every evening into the halls of the first floor of the *Garde-Meuble*, by help of the rusticated joints of the masonry and the ropes of the lantern at the corner of the Rue ST. FLORENTIN. After breaking open a window—whilst leaving intact and securing from inside the sealed doors of the halls—they forced the presses one after another, and gradually made off with nearly the whole of the treasure. The police were quite unconscious of the robbery until it was accomplished.

"During the night of 16th–17th September * certain men of the National Guard thought they saw a movement of the street-lantern attached to the colonnade, and on coming near saw a man clinging to the rope, and called out that unless he came down at once they would shoot. He made haste to come down, and they took him to their post.

"Another man sliding down in a fright fell on the pavement, and came likewise into the hands of the National Guard. These two thieves had diamonds in their pockets, besides carrying other portable valuables, such as a child's coral set with diamonds, which had been a gift of the Empress Catherine, and pieces of jewellery sent to Louis XVI. by Tippoo Sultan in 1790. Thus the captors became aware of the robbery, which had, in fact, been going on without disturbance since the 11th. Next day ROLAND, the then Minister of the Interior, related from the Tribune of the Assembly what had occurred, and declared that out of 25 (30) millions' worth of valuables scarcely half-a-million remained.

"Whilst the operation was going on, no regular patrol had been made ; the police in their rounds had discovered nothing; and yet the thieves had lights in the rooms of the *Garde-Meuble ;* they must have taken supplies of food, and passed successive nights there. For

---

* "Les tapissaries qui tendaient les murs, et les armures de nos rois de France, éclairées par des chandelles, devaient former un cadre saisissant à cette orgie de brigands qui fêtaient ainsi la réussite du plus beau coup que les temps modernes devaient, enrégistrer."—*Narrative by M. Bapst.*

when an entrance was eventually made after them, fragments of victuals, empty bottles, and candle-ends were found lying about, as well as burglars' tools, and diamonds.

" Nothing could illustrate the demoralisation of Paris at that time more thoroughly than the manner in which the news of this burglary was received by the various parties in antagonism, unless it was the way in which the trial of the captured criminals concerned was conducted.

" Madame ROLAND roundly ascribes the robbery to DANTON and his secretary FABRE D'EGLANTINE. Her husband took, or professed, the same view, and declared that his repeated demand for a proper guard over the valuables had always been treated with neglect.

" FABRE D'EGLANTINE, on the other hand, accused ROLAND of the crime ; and MARAT, in the *Ami du Peuple*, ascribed it to 'the aristocrats,' who had hired a gang of brigands to pillage the *Garde-Meuble*, in order to discredit the Municipality and the Committee of Public Security. LULLIER, the Public Prosecutor, in a violent and atrocious harangue, such as was the fashion of the day, denounced *une femme orgueilleuse, lascive et cruelle*, to wit, poor MARIE ANTOINETTE, as the author of the whole affair. One popular story ran that it was an act of the existing Government in order to obtain means for purchasing the retreat of the DUKE OF BRUNSWICK. And this has found an echo in the *Memorial of St. Helena.**

" The two thieves taken on the night of 16th–17th September were condemned and executed. But the crime with which all were charged, and for which the last were

---

* M. Bapst.

executed, was *un complot à main armée ayant pour but de renverser le gouvernement nouvellement constitué !* And the President (PEPIN) tried hard to make the accused admit that they had entertained relations with princes and other great personages attached to the late Court, who had set them upon this robbery. One of the executed was an unhappy Jew, against whom nothing was proved but his having sold to another Jew *un certain nombre de bijoux dont la provenance n'a pu être justifiée !* He also was put to death under the article of the penal code directed against *conspirations ou complots tendant à troubler l'Etat par une guerre civile !*

"Others, and leaders of the enterprise, who had succeeded in obtaining an appeal to the Court of Beauvais on the inapplicability of the article to their crime, whilst they admitted the burglary, obtained either release or commutation to imprisonment.

"A certain number of diamonds also were presently recovered, but the most important—the *Regent* and the *Sancy*—escaped the earlier endeavours to trace them. A man of the name of COTTET had stolen the *Sancy;* he passed it on to a comrade, who made off. As for the *Regent,* it was not found till twelve months later, and then in a *cabaret* of the FAUBOURG ST. GERMAIN. Other diamonds were recovered in the following years, and were carried to the credit of the *Caisse de l'Extraordinaire.*

"On the 20th Frimaire, An. II. (*i.e.,* 10th December 1793) *Voulland,* in the name of the Committee of Public Security, appeared before the Convention and reported the recovery of the *Regent* in these words :—

"'Your Committee of Public Security continues its search for the authors and accomplices of the robbers of the *Garde-Meuble,* and yesterday discovered the most valuable of the stolen property, viz., the diamond known as the *Pitt* or *Regent,* which in the last inventory of 1791 was valued at 12 millions.   To hide it they had made a hole of an inch and a half diameter in the timber-work of a garret.   Both the thief and the receiver have been taken, and the diamond, which has been brought to the Committee of Public Security, will serve as a *pièce de conviction* in bringing them to justice.   I move, in the name of the Committee, to decree that the diamond be carried to the General Treasury, and that the Commissioners of that establishment be directed to come and receive it during our sitting.'

" The *Procès-Verbal* proceeds :—

"'The National Convention, after having heard the Report of its Committee of Public Security, decrees that two Commissioners of the National Treasury shall come during the present sitting to the presence of the Convention, to receive and deposit in the National Treasury the diamond known as the *Regent,* discovered through the inquiries of the Committee of Public Security, and which shall be available at need as a *pièce de conviction* during the proceedings against the persons charged with the theft or the receipt of the property of the *Garde-Meuble.'*

"Another decree of the same date directed that two members of the Committee of Public Security should proceed to the National Treasury and deposit there, in a box with three locks, the diamond called the

Regent. A *Procès-Verbal* should be recorded, and one of the three keys should be placed among the National Archives.

"Three months later (1st Germinal, *i.e.,* 21st March 1794), among a number of stones seized in the possession of one TAVENEL and his wife, were recovered the *Sancy* and another important diamond known as *de la maison de* GUISE.

"In 1796 the *Regent* was pledged to German bankers, through the mediation of a cavalry officer,—Adjutant-General DE PARSEVAL,—as security for the cost of horse-furniture which had been advanced by TRESKOW. In 1797, TRESKOW having been paid off, DE PARSEVAL recovered the *Regent* and brought it back to Paris. But in 1798 the diamond was again pawned, through the same officer, for another supply of horse-furniture needed for the army of Italy, this time in the hands of VAN-DENBERG, a banker of AMSTERDAM. The first Consul BONAPARTE released it in 1802.

"These details, including the *Procès-Verbal* of VOUL-LAND, have been hitherto entirely unpublished.

"M. FAYE, ex-Minister of Public Instruction and Member of the Institute, has told M. BAPST that he often heard his father relate how VANDENBERG, the banker, when he had the *Regent* in his possession, put it in a glass case that all the world might admire it; and a considerable crowd came to his office to do so. His friends remonstrated with him on the danger of exposing before people, some of whom might be capable of evil designs, an article at once so valuable and so easily carried off. But the banker answered with a twinkle in his eye: 'The *Regent* that is in the glass case is a worthless sham; the real *Regent* is in my wife's stays.'

"At the coronation of Napoleon in 1804 the Crown jewels once more appeared in public; the *Regent* being set in the pommel of the Emperor's sword.*

"In 1814 the jewels were carried off to Blois by Marie Louise; but her father the Emperor Francis claimed them from her and sent them to Louis XVIII., who, on the night of March 20, 1815, took them on his flight to Ghent, and brought them back at the second Restoration.

"On the accession of Charles X. all the stones were reset for his coronation, and thenceforward remained unused till 1854, never having been worn by Louis Philippe or his Queen Marie Amélie. Between 1854 and 1870 they were several times remounted; and in August 1870 they were put up in a sealed box and deposited with M. Rouland, Governor of the Bank of France. In 1875 they were verified by an extra-parliamentary commission, which declared the record to have been kept with perfect regularity.

"In October 1886 the Chamber resolved that such of the Crown jewels as had no artistic value should be sold. They were then valued at twenty millions of *francs*, but

---

* "Napoleon had it placed between the teeth of a crocodile, forming the handle of his sword, unaware perhaps how much this gem had contributed towards raising up the most formidable opponent to his ambition and ultimate aggrandisement."—DAVIES GILBERT, *Parochial History of Cornwall*, under BOCONNSE, vol. i. p. 69.

[The reference here is to the fact that William Pitt was of the family of Thomas Pitt, and the diamond had had some share in making the position of the family, and done something to place William in his position.]

out of this the *Regent* was still reckoned at twelve millions. The diamonds which have been sold in consequence of the resolution of the Chamber are stated to have realised £289,000. There seems to be no present intention of selling the *Regent,* which, in spite of two small flaws or internal cracks, remains the finest diamond in the world.* The Crown diamonds which have not been sold have been distributed between the Louvre Museum, the School of Mines, and the Natural History Institution. It is intended that eventually a quadrangular receptacle of thick glass shall be placed in the Louvre, in which the diamond which has occupied so many of our pages, the Watch of the Dey of Algiers, the Dragon Ruby, and other similar precious objects shall be exhibited to the public. The *Regent* awaits this eventual destination in the cellars of the Treasury."

Among minor trials that beset Governor Pitt was the publication of many falsehoods regarding the means by which he had obtained the diamond. He was accused of having taken it from a slave who had stolen it from the eye of an idol, and had hidden it in a gash in his leg; another version was that he had given the murderer of this man £1000 for it, and similar extraordinary statements. Even Pope, the poet, seems to have had these rumours in his mind when he wrote certain lines in the "Moral Essays." A writer in the *European Magazine* says :—

"It was reckoned the largest jewel in Europe, and weighed 127 *carats.* The cuttings amounted to 8 or

---

* "The *Koh-i-Noor,* equal in quality, would have excelled the Regent in magnitude, but for its disastrous treatment."

£10,000. . . . It appears that the acquisition of this diamond occasioned many reflections injurious to the honour of Governor PITT, and Mr. POPE has been thought to have had the insinuation then floating in the world in his mind when he wrote the following lines" (in his episode of the history of " Sir Balaam," "Moral Essays," Ep. iii.) :—

> 'Asleep and naked as an INDIAN lay
> An honest factor stole a gem away ;
> He pledged it to the Knight, the Knight had wit,
> So kept the diamond, and the rogue was bit.' "

And on this Colonel Yule comments :—

" There could have been little doubt indeed that the stories floating about the world as to Pitt's having fraudulently acquired the diamond were in Pope's mind, however vaguely, when he penned these lines. And we now learn from Mr. Courthope's notes that in the Chauncy MS., which is (as we gather) in the poet's own handwriting, the last line runs—

> 'So robbed the robber and was rich as P——.'

" This allusion has been developed, in accordance with the fashion of a certain class of readers, into the suggestion that the whole story of *Sir Balaam* is founded upon the character and history of Pitt, the absurdity of which idea is manifest on the most cursory perusal of Pope's lines."

It was to meet these aspersions that Pitt drew up and published his narrative account of the whole transaction, which he has accompanied with his most solemn asseverations, given on a former page.

The world certainly owes Colonel Yule sincere thanks

for the manner in which he has presented the story of the
" Pitt" or " Regent " diamond—nothing could be more
satisfactory as to documents, nothing clearer and more
complete.   Many erroneous statements are here set at
rest, and Thomas Pitt's character completely vindicated.
We wish the same could be as undoubtingly said of
others who have speculated in diamonds.

XV.

ARTIFICIAL DIAMONDS.

"The one succeeds, the many fail," has seldom had a more striking illustration than in that of the manufacture of diamonds. It has been for long so well known that nearly every substance which exists in the solid state will, under certain conditions, crystallise, or present itself under definite geometrical forms, that it is no wonder attempts should have been simultaneously made in many laboratories to crystallise carbon and produce the diamond. Carbon, as every one knows, is what is called a simple element; that is, it resists all the efforts of the chemist to reduce it to yet simpler forms. It is found widely distributed throughout the world, entering largely into all animal or vegetable structures; so that when these are submitted to slow processes of decay after the favourite modes of old Mother Nature, time and rare combinations of circumstances give to us the "gems of purest ray serene" which shine in the crowns of kings and queens. The more common forms into which, for the good of the great world (since men could do without diamonds, but could not do without some other things), the carbon develops itself are coals and mineral oils. In an impure condition we find it in coke or charcoal. The common plumbago or blacklead with which the housemaid cleans the grate is very brother to the diamond; for there also we have pure carbon crystallised. Both—the one for use and the other for adornment—represent to us the carbonaceous matter of some dead fish or strange plant which was buried thousands of years ago in the slimy mud of some pre-Adamite shore.

Chemical analysis, however, here, as in many other things, fails to explain all; and there are some peculiar facts which nothing can explain. Diamonds almost perfect on being taken from the mine have, on being laid aside for some time before cutting, developed cracks and flaws which certainly were not present at first; and no cause can be given for the change. The chagrin of the possessors of such stones may be imagined. The skill which is acquired by experts in judging diamonds is very great, but they cannot quite foresee such contingencies. At Kimberley, at certain periods, the diamonds are sold in bulk—large and small, good and bad together, and are over-head valued at so much a carat—the value varying from 14s. or 15s. to 26s. or 30s. A great deal depends on colour—the pure white being more precious than those with a yellow tint, and it is said that by submitting the yellow-tinted stones to a high degree of heat a white colour is obtained temporarily, but long enough sometimes to effect a sale at a wholly deceptive price; and in this case the chagrin of the buyer may be imagined when he finds his white stone in a few days or weeks develop the yellow tint. There are tricks in all trades, and this is one in the diamond trade—unless we have been misinformed.

One great peculiarity of the diamond is, that it is octahedral, and that it crystallises with a curved face; and to this is attributed its great brilliancy, as well as the difficulty of imitating it. Many marks indicate pressure as one of the great processes used by Nature in the formation of the diamond, an idea which seems to have occurred to Faraday when he suggested magnesium minerals as associated with the diamond.

Seeing that products so very common as coal and blacklead are so near of kin to the most rare and the most beautiful and most precious, it is not to be wondered at that chemists in all periods should have endeavoured to forestall Nature, and to supersede her niggardliness by the bounties of human ingenuity. And such indeed has been the case.

Attempts at imitating real diamonds date from the Middle Ages; but no considerable trade was created until between the years 1762 and 1766, when three jewellers named Stras, Chéron, and Martin Lançon improved and purified the composition hitherto used in the manufacture, and produced the imitation stones or paste which are familiar to every one.

A century elapsed without any practical improvement. Modern appliances indeed had enabled the fusion of the alumina, potash, and other ingredients forming the *masse* to be carried to a degree of purity unattainable previously; but the finished stones, notwithstanding all the ingenuity and art lavished upon them, lacked brilliancy, durability, and reflective power, and could in no way compare with real diamonds.

The great stir that has been caused in this country

in recent years was due to the efforts of two Scottish chemists, both settled in the West. The first was Mr. Mactear of Glasgow, who, in a paper read before the Philosophical Society of that city, claimed to have produced diamonds. He went into an elaborate account of his labours, and specimens were sent up to London. They were examined and tested by Mr. Story Maskelyne and Dr. Flight, but were found to be wanting in some of the characters of the diamond, and to possess others of a very different kind. In fact, they were clever crystallisations, but not diamonds. Mr. Mactear, not content with this verdict, came up to London himself, and, provided with all requisites, conducted many experiments, with the idea of justifying himself; but he had finally to admit failure. After all his efforts, his " diamonds" no more stood the tests than before.

"Great minds jump." About the same time, or shortly after it, another Scottish chemist, Mr. J. B. Hannay of Helensburgh, read a paper to the Royal Society also claiming to have produced diamonds. Specimens were sent to London to be tested, and Mr. Maskelyne thus reported on them :—

" In lustre, in a certain lamellar structure on the surface cleavage, or refractive power, they accord so closely with that mineral that it seemed hardly rash to proclaim them, even at first sight, to be diamond. And they satisfy the characteristic tests of that substance. Like the diamond, they are nearly inert in polarised light, and their hardness is such that they easily scored deep grooves in a polished surface of sapphire, which the diamond alone can do. I was able to measure the angle between the cleavage faces of one of them, nothwithstanding that the image from one face was too incomplete for a very accurate result. But the mean of the angles so measured on the goniometer was 70° 29', the correct angle on the crystal of a diamond being 70° 31.7'. Finally, one of the particles, ignited on a foil of platinum, glowed, and gradually disappeared, exactly as mineral diamond would do."

A writer in the *Academy* of March 13, 1880, thus gives his account of Mr. Hannay's experiments :—

" Having noticed that many bodies like silica, alumina, and oxide of zinc, which are insoluble in water at ordinary temperature, dissolve to a very considerable extent when heated with water got at a very high pressure, it occurred to Mr. Hannay that a solvent might be found for carbon ; and as gaseous solution nearly always yields crystalline solid on withdrawing the solvent or lowering its solvent power, it seemed probable that the carbon might be deposited in the crystalline state. After a number of experiments, it was found that carbon would not dissolve, and that chemical action took the place of solution. A curious reaction was observed which appeared likely to yield carbon in the nascent state, and so allow of its being easily dissolved. When a gas containing carbon and hydrogen is heated under pressure in presence of certain metals, its hydrogen is attracted by the metal and its carbon left free. Hydrogen, it has been found, has at a very high temperature a very strong affinity for certain metals, notably magnesium, forming extensively stable compounds with it. When the carbon is set free from the hydrocarbon in presence of a stable compound containing nitrogen, the whole being near a red heat and under a very high pressure, the carbon is so acted upon by the nitrogen compound that it is obtained in the clear transparent form of the diamond. Mr. Hannay states that a great difficulty lies in the construction of an enclosing vessel strong enough to withstand the enormous pressure and high temperature; tubes constructed on the gun-barrel principle, with a wrought-iron coil, of only half-an-inch bore and four inches external diameter, being torn open in nine cases out of ten. He then proceeds to describe the properties of the crystals obtained by this method, crystals which satisfy all the tests that are peculiar to the diamond. They are as hard as natural diamond, they scratch all other crystals, and do not affect polarised light. They burn easily in platina foil over a blowpipe flame, leaving no residue; after two days' immersion in hydrofluoric acid they showed no signs of dissolving. A splinter heated in the electric arc turned black—a very characteristic reaction of the diamond. Last, fourteen millegrammes were burnt in a current of oxygen, and 97.85 per cent. of carbon obtained. The specific gravity was found to be 3.5."

Mr. Hannay's process was, however, so dangerous and costly that there was no likelihood of commercial result from it.

The reports in the newspapers of these enterprises, more particularly a letter in the *Times* from one of the descendants of the Jura manufacturers of precious stones, and signed " Fabricant," shortly after this led to the more general knowledge of the fact that some years previously artificial diamonds had been produced in France, and had been exhibited at the Great Exhibition in Paris in 1878, and there can be no doubt that in appearance these "*diamanté brilliantés*" are well calculated to be used as substitutes for diamonds, and evidently, judging from the prices at which they are quoted, are produced in a much less expensive and dangerous manner than were those of Mr. Hannay. They were introduced into England shortly after the letter of "Fabricant" appeared in the *Times*, and would appear to find many purchasers; they are sold at about one three-hundredth of the cost of real diamonds.

Ordinary imitation diamonds are either produced from "Strass," a superior kind of glass, or from natural transparent crystals. The latter are harder, but lack even the moderate brilliancy of the former. Both have been discarded as unreal, and in no way calculated to deceive even the most inattentive observer. These new "*diamanté brilliantés*" are said to be manufactured from a combination of the purest silica and other chemical ingredients intermixed with certain ascertained proportions of the precious metals, the whole being kept in a state of fusion at a high temperature for many days continuously.

The result is, at all events, a composition of great purity and transparency, and possessing high refractive power. This composition or *masse* cools in large blocks, and the various sizes of "*diamanté brilliantés*" are cut from them and polished preparatory to undergoing the process by which the refractive power is concentrated and permanently retained.

The perfection which artificial diamonds have reached in appearance, hardness, and brilliancy makes it more important to find a ready test of discriminating them. Nothing that can be said on this point would be absolutely reliable in the hands of an amateur; but that which is most likely is the temperature as tested by the tongue. To tell a real diamond from an imitation, says one, place the diamond on the tip of the tongue, the real diamond having a warmer feeling, which is missing in an imitation. And he goes on to say :—"Although a fair test, I would not advise an intending purchaser strictly to follow that rule. Real diamonds, when properly cut and finished, will have fifty-eight facets, thirty-three at the top and twenty-five at the bottom, and on looking through the top of the diamond there will be seen a small round spot, which is missing in an imitation; also, the facets of a real diamond will have a very smooth surface, which causes the brilliancy, for if the said facets are not properly polished the stone will have a dull appearance."

XVI.

POSTAGE-STAMPS.

FAMILIARITY, they say, breeds contempt; but that is not invariably true. We are all familiar enough with postage-stamps, but contempt for them is not likely to arise from handling, however frequent. They are potent as evidences of money paid to the State for services to be rendered in exchange; and since the days of "franking" have long ended (a blessing for which we should be thankful, since even that relic of privilege, most pertinaciously adhered to, did not a little to defer the era of cheap postage) everybody is on a pretty equal footing in the eyes of that modern Mercury, the penny post. When postage was very dear there was always a reason for claiming exemption; now that it is so cheap, exemption is hardly worth struggling for and privilege has died a natural death. But the higher classes in old days did struggle for their wrongful "rights"—oh, how they did struggle!—and the meaning of it simply was, that the poor and the less rich—the busy and the struggling, the industrious and the hard-working—should pay for the more rich, the idle, and the luxurious. And not only for letters carried free, but for all manner of commodities, articles of personal attire, bandboxes, and, it may be, guns and gun-cases! Such is always the case with the classes when they can get an advantage; they have sometimes stuck to small advantages, as they were pleased to name them, till they raised a spirit that brought down the fabric of constitution and State altogether. Well, when we look at a postage-stamp, value one penny, we may read a record there of the greatest social triumph, of equality, liberty, and fraternity, in the true sense; of equality, for rich and poor now fare alike at the hands of the Post-Office; of liberty, for there is nowadays no inspection of letters; of fraternity, for there is no agency more calculated to unite and bring together in sympathy and call forth and keep alive the feelings of kindred by force of circumstances or necessity separated and scattered in different parts than the penny post.

Postage-stamps, then, may tell some stories, if we care to listen; but on only one of these stories shall we dwell at present, and that is the story of their manufacture. When we think of the immense number of stamps that must nowadays be used, seeing that just as telegraphing increases and parcels post extends so more and more must stamps be in demand, we can realise that a great and growing industry must be active in the constant production of stamps. Probably the number of stamps now used has increased twofold during the last fifteen years.

The very idea of a postage-stamp marked a great advance in postal matters; for, simple as it seems, a long time went on before any one thought of attaching a thin ticket by gum to the outside of a letter, and in those

early days you had simply to pay hard cash over the
counter to the post-office clerk, who received the letters
and the money and passed and marked them for transit.
When stamps were first resolved on, the firm engaged
in making them employed for this purpose only some
ten or a dozen men, who managed to turn out quite as
many as were then wanted. Even that small staff was only
employed intermittently. Fifteen years ago some eighty
men were constantly employed; now there are more than
double that number; and they turn out something over
thirty thousand sheets per day of penny stamps, and some
£3000 worth of halfpenny stamps: in round numbers,
altogether about 3,000,000 stamps per year.

If we are to begin at the beginning in our description of
postage-stamps we must start with the paper, for the water-
mark was once of the greatest importance. It may not be
generally known that the paper for the penny stamp had
a water-mark of a crown in the centre of the head, while
the halfpenny sheets had the word "halfpenny" marked
across them in what was called water, though it was really
done by wires. All the paper comes to Somerset House,
and from thence it is issued to the printers. How often
the packages of 500 sheets each are counted before they
reach the firm we cannot say, but in their various stages
they are counted seven times during their process of
manufacture. We may say, however, that from the time
the parcels leave the mills until the sheets are issued to
the public they cannot be counted and receipted for
much less than twenty-five times.

Arrived at the printing-office, and, of course, after the
usual counting, the workmen have the paper given to

them in batches of four hundred, five hundred, or six
hundred sheets, according to their skill and known
rapidity of workmanship. The sheets are then put to
soak between two thick layers of felt. When thoroughly
saturated the water is squeezed out of them under a
powerful screw-press. They are thus reduced to the
requisite condition of dampness.

From this room they are taken to the plates in the
printing-room. They are printed from plates which are
made in this way, though we pretend to no more than a
slight and popular account of the process. A roller of
soft steel is placed over the die, and this roller being
forced upon the die by the pressure of a compound
lever, takes a complete fac-simile. The impression thus
got is then hardened by chilling the steel roller; this in
turn is rolled over the surface of the large soft steel
plates, which again in turn are hardened, and from these
the stamps are printed in sheets.

Before the plate went to press an initial letter was
punched on each of the four corners of the stamp, and
these so varied in their combinations that no two were
quite alike. Some five-and-twenty years ago this mark led
to the detection of a cruel murder in Ireland. A porter
secreted himself in a little country bank till all were gone
except the old cashier, whom he stunned so effectually
that he never spoke again. As the safe was effectually
closed and he could not find the key, he got but a few
pounds. But the deed was done, and he had to make
the best of a bad situation. He sat down and wrote a
letter to himself in a feigned hand, making an appoint-
ment at that same time at a place some miles distant

from the bank. Then he cut a postage-stamp from a small sheet in the dead cashier's desk, and leaving the bank, posted his letter. Suspicion, however, fell upon him, and he showed the letter to prove an *alibi*, but on comparing the number on the stamp with the number and letters on the sheet from which it had been cut it was traced like a bank-note till it was proved that the sheet had been sold to the cashier. At that time we believe there were only two stars in the uppermost corners of the stamp, and two letters at the bottom.

The life of a plate for printing is only about two years. Of course there is the usual variation in their time of durability, for that greatly depends on the quality of the metal. When any change of stamps takes place these plates have all to be renewed, and when the plates are worn out, the impressions on them are at once carefully obliterated by scoring them in all directions with a graver, so that by no possibility could they be used. With proper preparation the metal is susceptible of a fresh impression when it is wanted. Though the plates are not very thick, and therefore not very heavy, the metal is expensive. None of the workmen, under any excuse or pretence whatever, are allowed to bring or to connive at any white paper being brought into the building.

The white paper used for the stamps is in size and texture very like what is called "demy" in the trade. This can be got anywhere for 5d. a quire, though the stamp-paper is much more costly. It would, however, be a very risky business for any printer to try the manufacture of stamps.

Our readers must have observed that some years ago several changes took place both in the penny and half-penny stamps, the basis colour of the penny stamp having hitherto been a kind of reddish-brown, which had a peculiarly solid look, and was printed on thickish paper—a most useful-looking, characteristic, unmistakable stamp. But it was found that the basis colour of this stamp was too like ordinary white writing-paper, in so far as it resisted the action of certain acids that would remove the ink from the face of the paper, so that there was a chance that the stamps might be manipulated, and after having been defaced, might be used again and again. To render this impossible it was necessary to find a paper and a colour which would not resist any acid of the ink-removing kind, and the later recourse to colours of a very different kind has to some extent been determined by this consideration. Postage is certainly cheap enough, but if one stamp can be thus manipulated thousands may be, and in modern conditions of civilisation there are always, especially in an over-populated country like ours, a large class who will rather devote themselves to getting a living in this kind of way, in spite of all risks, than work hard and regularly day by day for their bread.

The recent changes in the stamps have led to some marked changes in the process of manufacture. The water-marks have gone, and instead of the alphabetical letters stamped in the corners, other devices have been adopted, as any one may see by scrutiny of the stamps.

Foreign stamps are well worth keeping and preserving and putting into albums, for not only do they present wide contrasts, but they are sometimes very suggestive of great events in history, or carry the mind back to a time when the whole aspect of political geography was different from what it now is. In Germany the different states issue their own stamps to those who desire them, with the head of their own sovereigns engraved on them, just as ours are; but there is an imperial stamp that is available in every state. France has once more reverted to its classical figure-head, the image of an ideal Republic personified in a beautiful Greek female head. The United States of America has a whole collection of its most famous presidents at different periods, by which the values of different stamps may be reckoned, as well as by other signs in colour, and so on. Any one who has a complete or even a good collection of United States postage-stamps has a little pictorial history of a great empire before him; and if it be true, as Berkeley said—

"Westward the course of Empire takes its way,"

then to America must be assigned a great place in the future history of the world; and if the deeds that they have done is but earnest of what they yet shall do, much is surely to be expected of them.

Looked at from this point of view, a postage-stamp album well filled may be one of the most interesting, instructive, and valuable books.

APPENDIX.

—•—

I.

THE following article from the *Ceylon Observer* puts the facts about H. Hasskarl and the Calisayas very effectively :—

THE INTRODUCTION OF CHINCHONAS INTO JAVA, AND THEIR CULTIVATION.

Amongst the contributions to the history of the great and beneficial enterprise of introducing the medicinal Chinchonas from South America into the Eastern world, an enterprise in which our Dutch neighbours had the honour of leading the way, not the least valuable is the long and interesting letter which last mail from Java brought us from Mr. Moens, the Director of the Chinchona plantations in that island. The perfect command which this gentleman possesses of the English language, although he has been eighteen years resident in Java, is explained by the fact of his having been thoroughly trained in the language of our country, a branch of his family being, indeed, settled in England. Our readers will recollect the case of the Mr. Moens who, about fifteen years ago, was seized by brigands near Naples and kept in durance for a long period, pending negotia-

T

tions for the payment of a ransom which the robbers demanded, and on the payment of which they indicated his life depended. Mr. Moens' extraordinary experiences while being carried from place to place by his captors were embodied in a book which is more interesting than many a romance. The father of this gentleman was brother to our correspondent. Mr. Moens of Java writes :—

"Enclosed I send you a packet of seeds of one of our best kinds of Ledgeriana. I write the analysis of the bark of the mother-tree on the paper, so you may see it is one of the best kinds."

The analysis to which Mr. Moens refers is as follows :—

C. *calisaya*, LEDGERIANA, No. 46, contains :—

Quinine	9.81	per cent.
Chinchonidine	0.40	,,
Amorphous alkaloids	1.04	,,

The courtesy which Mr. Moens has shown to us we cannot doubt he will be ready to extend, by the permission of his Government, to others, and as seeds of the best kinds of Ledgeriana are also being carefully collected from isolated trees in the Sikkhim gardens, we fear we could not hope for success in appealing to the Governments of India and Ceylon and to planters to raise £500 for a new seed-collecting expedition by Mr. Ledger, as suggested in a letter we recently received from his brother, as follows :—

"Some time since Mr. John Eliot Howard informed me you were making inquiries respecting obtaining some seed of the Chinchona tree for Ceylon, and that he had referred you to me as representing my brother, Mr. Charles Ledger, who had obtained the seed sent in 1865 to India and Java, which latter has proved to be the best and most productive sort, earning for itself, from the manager of the plantations in Java, the title of the 'Ledgeriana,' and the former, Mr. Howard (June 20th), now informs me he has bought the first importation of the product of this seed from the Neilgherries, and that 'it is good quality, reproducing one of the better South American kinds, but not "Ledgeriana."'

"I hear the Dutch Government are as jealous of their seed as the Bolivians are.*

"If it be your intention to procure Chinchona seed, I shall be glad of some communication from you, as I am contemplating an absence from London which I should desire to regulate, so as in due season to write to my brother, allowing ample time for him to make the necessary preliminary arrangements for procuring the seed.

"I think Mr. Howard informed you of my brother's terms, and advised their acceptance; but if not, it may save time if I inform you they are prompt payment to me on his account of £250 on account of labour and money expended, or to be expended, and £250 more on delivery of seed in London, my brother *to do his best* (and he has succeeded before) to get the *best* seed he can, and to get as *much* of it as its safe transit will permit."

If there are gentlemen who think Mr. Ledger should be subsidised, we should be glad to hear from them.

* Mr. Moens' courtesy to us disposes of this supposition.—ED. *Ceylon Observer.*

Meantime we quote the very important information with which Mr. Moens has favoured us :—

" I have to thank you very much for your kindness in sending me the very interesting numbers of the *Ceylon Overland Observer* of May last, which came duly to hand.

" But I think there are some corrections to make in the accounts of the introduction of Chinchona plants in Java.

" On page 449 (issue of May 13th) I read—' But Mr. Hasskarl, ignorant of the country and the languages, did not obtain any plant or seeds of the Calisaya, of which he was in quest.   All the kinds he collected were unfortunately either worthless or inferior.'

" Mr. Hasskarl was sent to Peru in December 1852. He stayed in Lima from February of that year till May 1853, chiefly to learn the Spanish language, and then proceeded inland, found the *Chinchona Pahudiana* and *C. officinalis* at Uchubamba, collected seeds and plants, and went to the southern provinces of Peru to obtain the Calisaya.   At Sandia, in the province of Caravaya, Hasskarl obtained the *C. calisaya, C. Pelleteriana, C. purpurea, C. magnifolia, C. erythroderma,* and *C. rufinerius ;* but he could not find a good supply of seeds, and therefore resolved to go back to Lima and to wait the favourable season of 1854.   The 8th of May (1854) he again travelled to Sandia, penetrated to Asalaya, where he found *C. calisaya,* with fruits and ripe seeds, but was compelled to go back, because the judge of Crucero, a friend of Hasskarl, warned him that an order to take him in custody had been issued, because he was taking away chinchona plants out of the country, which the natives would not allow. Hasskarl had made a contract with some Bolivian *cascarilleros* (bark-cutters) to bring him a supply of Calisaya plants, and he was fortunate enough to get five hundred plants of *C. calisaya.* Hasskarl then returned to the coast, where a Dutch man-of-war vessel was waiting for him, and landed his guardian cases at Batavia on the 13th of December 1854. Only seventy-eight of his plants were alive and could find a new home at Tji Budus on Gedeh mountain.

" This is the true account of the matter. It is true Mr. Hasskarl had not been in South America before, and was ignorant of the Quichua language ; but he had been a long time in Java, was accustomed to a tropical climate, was a botanist of some eminence, and, moreover, a practical gardener, had collected plants and seeds in the forests of Java, and knew how to help himself in a wild region.

" Mr. Clements R. Markham had a knowledge of the Quichua language, but was ignorant of botany and practical gardening. And whilst Hasskarl brought seventy-eight Calisayas to Java alive, *all* the plants of Mr. Markham were dead before they reached the Neilgherries.

" I think the great merit of Mr. Markham has been that he secured the services of men like Spruce and Cross, who succeeded in procuring the stock of plants and seeds from which all the *C. succirubras* and *C. officinalis* were obtained which are now grown in British India and Java. That the Calisaya collected by Hasskarl was the true Calisaya is beyond doubt. In 1855 Mr. Weddell paid a visit to the Botanical Gardens of Leiden, and saw there the Calisaya plants reared from seeds Mr. Hasskarl had sent from Sandia. As soon as he saw the young plants he exclaimed, '*La vraie calisaya, rien que cela, il n'y a pas le moindre doute.*' In 1874 I sent a case of dried specimens of our Chinchonas to that great quinologist, Mr. Howard. Amongst the specimens were some of the Calisaya varieties reared from seeds obtained from Hasskarl's original plants. Mr. Howard writes me about them :—'No. 1 may, and indeed *must*, be a rather fine kind. No. 2 is a form of Calisaya which I do not at present recognise. No. 4 resembles more my specimen of *C. calisaya vera.*'

"And the bark of these trees is also very good. I found in it 2 to 3 per cent. of quinine (= 2½ to 4 per cent. of sulphate of quinine), a yield as great as that of the common Calisaya bark of the Bolivia, and which was considered the *ne plus ultra* of quinine-yielding Calisaya barks until 1872, when I found that the Calisaya variety we obtained (bought) of Mr. Ledger holds *at least* two times as much.*

"In 1875 we have sold 25,552 lbs. of the Calisaya bark, which resulted from Mr. Hasskarl's mission, for 35,360 f., and in 1876, of the same bark, 37,335 lbs. for 54,828 f. Before this time we had sold about 34,000 lbs. for 40,000 f. The highest prices were, in 1875, 1.91 f. per half-kilogram ; in 1876, 2.11 f. per half-kilogram ; whilst Ledgeriana fetched at the same time—

Highest price in 1875	.	.	.	.	.	4.55
Do. 1876	.	.	.	.	.	4.40

---

* I remember also the discovery of *C. condeminea*, var. *Angustifolia*, by Broughton (in 1868), with 7 to 9 per cent. of quinine, but this was no calisaya.

"You know that 1 guilder (1 f.) = 1s. 8d., and that your lb. is a little lighter than our half-kilogram.

1 lb.	equals	.	.	.	.	.	0.4536 kilogram
½ kilogram	,,	.	.	.	.	.	0.5000 ,,

"I hope the above will convince you that Mr. Hasskarl undoubtedly succeeded in bringing a good (not the best) kind of Calisaya to Java.

"In the Amsterdam market we have sold, in all, a quantity of alkaloids and almost no quinine. But it is as true that this poor bark has been sold till now for a price as high and sometimes higher than that of *succirubra*.

Before and in 1874 ...	11,000½	kilograms	.	.	f. 4700.00
,, ,, 1875 ...	3,704½	,,	.	.	5053.71
,, ,, 1876 ...	1,654½	,,	.	.	2352.62
Or 1.36 f. and 1.42 f. per kilogram in the last years.					

"This 'worthless' kind, you see, has been worth 22,100 f. And there are many thousands of trees left, planted out in the dense forest shade before 1864, the bark of which is still very thin, but may perhaps, after ten or twenty years, repay the cost of planting, as they require no care at present and are left to themselves.

"I wonder how Mr. M'Ivor, in his half-yearly reports, continues, since 1864, to put down the *C. Pahudiana* bark as 'worth unknown.' He might know the worth, however, as we have sold Pahudiana bark since 1872.

"As to the question of the Calisaya being so very much given to sporting, I think you ought not to fear this so much as you appear to do. In the Neilgherries and in Java different species of Chinchona have been planted near to each other, and as the genus Chinchona is particularly apt to form hybrids, the occasion being given, it was no wonder that the offspring of your and of our Calisayas consisted for the greater part of hybrids. With us the hybrids have the type of *C. calisaya* mixed up with *C. Pahudiana;* with you of *C. calisaya* mixed with *C. micrantha* and *succirubra.* So Calisaya could not help sporting; but it was not her own fault, but the fault of the growers, who at that time were not sufficiently aware of the danger of the better sort being hybridised by the worse. Our seed-bearers of Ledgeriana are kept strictly isolated; and till now the young plants have a strong resemblance with young shoots of the mother-trees, and there is almost no difference between the individuals of the same origin.

"Then it is not at all certain that those which do not resemble the mother-tree will be found degenerated. Amongst our oldest trees of Ledgeriana you may find perhaps five or six varieties. And they are *all* very good. Only one variety has no more than 3 per cent. quinine in the bark; but then it holds 1.5 to 2 per cent. of quinidine, an alkaloid which is coming into large demand and is much sought after, the price approximating more and more to that of quinine. It is not correct when you say (issue of 2nd May, page 4), that the narrow-leaved *C. Ledgeriana* is the best. I have found broad-leaved varieties with 11 per cent. of quinine = 14.82 per cent. of sulphate of quinine.

"I have just received a report about the sale of our bark-crop of 1875, which took place on the 1st of June 1876. The prices were :—

Per ¼ Kilogram.

		s. d.	*s. d.*
C. succirubra . . .	f. 1.10 ... 1.61 = 1 10 ...	2 8
,, *pahudiana* . . .	. 1.10 ... 1.68 = 1 10 ...	2 10
,, *micrantha* . . .	. 1.28 ... 1.34 = 2 2 ...	2 3
,, *officinalis* . . .	. 2.55 ... 2.65 = 4 3 ...	4 5
,, *calisaya Anglica* (*) .	. 1.36 ... 1.52 = 2 3 ...	2 6
,, ,, *Schuhkraft* (†)	. 1.21 ... 1.53 = 2 0 ...	2 6
,, ,, *Ledgeriana* .	. 3.00 ... 4.40 = 5 0 ...	7 4
,, ,, *Javanica* (‡) .	. 0.71 ... 2.11 = 1 2 ...	3 6
,, *Hasskarliana* . .	. 1.21 ... 1.61 = 2 0 ...	2 8
,, *Ledgeriana*, powdered .	. 2.30 ... 2.51 = 3 10 ...	4 2
,, *calisaya Jav.* . .	. 0.30 ... 0.80 = 0 6 ...	1 4

" I hope the above will be of some interest to you."

We are glad, on this, the very best authority, to do justice to Mr. Hasskarl, whose arrival with the first Chinchonas which had ever reached the Eastern world well remember being chronicled in the Straits papers (quoting those of Java), and our own puzzlement, in copying the intelligence, by the Dutch form " Kina " used as descriptive of the plants. The enterprise initiated by Mr. Hasskarl, and carried forward by Junghuhu and his successors, has been persevered in, much to the credit, and, we are glad to learn, ultimately to the considerable profit, of the Dutch Colonial Government. It would really seem as if soil and climate in Java were so favourable that no description grown there can be regarded as worthless. Even *C. Pahudiana*, it appears, has

* *Calisaya Anglica:* a hybrid reared from seeds we obtained from Madras.

† *Calisaya Schuhkraft:* reared from seeds obtained of Mr. Schuhkraft, the Dutch Consul at La Paz (Bolivia), appears to be *C. calisaya Josephiana.*

‡ *Calisaya Javanica:* the offspring of Mr. Hasskarl's trees. The whole amount of the sale was 118,080 f.—the cost in 1875 of Chinchona culture, 49,857 f.

yielded bark which fetched prices in the Amsterdam market equal to those got for the produce of *C. succirubra.* *C. calisaya, var.* JOSEPHIANA, which, if we recollect aright, Mr. Howard pronounced "worthless," sold in the latest Amsterdam auction at no less than 2s. to 2s. 6d. per lb. In Java, with Calisayas, as with all the other Chinchonas, the question seems to be one merely of degree of value ; of the half-dozen varieties cultivated, all are good. That climate and soil must exercise great influence seems obvious from the fact that in British Sikkhim Calisayas grown from a portion of the seed collected by Mr. Ledger, and which has given such wonderful results in Java, turned out a few exceedingly good, and others (the bark in every case carefully analysed by Mr. Wood, the Government chemist) *absolutely* "worthless." The good trees are distinguished there, we feel pretty certain, by narrow leaves, as well as a pure *white blossom*, to which latter characteristic supreme importance is attached. But as most of the Calisayas we have yet seen in Ceylon are broad-leaved, it is reassuring to learn from Mr. Moens that largeness of size in leaf is quite compatible with richness of quality in bark. The results in Java, too, rebut Mr. Broughton's statement that Chinchona hybrids partake only of the bad qualities of both parents. Indeed it seems quite probable that hybridising in India and Java may produce varieties of unsurpassed richness. *C. Angustifolia*, the variety of *officinalis* grown on the Neilgherries, which equals *C. calisaya* itself in amount of quinine, seems referable to a process of hybridisation, and the kind obtained from Ceylon, and to which so much attention is now devoted in Sikkhim (*ignota*), may, we believe, be placed in the same category. The fate of the seed obtained by Mr. Ledger and the varying results it gave form a curious chapter in the history of the Chinchona enterprise. Mr. Howard sowed a small quantity in his conservatory, and he got about a dozen varieties of plants, which he referred not to hybridisation but to "sporting." If hybridisation there was, the process must have taken place in the forests of South America, for, as we understand it, the seed obtained by Mr. Ledger was divided between Mr. Money and the Java Government; while Mr. Money (Mr. M'Ivor's partner in a Chinchona plantation) gave a portion of his to the Madras Government in exchange for *succirubra* seed. On the Neilgherries, according to the emphatic and oft-recorded opinion of the late Mr. M'Ivor, Calisaya was not a success, the trees growing with a spindly habit. Mr. Broughton, however, differed from Mr. M'Ivor, and urged special attention to the cultivation of the Calisayas; while, according to Mr. Ledger's letter to us quoted above, Mr. Howard reports favourably on the first specimens of bark of this kind he has obtained from the Neilgherries. The great quinologist, however, pronounces the bark not to be that of true Ledgeriana. So that climate and soil on the Neilgherries would seem not to be very favourable. In Sikkhim, on the other hand, where *C. officinalis* proved an entire failure, the Calisayas grew well enough; but, as we have already indicated, a large proportion turned out worthless, and propagation there, by means of cuttings from the good trees, has to be carried on under glass, as the cuttings will not strike and grow in the open air. Seed from carefully isolated trees (white-blossomed, and the bark of which has given good results) is also being tried on an extensive scale. In Java all the seed obtained seems to have resulted in trees all good, and some supremely excellent. Our conditions of climate, at least in Ceylon, so closely resemble those of Java, that we have reason to hope every kind of Chinchona will succeed in our island, from *C. succirubra*, which at the late Dutch sale sold for 1s. 10d. to 2s. 8d. per lb., up to *Calisaya Ledgeriana*, which realised from 5s. to 7s. 4d.

II.

SYNDICATES OF DIAMONDS AND SALT.

It appears that, as we write, there is a movement to form a Diamond Syndicate. This would seem to imply that there *is* something in the fact of over-supply being likely to reduce the value of, at all events, the smaller diamonds, though, talking the other day to a gentleman who has been for many years in South Africa, and interested in the diamond-trade, he assured us that the area of sale and the demand were so wide, that this was all "moonshine," and got up merely in the interest of a limited few. But this gentleman also admitted that much might have been done to control the market, and to keep out certain classes of middle-men, if it had only been done in time at the South African diamond-fields. Syndicates, as we all know, can do much to maintain prices, though whether even Syndicates ultimately will realise all the good expected from them by those who combine to form them may be questioned, and that not merely in the line of the meaning of the maxim that "Competition is the life of trade." Prices artificially kept up by such combinations will react in two ways:—(1) on those concerned in the industries connected with the product, particularly in the finer departments; and (2), on the area of purchasers, more especially if scientific invention realises what may not unreasonably be expected of it, in the production of still more perfect imitations.

The elements bound up in the question of Syndicates touches us still more closely as regards salt. Salt is a necessity of life, which the diamond certainly is not. It is true that in past times, as even now, a few have questioned whether salt was essential to the well-being of the human system, and some of the most curious literature existent is to be found in connection with this point—one ingenious author even endeavouring to prove that salt was the forbidden fruit !—but the imperious necessity that impels both animals and men to indulge in it seems conclusive on that point for practical purposes. The Salt Syndicate has already made itself felt in the advance of prices; and it may be that this will by-and-by lead to greater care and economy in the use of the article. It certainly will do so if the Syndicate's work should be effective, and raise prices further still—as far as they would, of course, wish to raise them; and, perhaps, in this respect also may do good; for, from its cheapness,

salt had come to be regarded as a very "common creature" indeed.

But already one of the effects we have hinted at has
made itself felt, if we may trust to the following paragraph
which we notice in a London evening newspaper as we
write. It tells us that—

"The irritation in the salt trade is increasing, and is
all the more general because the workmen thought that
they were to share in the benefits which the Salt Syndicate promised. Since the Syndicate started it has not
increased wages, but it has increased the quantity of
work demanded from the men, and has augmented their
hours of Sunday labour. The Trades Union recently
formed has now 2250 members; their chief difficulty
appears to be that a surplus labour population is in
existence in the salt district. In Northwich and Winsford
alone some 600 men are out of employment. That being
the case, the success of the salt unionists is doubtful,
though their cause is a good one."

Syndicates and Conventions have their own uses, of
course; and any legitimate action in the way of protecting interests and industries is quite allowable, and may
be very praiseworthy; but one thing is clear, that legislative sanction in such matters wants to be very jealously
safe-guarded, and not overdone. The agricultural interest
is now deeply paying the penalty for its persistence in
the case of the Corn-Laws. The Sugar Convention has
already had its own effect, and as we write we cut this
from the same paper as the foregoing :—

"'Sugar, Mr. Speaker—(laughter)—Sugar, Mr. Speaker
—Sugar, Mr. Speaker, who will laugh at sugar now?'

So spoke an English statesman nearly a hundred years ago, and I am inclined to borrow his words. This Sugar Convention is no laughing matter. We have treated the Sugar Bounty agitators with contempt too long, and at last they have succeeded in persuading Conservative statesmen that they have a great following at their back. I am confident that they have not sufficient following to turn the scale at half-a-dozen elections. There are signs that the country is waking up to the danger of this insane Convention at last, and that the Government is not disposed to run any serious risks on account of the Convention. Ere long the utter hollowness of the agitation will be apparent to Lord Salisbury himself."

III.

ARSENIC.

We cut the following, which appears in Answers to Correspondents, from the *Echo*, more especially for the simple hint about the detection of the presence of arsenic in wall-paper or muslin fabric :—

"A great deal of nonsense is often written about 'poisonous' this, that, and the other. Poison is a relative term, and its death-dealing power depends on quantity. Arsenic is present in many dyes in small quantities, and some pigments are made up almost entirely of a compound of arsenic. A dress of muslin of a pale green-blue colour might be dangerous if the colour was in powder, and so could be shaken off, but if 'fixed' there is no harm in it. A simple test for arsenic is to burn a portion of the fabric, and if a smell of garlic is perceived arsenic is no doubt present.—S. R."

THE END.

PRINTED BY BALLANTYNE, HANSON AND CO.
EDINBURGH AND LONDON.

www.ingramcontent.com/pod-product-compliance
Lightning Source LLC
Chambersburg PA
CBHW021033030726

* 9 7 8 3 7 4 4 6 6 1 6 2 1 *